"A Curious Machine"

"A Curious Machine"

Wesleyan Reflections on the Posthuman Future

EDITED BY
Arseny Ermakov
AND
Glen O'Brien

WIPF & STOCK · Eugene, Oregon

Wipf & Stock
An Imprint of Wipf and Stock Publishers
199 W. 8th Ave., Suite 3
Eugene, OR 97401

www.wipfandstock.com

PAPERBACK ISBN: 978-1-6667-6259-4
HARDCOVER ISBN: 978-1-6667-6260-0
EBOOK ISBN: 978-1-6667-6261-7

VERSION NUMBER 09/01/23

To the Rev Dr Rob Fringer and Major Dr Dean Smith, previous Directors of the Australasian Centre for Wesleyan Research, in appreciation for their dedicated leadership.

Contents

Acknowledgments

WE WISH TO ACKNOWLEDGE that the conference from which most of the material for this book is derived, was held on the unceded lands of the Wurundjeri people of the Kulin nation, who have cared for their land since ancient times. We pay our respects to their elders, past and present, and commit to reconciliation and justice for all Indigenous people.

This book is one result of the scholarly work undertaken by the Australasian Centre for Wesleyan Research (ACWR). Established in 2000, the ACWR is a diverse and multidisciplinary community of both early career and established scholars united by a desire to foster and promote Wesleyan research and scholarship in Australia and New Zealand. The Centre's main activities have been in publishing the peer-reviewed journal *Aldersgate Papers*, as well as collections of essays, and in the running of an annual scholarly conference. The ACWR is a working partnership formed by the following theological institutions, denominational partners, and libraries: Asia-Pacific Nazarene Theological Seminary (Manila, Philippines), Booth College of Mission (Wellington, Aotearoa New Zealand), Kingsley Australia (Melbourne, Australia), Nazarene Theological College (Brisbane, Australia), The Sugden Heritage Collections, Queen's College, University of Melbourne, Pilgrim Theological College (Melbourne, Australia), United Theological College (Sydney, Australia), and The Wesleyan Methodist Church of Aotearoa New Zealand.

We acknowledge the support of these partner institutions in making the publication of this book possible, especially our home institution, Eva Burrows College (University of Divinity), and Academic Dean, Terry Grey.

We are grateful to the present ACWR Director, Joseph Wood, and our fellow past and present members of the ACWR executive committee, Tony Franklin-Ross, Rob Fringer, Jemila Isaacs, Caroline Jewkes, Emma Moore, Pam Reed, Matthew Seaman, Dean Smith, and David Wilson for the support and guidance they have offered this project. Finally, we thank each contributor, each peer reviewer of the chapters, and Wipf and Stock Publishers for their patience and commitment to the production of the volume.

List of Contributors

Jonathan P. Case is Professor of Theology at Houghton University, New York, USA.

Arseny Ermakov is Senior Lecturer in Biblical Studies at Eva Burrows College, University of Divinity, Melbourne, Australia.

Francesca Ferrando is Adjunct Assistant Professor at NYU Liberal Studies, New York, USA.

Stephen Garner is Academic Dean and Senior Lecturer in Theology at Laidlaw College, Auckland, New Zealand.

Grenville Kent teaches Old Testament and Christian Apologetics at Morling College and the Australian College of Ministry, Sydney, Australia.

Sandra Godde is an Independent Researcher, and formerly a Lecturer in Theology at Christian Heritage College, Brisbane, Australia.

Glen O'Brien is Research Coordinator and Professor of Christian Thought and History at Eva Burrows College, University of Divinity, Melbourne, Australia.

John McDowell is Associate Academic Dean, and Professor of Philosophy, Systematic Theology, and Moral Theology at Yarra Theological Union, University of Divinity, Melbourne, Australia.

Caleb Smith is an Auxiliary Lieutenant at the Temora Salvation Army Corps, New South Wales, Australia.

Introduction

Arseny Ermakov and Glen O'Brien

THE ONSET OF THE digital era has been as significant to human societies as the technological breakthroughs that have preceded it, including the invention of stone tools by early humans, the domestication of wildlife, the control of crop cycles, the invention of the printing press, and the industrial revolution. Each of these technological advancements had massive implications for the development of human society. Each raised new opportunities and new problems, while leading to the creation of entire civilizations and empires. The technological revolution brought on by the invention of personal computers and the Internet is proving to be just as determinative as these earlier epochal shifts in the course of the human experience.

The rapid rate of technological change and the impact of increasingly sophisticated forms of Artificial Intelligence (AI) on human society have forced philosophers, theologians, and ethicists to explore their implications for human experience. Human enhancement, genetic modification, remotely controlled weapons, the replacement of human labor and skill by robots, the commodification of data, and the possibility of independent reasoning powers in artificial intelligence all carry both promise and risk.

The Technological Singularity

Many futurists anticipate a moment known as "the Singularity"—the point at which artificial intelligence becomes self-determining and self-perpetuating, able to program and develop itself without human interaction or control.[1] AI will not necessarily need to develop consciousness for this to occur; sufficient levels of "superintelligence" will be enough. According to Kevin Kelly, the Singularity is the point at which "all the change in the last million years will be superseded by the change in the next five minutes."[2] Some AI experts ambitiously anticipate that as early as the year 2047, the technology will have reached a stage of development capable of producing human-level intelligence in machines.[3] Transhumanists claim that we will eventually be able to leave our bodies and live forever inside a computer simulation program (silicon-based enhancement) or have such advanced technology applied to our bodies that we will experience god-like capacities and virtual immortality (carbon-based enhancement). Such hopes have a weirdly religious vibe though they often rely on outmoded theological ideas. Milad Doueihi claims that "digital culture is the only rival to religion as a universal practice [and is] a world religion with its prophets and priesthood, its institutions and sects and believers, its dissenters and schismatics."[4] Of course, technology experts are already theorizing about "quantum computing"—a new technology that may leave digital modes of computing behind just as digital earlier replaced analog technology. Like many eschatological theories before it, the Singularitarian utopia may end up proving to be an illusion.

Max Tegmark in his book *Life 3.0* outlines three broad responses to the onset of "the Singularity" or something very like it. Techno-skeptics hold to the view that it will not happen for hundreds or thousands of years, if ever, so there is no need to worry about it now. Digital utopians believe it will happen soon, probably in this century, and that it should be welcomed as the next stage in cosmic evolution. The Beneficial AI movement agrees it will happen in this century but argues for careful protections through AI safety research to ensure only beneficial outcomes.[5] Christians

---

1. Mohan, *Posthumanism,* 246.
2. Mercer and Trothen, *Religion and the Technological Future,* 186.
3. Tegmark, *Life 3.0,* 157.
4. Doueihi, *Digital Cultures,* 3.
5. Tegmark, *Life 3.0,* 48.

who take seriously the possibility of dangerous levels of AI superintelligence being reached will likely be in sympathy with the Beneficial AI movement and support AI research aimed at beneficial use, not only for human beings but for all of creation.

The Social Impact of Robotic Technology

People seem to have a love-hate relationship with the idea of artificial humans. We are drawn to them with deep fascination but at the same time fear their potential to harm us. Of course, most robotic devices currently employed in industry, manufacturing and medical technology are not human-like at all, and we seem quite comfortable with those. Experiments have shown, however, that the more life-like a humanoid robot appears the less comfortable we are in its presence. This phenomenon, known as "the uncanny valley," first identified in the 1970s, refers to the hypothesis that humanoid objects which imperfectly resemble human beings provoke strangely familiar feelings of eeriness and revulsion in observers. Two instinctive responses to robots that have found expression in the arts are the idea that the creation of a human-like being is an act of blasphemy and that the creation of robots will lead to the inevitable destruction of the human race. These two fears may even be seen as causally connected with the blasphemous usurping of the divine prerogative of creation being punished by our extinction.

Erik Brynjolffson at the Massachusetts Institute of Technology has a vision of the future that he refers to as "Digital Athens."[6] In Brynjolffson's utopia, human drudgery and stress would be eliminated by a robot workforce that freed us all up to be dreamers, musicians, artists, and philosophers. Of course, such a reality would require a very different kind of economic system. For one thing, a guaranteed income, one not based on a return for labor, would be required, raising important questions about equitability and access. In the time it took to develop such a robot utopia, only those in wealthier parts of the world would have access to the technology that frees them from drudgery, leaving the world's poor open to exploitation as an underclass grinding away at soul-destroying physical labor for the benefit of the world's wealthy and privileged technocrats. It doesn't take too much thought to realize that we are, to a great extent, already in that situation. Would progress toward a digital utopia simply reinforce the present system

6. Tegmark, *Life 3.0*, 118–21.

of the exploitation of the labor of the world's poor to serve the acquisitive needs of a wealthy technocracy? We are already seeing the social impact of AI and robotics in the workplace. Automatic checkouts at the supermarket, automatic teller machines in banks, and automated assembly lines in manufacturing plants, all mean fewer jobs for people. At least, that is, fewer jobs of particular kinds. As employment patterns shift, new kinds of jobs become necessary, putting pressure on people to retrain in order to remain employable. We are seeing the emergence of a "precariat" in which people's sense of vocation is being negatively impacted in a dehumanizing process brought on by a more technological workforce.

More positively, robots can be used in very helpful ways to assist us, for example in manufacturing, in medical care, and in elder care. AI researchers are currently attempting to teach machines to infer goals from behavior. If an elderly person needed to explain to a home care robot that they needed to move out of a sedentary position once an hour to reach their health goals, it would be helpful if they didn't have to create a computer program to enable it. What if the robot could independently learn our needs and preferences and then prompt, remind, and assist the person as and when needed? This is not as easy and straightforward as it might sound, however. The ability to understand the purpose or goals of behavior is known as "inverse reinforcement learning," a very sophisticated learning function. Designing a robot with that capacity is a problem that will need to be solved before robots can offer consistent, reliable, and safe assistance to people. It will also be very important as robotic intelligence advances to higher levels to ensure that robot goals are always aligned with human goals. One of the most beneficial uses of robots is in manufacturing, where robots are used to build planes, cars, and other machines with much greater precision and efficiency than previously possible. Cottage-level manufacturers now use 3D printers to design and create anything their imaginations can devise. While there have been some deaths from industrial accidents involving robots, these are small compared to similar deaths in the pre-robotic era of manufacturing. It is likely that AI-controlled cars will reduce road fatalities by eliminating accidents caused by human error.

Robots are no real threat to human beings at present (though AI researchers are aware of the need to anticipate that possibility). Robot vacuum cleaners cannot even cope with upturned rugs, so it is doubtful they will be overthrowing us any time soon. The rationality of machines is at present very limited without anywhere near the sophistication and flexibility of the human brain. The rules a machine has to learn in order to figure out what to do in any given circumstance are too simplistic to allow them what we might consider "agency." As techno-skeptic Andrew Ng puts it, "Fearing a rise of killer robots is like worrying about overpopulation on Mars."[7] Remote-controlled weapons systems, however, do raise important ethical challenges, especially the possibility of their becoming autonomous. Autonomous Weapons Systems, sometimes referred to as Lethal Autonomous Weapons Systems (LAWS) are military weapons that can independently search for and engage targets through programming rather than human triggering (though, at present, most still involve a human element). Such "slaughterbots" naturally raise fears and ethical concerns. An Open Letter on Autonomous Weapons has so far attracted over 4,500 signatures from AI and Robotics researchers as well as over 2,600 others.

> Just as most chemists and biologists have no interest in building chemical or biological weapons, most AI researchers have no interest in building AI weapons—and do not want others to tarnish their field by doing so, potentially creating a major public backlash against AI that curtails its future societal benefits . . . Starting a military AI arms race is a bad idea, and should be prevented by a ban on offensive autonomous weapons beyond meaningful human control.[8]

In 2020, the Catholic Church signed *The Rome Call for AI Ethics*, along with European Union and United Nations officials as well as IBM and Microsoft representatives. It outlines the principles that should guide the development and implementation of AI technologies with the end purpose being to "benefit humanity and protect human rights and dignity."[9]

The Information Revolution

The impact of the Internet is being felt in all aspects of modern life. It has not only changed the way we create, share, and consume information, but is also reshaping the way we live as individuals and society: entertainment, politics, business, learning, trade, social life, relationships, church life, the list continues. Relational connections are now often forged in a disembodied

---

7. Cited in Tegmark, *Life 3.0*, 33.
8. "Autonomous Weapons."
9. RenAIssance Foundation, "Rome Call for AI Ethics."

digital space well ahead of any physical or material connection. This raises many interesting theological questions for Christians, who affirm a materially based and incarnational view of reality. By "materially-based" we mean that in Christianity, matter matters. Because mainstream Christian thought rejected the spiritualized, disembodied approach of Gnosticism in favor of stressing the goodness of the material creation and the central mystery of the Word-become-flesh, it has always been nervous about the disembodied nature of the digital world and the identities and communities that are created there. Think, for example, of the flurry of theological comments that arose in light of the global pandemic and the consequent shifting of worship into a digital space. How do we "go to church" online? How are we present to each other in a Zoom meeting? Most seem to agree that the physically distanced conditions created by the global pandemic have forced churches not only to introduce "emergency measures" to stay connected online but also that church life post-COVID will significantly change as a result of lessons learned from new digital practices and experiences.

The question of digital identities is also of great importance for Christians. Social media, in particular, is a place where personal identities are formed and curated. To what extent are our online identities congruent with our "real" identities? And what of social media etiquette? It seems that social media brings out the best and the worst in human nature as cooperative and supportive activities sit right alongside the worst kind of bullying, hate speech, misogyny, homophobia, misinformation, and dissemination of flaky conspiracy theories, with Christians often seeming to be the worst culprits (or at least just as bad as everybody else). Part of the problem is that social media platforms encourage us to think that our viewpoints and opinions are of such importance and value to the world that they simply must be shared. (This is particularly intoxicating to preachers who are always looking for an audience.) In expressing ourselves so frequently we sometimes forget that social media platforms are not just sites of private opinion but also of public pillorying; in that intersection of the public and the private, we can find ourselves entangled in toxicity and malice. Little wonder that many Christians find that a periodic "fast" from social media is a necessary spiritual discipline, or that opting out altogether is the best choice for them.

Another set of concerns arises out of the increasingly sophisticated technology behind "Big Data," defined as "extremely large data sets that may be analyzed computationally to reveal patterns, trends, and associations, especially relating to human behavior and interactions."[10] It is these data sets that enable companies to identify consumer buying patterns and target them with their products. You may have purchased an item online and then noticed that, almost immediately, advertisements for related products begin to pop up on your Facebook feed. That is Big Data at work in a closely-knit alliance with consumer capitalism. This is often experienced as if, "someone is watching me," but this is only true in a metaphorical sense, since this information is generated by an automated set of algorithmic zeroes and ones. There is no "evil genius" sitting at a computer terminal watching what you buy, or what movies you watch, or whether you "like" more memes that support conservative or progressive values. However, there certainly are real people in the businesses and corporations on the receiving end of such data who want to use it in ways that directly affect our lives.

Digital natives who have grown up with this technology have accepted what older people might consider the invasion of privacy as a small price to pay for the obvious benefit and convenience that Big Data brings. If you grew up carrying a street directory in your car, you had to learn to read road maps in order to arrive at your destination. Now the built-in GPS system in your car will guide you exactly to where you want to go (and in a pleasant voice) without having to balance a map turned upside down on the steering wheel. The fact that the GPS "knows" exactly where you are at all times seems to be a small price to pay for the convenience gained.

Theologians, philosophers, and ethicists need to think carefully about the era of Big Data especially around questions of hermeneutics (the theory of interpretation). What worlds of meaning are being constructed in the digital worlds with which we engage on a daily basis? How do we balance our privacy needs with our desire for the convenience and creative opportunities that digital technology enables and enhances? What strategies should governments, media outlets, educational institutions, churches, and other agencies put in place to preserve the values and behaviors that contribute to healthy, cohesive, and compassionate societies? Or should such agencies remain out of that process, leaving such choices entirely up to the individual?

One of the ways that digital technology is used maliciously is in the creation and distribution of "deep fakes"—digitally created images and videos that are becoming increasingly more sophisticated and difficult to

10. McAfee and Brynjolfsson, "Big Data."

distinguish from the real thing. In an era in which trusted mainstream media is dismissed by political leaders as "fake news" and where media start-ups do not always have well-developed moral scruples, but have access to the distribution of content on a massive scale, it is little wonder that people are becoming confused about what can be trusted in the media space. Paul Ricoeur's concept of a "hermeneutic of suspicion" is helpful when applied to the new digital landscape.[11] A "hermeneutic of suspicion" questions the meaning of any discourse and asks questions about "what's really going on" behind it. What are the hidden purposes, agendas, and power plays that underlie any and every piece of information we encounter on the Internet? What remains hidden from view lest it disrupt the intended narrative of the text and how might we unmask that? In an age in which digital media is so easily manipulable, a hermeneutic of suspicion is made perhaps more necessary than ever.

Christians should consider technology among the good gifts of God, a gift that draws on divinely given knowledge, wisdom, and skill for the benefit of creation. Like all divine gifts, however, a danger lies in their misuse and misapplication arising out of the fallenness of the human condition and the debilitating impact of sin on all human endeavor. Technology is power, and power is a seductive capacity that is open to prideful and idolatrous misuse. Jesus taught us to be "harmless as doves" but also "wise as serpents" (Matt 10:16). The appearance of increasingly sophisticated forms of AI will require us to seek this wisdom with ever greater urgency. We need not be fearful, however, because we also see divine purpose in the development of that same technology, especially in its therapeutic applications and in its capacity to address real human problems. To the extent that advanced technology contributes to human flourishing which will find its ultimate fulfillment in the new creation, we may embrace it with gratitude as a good gift of God.

Negotiating the Posthuman Future

Michel Foucault famously said that "man is an invention of recent date."[12] What he meant by this was that the category of "humanity" only came into focus during the modern period when "man" came to be thought of as both a subject and an object. When Descartes said, "I think, therefore I

11. Ricoeur, *Freud and Philosophy*, 32.
12. Foucault, *Les mots et les choses*, 387.

am" he was speaking (in a manner foreign to the classical world) of a human being as one who is simultaneously a transcendental subject and an empirical object. It is this "epistemological human" that Foucault believed to be of recent invention. Where Humanists had believed passionately that human beings generated knowledge more or less innately out of "human nature," posthumanists have generally followed Foucault in holding that the very idea of something called "human nature" is derived from structures that are policed and controlled by social power. No "essential human nature" can be found outside of this system of power and control. This move has had the effect of dislodging the concept of "humanity" from its hegemonic power at the center of rational discourse. N. Katherine Hayles, a postmodern literary critic at Duke University, argues, similarly to Foucault, that there is no fixed notion of "the human"; it is simply a concept produced by modernity. The "posthuman" comes into being with the coproduction of human and machine intelligence. She conceives of the human body as a kind of prosthesis of the mind, so that bodily existence is equivalent to a computer simulation.[13]

Responding to posthumanism can be challenging, partly because the term is used in a number of different ways. For some, it sits under the broader category of transhumanism. For others, it is an entirely different, almost opposing philosophy to transhumanism. philosophical posthumanism, critical posthumanism, and cultural posthumanism are not exactly the same thing, though they are all thrown up by posthuman ideas.[14] Complicating things further, some of the thinkers who are identified with posthumanism, including Friedrich Nietzsche, Jacques Derrida, or Michel Foucault, did not identify themselves as "posthumanists," even though their ideas are often drawn on in posthumanist discourse. Was Nietzsche's concept of the *Übermensch* (Overman) (an ideal form of the human with this- world, more than next-world concerns) a transhuman, posthuman, or antihuman construct? Perhaps it was a little of all three, but Nietzsche was not himself a "posthumanist," even if his ideas anticipated posthumanism in many respects. This is especially so if we consider philosophical posthumanism as a natural development of postmodernism.

It is important to remember that posthumanist thought is not "antihuman." Dislodging human beings from the center of discourse is not only good for the planet; it is good for human beings as well. People flourish

13. Hayles, *How We Became Posthuman*.

14. For a helpful guide to the various terms see Sorgner, *On Transhumanism*, 31–56.

best when they do not stand in an exploitative or hierarchical stance over nature or each other but work harmoniously within ecosystems to assure sustainability for all organisms. When applied to technology, should machines ever develop consciousness or human-machine cyborgs emerge (the nearness of both eventualities is routinely over-exaggerated), posthumanists would argue for a shared and non-exploitative set of relationships between the variety of sentience-bearing beings for the mutual benefit of all. It is the posthuman conviction that without the toppling of humanity from the top of the pyramid of existence such mutually beneficial co-existence would be impossible.

When transhumanists talk about "the posthuman" they are usually referring to an evolutionary stage of human enhancement, whether the dualistic idea of uploading the mind to a computer, or the biological enhancement brought about by genetic engineering, the use of nanotechnology, or even mind-altering or body-altering drugs. On the other hand, a philosophical posthumanist uses the term to refer to *a different way of thinking about* human beings, as distinct from *a different type of* human being. One reason for this difference lies in the sources of the two movements. Transhumanism stands in the Anglo-American tradition of science with a commitment to progress based on the Darwinian concepts of evolution. Philosophical posthumanism, on the other hand, emerges from the Continental literary tradition which is not deeply committed to the idea of scientific progress. Broadly speaking transhumanists are interested in what people are becoming and posthumanists in how people are to be understood.

As in all critical discourse, any response to posthumanism must be more than a simple, blank, unthinking rejection, like Australian right-wing politician Pauline Hanson's famous xenophobic dismissal, "I don't like it!" The various responses we are highlighting in this book each in their own way engage with posthuman ideas, not via wholesale rejection but by a more nuanced response of questioning, probing, and appropriating some ideas as valid while rejecting others as problematic or untenable. Ideas we might now consider posthuman can be found in older, and even ancient, theological sources. In the Bible, humans play an important role in the history of salvation but it is not a completely human-centric story. People take their place in a much bigger interrelated cosmos filled with other sentient beings, "living souls," and "powers and dominions." At the center of the biblical story is the Triune God who is on a mission to reconcile and restore the whole of "groaning creation" including, but not limited to, suffering humanity, and bring about "a new heaven and a new earth."[15] The Patristic concept of "theosis," which sees humans transformed into beings possessing more divine qualities through perfecting grace, is another example. As is John Wesley's broadening of divine purpose beyond human beings to include animals with heightened powers of rationality in the new creation, so that they also bear aspects of the image of God. Posthuman discourse is helpful in reminding us to ask the question, "What have we lost in the centering of purely anthropological concerns?" Of course, it is also appropriate to ask, "What might be lost to us if the traditional preferencing of human beings is set aside?" For example, the Christian doctrine of human beings as made in the image of God has often formed the basis of universal human rights. If every person bears the stamp of the divine image, then every person is worthy of respect and protection. To lose that may result in the loosening of the foundations of the concept of human rights (though of course the latter may be established in other ways).

Since it is possible to be a Christian theologian and also a posthumanist thinker, framing the discussion as "theology versus posthumanism" or "Christianity versus posthumanism" does not work. It is better to think in terms of a conversation with posthumanists in which theological ideas are engaged, rather than in terms of debate or opposition. Our conversation with Francesca Ferrando in chapter 9 is a good example of this. Certainly, there is room for contestation, critical reflection, and analytical exploration, and not all contributors to this volume are agreed on the relationship between theology and posthumanist thought. However, it is not a zero-sum game where one voice wins out while others become losers. We invite you as a reader to enter into and enjoy the conversation in a manner that reflects the Wesleyan tradition of openness to the ideas of others, based on the conviction that prevenient grace reaches all persons and informs all areas of human intellectual inquiry.

This book has been developed from papers delivered at the Australasian Centre for Wesleyan Research Conference on *"A Curious Machine": Wesleyan Reflections on the Posthuman Future*, held in Melbourne, Australia, in August 2019. Not every contributor writes explicitly from a Wesleyan framework, though each reflects in their own way a Wesleyan openness to science and technology, as well as the Wesleyan conviction that divine

---

15. See Koosed, *Bible and Posthumanism*, for more explorations of intersecting themes.

grace is preveniently at work in the world. There is a teleological shape to Wesleyan discourse because it looks in the forward direction of perfecting grace rather than backward to a lost innocence. It moves from creation to new creation, exploring the intersection of divine grace and human response in a manner that embraces the future. Christian experience is an anticipation "of heaven below" as the powers of the world to come are tasted pre-emptively in the present life through sanctifying grace.[16]

Bibliography

"Autonomous Weapons: An Open Letter from AI & Robotics Researchers." *Future of Life Institute*, February 9, 2016. https://futureoflife.org/open-letter-autonomous-weapons/.

Doueihi, Milad. *Digital Cultures*. Cambridge, MA: Harvard University Press, 2011.

Foucault, Michel. *Les mots et les choses*. Paris: Gallimard, 1966. Translated by Alan Sheridan as *The Order of Things*. New York: Vintage, 1973.

Hayles, N. Katherine. *How We Became Posthuman: Virtual Bodies in Cybernetics, Literature and Informatics*. Chicago: The University of Chicago Press, 1999.

Koosed, Jennifer L, ed. *The Bible and Posthumanism*. Society of Biblical Literature. Semeia Studies 74. Atlanta: Society of Biblical Literature, 2014.

McAfee, Andrew, and Erik Brynjolfsson. "Big Data: The Management Revolution." *Harvard Business Review* 90 (2012) 60–68.

Mercer, Calvin and Tracy J. Trothen, *Religion and the Technological Future: An Introduction to Biohacking, Artificial Intelligence and Transhumanism*. New York: Springer, 2021.

Mohan, Peter. *Posthumanism: A Guide for the Perplexed*. London: Bloomsbury, 2017.

RenAIssance Foundation. "The Rome Call for AI Ethics." https://www.romecall.org/the-call/.

Ricoeur, Paul. *Freud and Philosophy. An Essay on Interpretation*. Translated by Denis Savage. New Haven, Connecticut: Yale University Press, 1970.

Tegmark, Max. *Life 3.0: Being Human in the Age of Artificial Intelligence*. London: Penguin, 2017.

Wesley, John. *The Works of John Wesley: Volume 7: A Collection of Hymns for the Use of the People Called Methodists*. Edited by Franz Hildebrandt and Oliver A. Beckerlegge. Nashville: Abingdon, 1983.

---

16. The phrase "anticipate your heaven below" is found in the final stanza of the Charles Wesley hymn, *O For a Thousand Tongues* (Wesley, *Works*, 7:79).

1

"Creatures Capable of God"

John Wesley's Theological Anthropology
and the Posthuman Future

GLEN O'BRIEN

Introduction

FRANCESCA FERRANDO DEFINES "PHILOSOPHICAL Posthumanism" as
a decentering of the human from modes of discourse. This move is appropriate to the age informally known as "the Anthropocene," an epoch
of human devastation of the planet which has almost reached its limits.[1]
Where humanism placed human rationality, consciousness, and culture at
the center of existence, posthumanism disrupts this discourse by claiming no special place for humans at the top of the hierarchy of being. According to Stefan Lorenz Sorgner, a central element in posthumanism is
that, "people are no longer regarded as the crowning glory of the natural
world or as entities that categorically differ from nature in its purity, but are
understood as only *gradually (rather than essentially)* differing from other
natural beings."[2] Cary Wolfe has highlighted what he considers a prejudice
in bioethics that is based on "species difference" and a failure to acknowledge

1. Ferrando, *Philosophical Posthumanism*, 22.
2. Sorgner, *On Transhumanism*, 32.

the "dramatic changes over the past thirty years in our knowledge about the lives, communication, emotions, and consciousnesses of a number of nonhuman species."[3] He argues that "the human occupies a new place in the universe" no longer dominant or able to claim sovereignty over "nonhuman subjects."[4] For Ferrando, posthumanism is "the philosophy of our time," a second stage in Postmodern discourse that "destabilizes the limits and symbolic borders posed by the notion of the human. Dualisms such as human/animal, human/machine, and . . . human/nonhuman are reinvestigated through a perception which does not work on oppositional schemata."[5] In other words, posthumanism seeks to conceive of humanity not as hovering above all other existences but as part of the matrix of being, embedded within it alongside of others. All of this can be a challenge for a traditional theological anthropology that views human beings as "the crown of creation," uniquely made in God's image.

John Wesley's thought was "Humanist" in the sense that it was deeply embedded in human reason and religious experience. At the same time, in his fascination with science and technology as instruments of human flourishing and in the teleological direction of his new creation anthropology, his thought can inform both posthuman and transhuman discourse. Wesley was something of a polymath—interested, though not always adept, in a wide variety of scientific and mechanical experiments and remedies. His best-known dalliance in these areas is his *Primitive Physic* (1747) which went into numerous editions in his lifetime and included his recommendation of electrification for the cure of melancholy, an interesting precursor to the use of electro-shock therapy.[6] It would be a stretch to say he was a "futurist" but when we couple his interest in emerging technologies with his later eschatological sermons on the nature of the new creation, we discern a teleological direction in the broad shape of his theology. This chapter will consider a number of Wesley's sermons on theological anthropology as well as two later sermons on eschatological themes and argue that he anticipated a cosmic renewal that was not limited to the salvation of human beings. For Wesley, the future of humanity, of non-human animals, and of the very constituent elements of the organic world were caught up together in God's preparing, birthing, and perfecting grace.

3. Wolf, *What is Posthumanism*, 56.
4. Wolf, *What is Posthumanism*, 47.
5. Ferrando, *Philosophical Posthumanism*, 1–6.
6. Wesley, *Works*, 32:97–266.

Human Understanding and the Image of God

Two of Wesley's earliest sermons deal directly with questions of theological anthropology. Sermon 140, "The Promise of Understanding," was preached at All Saints, Oxford on 1 November 1730.[7] The sermon was based on the words of Jesus spoken to Simon Peter when he washed his disciples' feet, as recorded in John 13:7, "You do not know what I am doing, but later you will understand." A rebuke to the sin of intellectual pride, it sets forth a rigorous body-soul dualism and stresses the limitations of human knowledge and the consequent need to depend, in humility, upon divine revelation. Wesley shares the Aristotelian conviction that the desire for knowledge brings great pleasure and is a "delightful" and "useful inclination." He warns, however, that it should be "contained within proper bounds and directed to proper objects."[8] The desire to know all that could be known of God would be a futile exercise since God's ways are unsearchable. Though we daily observe the natural world all around us, we cannot know how it is held together by divine wisdom and power. Wesley conceded that it is the force of gravity that holds the stars and planets in place but insists that we cannot know *how* it does so. "We know it is the law of nature; it is the finger of God, and here our knowledge ends."[9] This principle of the limits of scientific investigation holds true also for the attempt to understand the connection between the body and the soul.

> Who knoweth how God holds his soul in life? How he encloseth spirit in matter? How he so intimately joins two substances of so totally different natures? How he who establishes it at first, so still preserves that exact dependence of one on the other? Who knows how the thought of his inmost soul immediately strikes the outmost part of his body? How an impression made on the outmost part of his body immediately strikes his inmost soul? How a consciousness in the mind of having done anything amiss instantly spreads a blush over the cheek? How the prick of a needle on the hand immediately occasions a painful thought in the soul?[10]

Only in the eschaton will humanity understand how God, "effected and maintained that amazing union between the body and the soul of

---

7. Wesley, *Works*, 4:279–91.

8. Wesley, *Works*, 4:281–82.

9. Wesley, *Works*, 4:283.

10. Wesley, *Works*, 4:283.

man, that astonishing correspondence between spirit and matter between perishing dust and immortal flame!"[11] This may seem naïve today when the science of neurobiology has taken us so much further down the road toward understanding the connection between the mind and the body, the thoughts and the feelings.[12] Early psychological studies such as Burton's encyclopedic *Anatomy of Melancholy* (1621) had explored emotional states and their affects upon the body but works that approached a more modern scientific approach such as William Murray's *Treatise on Emotional Disorders* (1866) were still more than a century away.[13]

Sermon 141, "The Image of God" was preached at St. Mary's, Oxford on 15 November 1730, only two weeks after "The Promise of Understanding." It is based on the simple and elegant statement of Gen 1:27, "So God created humankind in his image." Wesley follows the Cambridge Platonists in attributing an "original righteousness" to Adam, and medieval thinkers such as Maimonides in assigning a high degree of intellectual and moral perfection to the human progenitors described in the book of Genesis. The fall of humanity is understood as a loss of its original goodness in terms of the intellect, the will, and the affections.

Recent discussion among theologians on the image of God has broadened beyond identifying certain qualities such as reason, conscience, or will, as constituting the image of God in humanity. Instead, the focus has been on a more functional and relational approach, insisting on seeing the image of God as a way of being and acting in the world.[14] Marc Cortez proposes a way forward by bringing the functional and relational models together through a consideration of the themes of Representation, Presence, and Covenant. The human person represents God in creation and has the responsibility of stewardship toward it.[15] This representative function is more than merely symbolic; God is actually personally present in creation through human beings, most definitively (and in a unique way) in the person of Jesus Christ. On this understanding, the image of God becomes

11. Wesley, *Works*, 4:288.

12. Frijda et al., *Emotions and Beliefs*.

13. Burton, *Anatomy of Melancholy*; Murray, *Treatise on Emotional Disorders*; Trotter, *View of the Nervous Temperament*.

14. Cortez, *Theological Anthropology*, 13–40, helpfully outlines areas of agreement and disagreement on the image of God among theologians.

15. Cortez uses the terms "dominion" and "rulership," but these are problematic from an eco-theological perspective with the connotation of environmental exploitation and degradation.

a task (or even a mission) rather than a static quality or set of qualities. God continues to unfold God's purposes in and through the covenantal relationships established in the Gospel narrative. This should not be understood, however, to be confined to what the church does or what Christians do, since God's covenant is with all creation.[16]

The sermon begins with the insistence that "the image of the Divine parent" remains visible upon humanity, in spite of its evident imperfections and suffering, and with a rejection of the idea that human beings should be classed among the other animals. Wesley then sets out to enquire, "how man was made in the image of God . . . how he lost that image, and . . . how he may recover it."[17] The image of God consisted in certain divine capacities being shared with human beings, including an unfailing capacity to see things as they really were, without errors of thought of any kind. This faultless comprehension was something swift, almost immediate, as evidenced by Adam's naming of the animals.

Alongside these perfect reasoning capacities sat an even more noble quality—affections ruled by love. "[M]an was what God is—Love. Love filled the whole expansion of his soul; it possessed him without a rival. Every movement of his heart was love; it knew no other fervour. Love was his vital heat; it was the genial warmth that animated his whole frame." This love flowed not only toward God but to "all sensitive natures inasmuch as they too were [God's] offspring," and especially toward fellow human beings who shared the divine image.[18]

One final quality in this suite of perfections was perfect liberty—a freedom unencumbered by any outside influences or determinants. Not even God, much less any fellow creature, could force the original human pair to act in any way whatsoever. Every choice, every action, was their own, freely made without compulsion of any kind. These perfections of understanding, affections, and will were then crowned with happiness—"to live was to enjoy . . . to indulge in rivers of pleasure, ever new, ever pure from any mixture of pain."[19] How was it, then, given such evident perfections and happiness, that humanity fell from its original state and experienced the shattering

16. See also Green, *Body, Soul and Human Life,* 61–71.

17. Wesley, *Works,* 4:292–93. For a good discussion of Wesley's doctrine of the image of God including the Natural Image, Political Image, and Moral Image see Collins, *Theology of John Wesley,* 49–86 and Runyon, *New Creation,* 13–25.

18. Wesley, *Works,* 4:294–95.

19. Wesley, *Works,* 4:295.

of the perfect image of God? It was necessary, argued Wesley, that Adam should be tested, as liberty requires the power of contrary choice.

Of course, Wesley takes the Genesis account quite literally, and one of the more interesting and curious elements in the sermon is the connection drawn between the eating of the forbidden fruit and atherosclerosis, the building up of fats and cholesterol on the walls of the arteries. This speculation arises out of the prior claim that "man even at his creation was a compound of matter and spirit."[20]

> [I]t was ordained by the original law that during this vital union neither part of the compound should act at all but together with its companion; that the dependence of each upon the other should be inviolately maintained that even the operations of the soul should so far depend upon the body as to be exerted in a more or less perfect manner, as this was more or less aptly disposed.[21]

This psychosomatic union forms the basis of Wesley's explanation (admittedly speculative) of how the eating of the forbidden fruit may have led to physical death. The fruit of the tree, about which Adam was warned by God, may have possessed some agent that caused the juice to cling to "the inner coats of the finer vessels" of the human body. This, combined with the build-up of other particles floating loosely in the blood, laid "a foundation for numberless disorders in all parts of the machine," leading ultimately to death. Had Adam eaten of the corresponding Tree of Life, its fruit would have introduced an "abstersive" (that is, "cleansing") agent that would have functioned as a curative thus preserving his original immortality.[22] But before physical death achieved its destructive end, the human creature lost its perfect understanding, affections, and freedom, to be replaced by error, ignorance, "vile affections," and an enslaved will.[23]

We may well smile at this explanation, with its assumption of a literal reading of the text that depends upon the naïve acceptance of a narrative that is now understood in mythic rather than historic terms. Such a view of an originally perfect human state corrupted by the physical properties of a species of fruit certainly does not match with the present scientific account of human origins. What is of greater interest, however, is the way that Wesley attempts a scientific explanation (by necessity an eighteenth-century

20. Wesley, Works, 4:296.
21. Wesley, *Works*, 4:296.
22. Wesley, *Works*, 4:296–97.
23. Wesley, *Works*, 4:297–99.

one) of the events recounted in the text. He receives the canonical authority of the Scriptures but wants at the same time to think through its scientific implications. Far from religion and science being pitted against each other, it is the very fact that Wesley accepts the Genesis account of creation and fall as literal history that he is able to attempt a scientific explanation. When the account is treated as myth or saga there is no need for any scientific exploration of the text at all, and the kind of creative and constructive interpretive path that Wesley makes is never even opened up.

Such an exalted view of the original human condition might suggest a backward-looking orientation toward a pristine paradise as if the perfected human being were situated in a now irretrievable past. We will see, however, that Wesley's concept of the divinely perfected human being lies in the future and that such a human being will exhibit even higher qualities. Eve and Adam possessed an original innocence but in the new creation their daughters and sons will exhibit holiness, understood not simply as the absence of imperfection but as the superabundance of love.

What is a Human Being?

Wesley wrote two sermons with the title "What is Man?" both based on selected verses from Psalm 8. Neither were actually preached by Wesley (at least as far as we know); they are instead essays setting forth his theological anthropology.[24] The first was written in Manchester in July 1787 and is based on Ps 8:3–4 in the Authorised Version, "When I consider thy heavens; the work of thy fingers, the moon and the stars, which thou has ordained; What is man, that thou art mindful of him? And the son of man that thou visitest him?" On the one hand, humanity is described in this sermon as an insignificant speck in the midst of a vast universe. On the other, human beings are the objects of God's redeeming love and as such have eternal significance. Certain features of the sermon suggest that it may have been influenced by Joseph Addison's essay on Psalm 8 which had been published in The Spectator in July 1714. Albert Outler noted how this, in comparison with the earlier (1730) sermon on "The Image of God," shows a late career Wesley returning to theological anthropology, "having neglected it in his oral preaching during the years between."[25]

---

24. Wesley, Works, 3:454–63.

25. Outler, "Introductory Comment," in Wesley, Works, 3:455.

Wesley sets out to consider humanity in two respects—as to "magnitude" and as to "duration." Rejecting the popularly held world population figure of 400 million, he suggests a much larger estimate of "four thousand millions."[26] What is one person in the face of such numbers? The earth itself is a small planet compared with others in the solar system, and the solar system, in turn, but a tiny corner of the visible galaxy which, for all we know, may be dwarfed by a larger unseen universe. In the light of infinity, "would not reason suggest to us that so diminutive a creature would be overlooked by [God] in the immensity of [God's] works?"[27]

Turning to a consideration of humanity's duration, Wesley notes the temporary nature of life and the shortness of our days. Citing the biblical seventy years (the "threescore years and ten" of Ps 90:10) and Methuselah's 960 years (Gen 5:25, 27), he observes that such lifespans are less than nothing compared to eternity.[28] What the Psalmist appears not to have noticed is, "that the body is not the man; that man is not only a house of clay but an immortal spirit, a spirit made in the image of God, an incorruptible picture of the God of glory; a spirit that is of infinitely more value than . . . the whole material creation . . . more durable, not liable to either dissolution or decay."[29] The greatest proof of God's loving concern for "little, short-lived man," and "especially to his immortal part," is the coming to earth of God's Son "in fashion as a man," to die "for us . . . and for our salvation."[30]

There follows a consideration of whether there is life on other worlds and therefore other beings for whom God has a special concern. At one stage convinced that this was the case, in the end it was the finding of a Dutch scientist that convinced him otherwise. He was aware (and at one point convinced by) the claims of those like Louis Dutens and Bernard Le Bovier de Fontenelle who believed in the plurality of worlds and therefore, in extra-terrestrial life, but came to reject this hypothesis on the basis of an absence of scientific evidence.[31] "Suppose there were millions of worlds," Wesley argues, "yet God may see, in the abyss of his infinite wisdom, reasons that do not appear to us why he saw good to show this mercy to

26. Wesley, *Works*, 3:456.

27. Wesley, *Works* 3:458.

28. Wesley, *Works* 3:458–59.

29. Wesley, *Works*, 3:460.

30. Wesley, *Works*, 3:460–61.

31. Wesley mentions Bernard Le Bovier de Fontenelle's *Conversations on the Plurality of Worlds* in his *Survey of the Wisdom of God in Creation* (1763). See *Works*, 3:461 n. 47.

ours in preference to thousands of millions of other worlds."[32] Wesley's rejection of the "plurality of worlds" hypothesis was, at least in part, motivated by the fact that many of those who opposed Christianity supported the idea. However, he had also read (in 1759) the Dutch mathematician Christiaan Huygens (1629–1695) whose *Celestial Worlds Discovered, Or Conjectures on the Planetary Worlds* (first translated into English in 1689) had originally argued that rational creatures inhabited the moon and other planets in the solar system. Huygens later recanted that view (at least in regard to the moon) because he believed he had demonstrated on the basis of his study of lunar and solar eclipses that the moon had no atmosphere. Wesley concluded, "I *know* the earth is [inhabited]. Of the rest I know nothing."[33] Wesley's pious conclusion is that it is useless to speculate on how many inhabited worlds God *may* have created. It is enough to know that 'the almighty Creator hath shown [greater] regard to these poor little creatures of a day' than even to angels, by giving his Son to live and die for them.[34] What is really interesting here is the blending of theological and scientific claims. The privileging of humanity as made in the image of God and therefore significant no matter how infinitesimal within the vastness of the universe is a theological conviction. But the question of whether there are other inhabited worlds is settled in equal measure by a scientist's observations of the lunar and solar eclipses.

In May 1788, four months after Arthur Phillip sailed his eleven ships into Botany Bay, opening up the final leg of the British overseas expansion into the Antipodes, John Wesley wrote his sermon "What is Man?" in the midst of a preaching tour through the Midlands.[35] Based on Ps 8:4 in the 1611 Authorized Version ("What is man, that thou art mindful of him? and the son of man, that thou visitest him?"), sermon 116 especially reflects eighteenth-century scientific views of human biology, including the idea that the body is interlaced with fibers that carry "various fluids constantly circulating through the whole machine."[36]

Albert Outler identified this sermon's view of the body as a complicated machine as reflecting the "third-generation Cartesianism" found in such works as Julien Offray de La Mettrie's *L'Homme Machine* (1748), Paul-Henri

32. Wesley, *Works*, 3:461.
33. Wesley, *Works*, 21:229–30.
34. Wesley, *Works*, 3:463.
35. Wesley, *Works*, 4:20–27.
36. Wesley, *Works*, 4:20.

Thiry, Baron D'Holbach's *Systeme de la Nature* (1770) and David Hartley's *Observations on Man* (1749).[37] Where these writers (with the probable exception of Hartley) denied the existence of the soul, Wesley maintained his usual body-soul dualism. In this he followed the tradition of the Cambridge Platonist John Norris (1657–1712) and the French philosopher Nicholas Malebranche (1638–1715) who both in their own ways offered creative and original developments of Cartesian ideas.

For Wesley, the human body was a "curious machine," something that one finds fascinating and puzzling. He describes how "a little portion of earth, the particles of which cohering I know not how, lengthen into innumerable fibres, a thousand times finer than hairs. These, crossing each other in all directions, are strangely wrought into membranes; and these membranes are as strangely wrought into arteries, veins, nerves, and glands; all of which contain various fluids, constantly circulating through the whole machine." The elements of air, fire, and water circulate through the body via an "engine fitted for that purpose." Every particle of air contains also an "ethereal" particle of water and of fire, and these are mingled with the blood.[38] Interestingly, Wesley attributes the circulation of the blood not to the heart but to the lungs, or more precisely to the ethereal fire produced by the lungs, which are described as a "curious fire pump."

> [T]he cause usually assigned for [the circulation of the blood], namely, the force of the heart, is altogether inadequate to the supposed effect. No one supposes the force of the heart, in a strong man, to be more than equal to the weight of three thousand pounds. Whereas it would require a force equal to the weight of a hundred thousand pounds, to propel the blood from the heart through all the arteries. This can only be effected by the ethereal fire contained in the blood itself, assisted by the elastic force of the arteries through which it circulates.[39]

In addition to this scientific description, Wesley posits also the existence of a soul, "something in me that thinks . . . and feels," an "inward principle" consisting of thought, will and affections situated (it is speculated) "in some part of [the] head; but whether in the pineal gland, or in any part of the brain, I am not able to determine."[40] Wesley's body-soul dualism is

37. Outler, "Introductory Comment," in Wesley, *Works*, 4:19.
38. Wesley, *Works*, 4:20–21.
39. Wesley, *Works*, 4:21.
40. Wesley, *Works*, 4:21–22.

expressed nicely in the following rhetorical flourish, which is also helpful in opening up reflection on the future state of human beings.

> Unquestionably I am something distinct from my body . . . For when my body dies I shall not die; I shall exist as really as I did before. And I cannot but believe this self-moving, thinking principle, with all its passions and affections, will continue to exist although the body be mouldered into dust. Indeed at present this body is so intimately connected with the soul that I seem to consist of both. In my present state of existence I undoubtedly consist both of soul and body. And so I shall be again after the resurrection to all eternity.[41]

This last observation should not be passed over too quickly. Wesley's body-soul dualism is not a Platonic separation in which the soul is ultimately the only truly valuable thing and the body simply a prison for the soul, destined for an ignoble end in disintegration. Rather, body and soul are designed to be joined in a union which, though sundered temporarily at death, will be reunited and preserved at the resurrection. As Randy Maddox (among others) has convincingly shown, "John Wesley consciously challenged the restriction of a Christian's present concern to spiritual dimensions of salvation."[42] The new creation will be an embodied, material creation and human beings will participate in it, not as disembodied souls floating on ethereal clouds, but in a union of body and soul that will interact with and impact upon a range of other material life forms. The purpose of life being bestowed upon human beings is that they might "prepare for [this] eternity."[43]

On the cusp of what came to be known as the industrial revolution, the idea that the human body was a finely wrought machine perfectly matched the mentalité of the age. The attempt to locate the soul in a particular part of the brain indicates a scientific concern that matches the theological affirmation of the soul's existence. Wesley's body-soul dualism also points teleologically toward an embodied new creation.

---

41. Wesley, *Works*, 4:23.

42. Maddox, "Salvation as Flourishing," 13.

43. Wesley, *Works*, 4:25–27.

The New Creation

Placing Wesley into precise eschatological categories is difficult but, generally speaking, his views may be described as "postmillennial," in that he anticipated a gradual conversion of the world to Christianity taking place before Christ's return. He anticipated that a global revival would take place which would spread from nation to nation until the whole globe was Christianized and only then would Christ return.[44] Wesley believed that God would accomplish a global renovation, restoring the world and all its inhabitants to the condition designed for them by God, not to be accomplished by irresistible grace but by God's persuasive grace working in the hearts of all so that they would be drawn to co-operate with the offer of transformative grace in both the personal and political spheres.[45] He placed the revival taking place in his own time in the context of this anticipated cosmic renewal, seeing it as the birth pangs of such a universal renovation.[46] Wesley's broadly postmillennial eschatology might suggest a rigid determinism as if the shape of the future were divinely determined, which would conflict with futurist anticipations of the diversity of possible worlds that may emerge. Wesley's rejection of Calvinistic determinism in favor of an Arminian understanding of grace-enabled freedom is helpful here. While the final telos of the cosmos is secured by divine omnipotence, the range of possible futures is limitless, due to the genuinely free human choices that are made in response to God.

There are a number of late-career sermons that give us insight into Wesley's eschatological views, a number of which will be examined here. Sermon 60, "The General Deliverance," first appeared in *The Arminian Magazine* in 1782.[47] Based on Rom 8:19–22, with its picture of creation groaning to be delivered from its present bondage to share in the "glorious liberty of the children of God," it is, in part, a theodicy, asking how the love of God to all creatures is compatible with the suffering we see around us. Wesley borrows the title from a 1742 essay by John Hildrop (c. 1680–1756), who had applied the Platonic concept of a "chain of being" to explain the degradation of animal species as a result of human sin. Where Hildrop

---

44. The more pessimistic Premillennial system (at least the Dispensational variety) which saw everything getting worse and worse until Jesus came to "rapture" the church and judge the world had yet to make its appearance.

45. Wesley, *Works*, 2:488–90.

46. Wesley, *Works*, 2:491–95.

47. Wesley, *Works*, 2:436–50.

placed human beings and animals on a continuum, Wesley gives humanity the role of "conveying" God to animals.[48]

Wesley begins by asserting the mercy of God over all creation, and God's awareness of the pleasure, pain, happiness, or misery of every living being.[49] How is this mercy consistent with the obvious suffering experienced by animals? The problem of animal suffering is especially acute, since they are not moral beings, yet they experience suffering along with humanity as a result of the fall. Wesley then considers, "the original state of the brute creation" and concludes that animals shared with human beings, self-motion, understanding, will, and liberty. This is significant in that these qualities are designated, "the natural image of God," suggesting that, at least in some sense, animals possessed this natural image. The only difference between humanity and other creatures is that "man is capable of God; the inferior creatures are not."[50]

These capacities in humanity were perfect in every way, enabling the first humans to derive immense pleasure and happiness from the natural world.

> He saw with unspeakable pleasure the order, the beauty, the harmony of all the creatures; of all animated, all inanimate nature—the serenity of the skies, the sun walking in brightness, the sweetly variegated clothing of the earth, the trees, the fruits, the flowers, "And liquid lapse of murmuring streams [uninterrupted] by evil of any kind."[51]

Humanity functioned as the channel of conveyance between God and the "brute creation," and when this channel was blocked or broken the great diversity of animal species was plunged into the Fall along with humanity. Wesley points to the loss of reason among the lower animals, even suggesting that prior to the Fall, "Perhaps insects and worms had

---

48. See the discussion by Outler in the "Introductory Comment" to the sermon for the background in Wesley, *Works*, 2:436.

49. Wesley makes this point also in sermon 67, "On Divine Providence," asserting that God is concerned "every moment for what befalls every creature upon earth; and more especially for anything that befalls any of the children of men." This may seem hard to believe considering the "complicated wickedness" and "complicated misery" we see on every side. Yet it remains true that all God's wisdom is employed for the good of all creatures, both human and non-human. Wesley, *Works*, 2:540.

50. Wesley, *Works*, 2:438–42.

51. Wesley, *Works*, 2:439–40.

then as much understanding as the most intelligent brutes have now."[52] Extrapolating from that hypothesis, higher, more complex species might have possessed rational capacities we now associate with human beings. In the present dispensation, the brute creation groans in mutual predation and though we close our eyes to their pain, God does not. "[God] knoweth all their pain, and is bringing them nearer and nearer to the birth which shall be accomplished in its season," when "the whole animated creation" will be delivered from its present frustration.[53] The promise in Rev 21:3–5 that God will "make all things new" and eliminate all death and pain will take place "not only on the children of men—there is no such restriction in the text—but . . . on every creature according to its capacity."[54] That Wesley sees animals as participating in the bodily resurrection is made clear in his description of their enhanced physical powers, their peaceful temperament, their beauty, and their happiness, to be enjoyed in a future perennial spring, when "their corruptible body has put on incorruption."[55]

Though he maintains that God has a special concern for human beings, Wesley nonetheless insists that, "God regards everything that he hath made in its own order, and in proportion to that measure of his own image which he has stamped upon it."[56] He foresees the possibility of animals being exalted to the present intellectual ability of human beings, speculating that God might even give animals the capacity to know and love God.

> May I be permitted to conjecture concerning the brute creation? What if it should then please the all-wise, the all-gracious Creator to raise them higher in the scale of beings? What if it should please him, when he makes us "equal to angels," to make them what we are now? Creatures capable of God? Capable of knowing, and loving, and enjoying the Author of their being? If it should be so, ought our eye be evil because he is good? However this be, he will certainly do what will be most for his own glory.[57]

Remembering that it was the enjoyment of God that was earlier said to be the one aspect of the image of God that animals did not bear, what we have here is an astonishing anticipation of the stamping of the image

52. Wesley, *Works*, 2:442.
53. Wesley, *Works*, 2:445.
54. Wesley, *Works*, 2:445–46.
55. Wesley, *Works*, 2:446–47, citing 1 Cor 15:53–54.
56. Wesley, *Works*, 2:447–48.
57. Wesley, *Works*, 2:448.

of God on non-human animals in the new creation. Here, then, lies the answer to the problem of affirming a God of mercy in the face of the suffering of animals who are not moral agents. "[T]he objection vanishes away if we consider that something better remains after death for these poor creatures also [and that they] shall then receive an ample amends for all their suffering."[58] Such an enlarged vision takes Wesley's theology well beyond anthropocentrism into a teleology that embraces the entire creation as the arena of divine purpose and cosmic renewal.

The inclusion of non-human animals in the new creation may also provide a foundation for opposition to animal cruelty and ethical choices such as vegetarianism and veganism. At very least, it necessitates an opposition to any form of animal cruelty.

> One more excellent end may undoubtedly be answered by the preceding considerations. They may encourage us to imitate him whose mercy is over all his works. They may soften our hearts towards the meaner creatures, knowing that the Lord careth for them. It may enlarge our hearts toward those poor creatures to reflect that, as vile as they appear in our eyes, not one of them is forgotten in the sight of our Father which is in heaven. Through all the vanity to which they are now subjected, let us look to what God hath prepared for them. Yea, let us habituate ourselves to look forward, beyond this present scene of bondage, to the happy time when they will be delivered therefrom into the liberty of the children of God.[59]

Sermon 63, "The General Spread of the Gospel" based on Isa 11:9, "The earth shall be full of the knowledge of the Lord, as the waters cover the sea," was written in Dublin in April 1783.[60] It first describes the utterly miserable condition of the world in Wesley's own time and then goes on to describe his hopes for universal redemption. Wesley's description of the "heathen" of the South Seas significantly contrasts with Rousseau's "noble savage" ideal. Far from living in an untouched paradise of innocence they are shown to be as corrupt in morals as any European. Moslems, Orthodox Christians, Catholics, and Protestants are in no better condition.[61] In spite of this very negative view of a humanity steeped in sin, Wesley nonetheless

58. Wesley, *Works*, 2:449.
59. Wesley, *Works*, 2:449.
60. Wesley, *Works*, 2:485–99.
61. Wesley, *Works*, 2:485–88.

holds a postmillennial theology of hope (though "theology of hope" is not a term he or his contemporaries would have used). Perhaps drawing on his own experience as a field preacher as much as on the scriptures, he asserts that, "The wise, the learned, the men of genius, the philosophers" will be the last to enter the kingdom. Wesley describes this time as "the grand Pentecost," where there will again be that quality of life described in the early chapters of the Book of Acts. Muslims, Jews, Native Americans, and all other peoples will be convinced to convert to the Christian faith as a result of the holy lives exhibited by Christians.[62] There is a "colonizing" element here, that is difficult for us to accept without challenge, and more contemporary approaches have found ways to see prevenient grace operating *within* other religions, without the need for conversion to Christianity in order to bring about God's renewing purposes for the planet.[63] But leaving aside the claims of exclusivity, the vision of universal restoration remains a compelling anticipation of a new and better world. Behind this sermon is an attempt to offer a theodicy as well as to instill confidence in a future state of "universal holiness and happiness."

> This I apprehend to be the answer, yea, the only full and satisfactory answer that can be given, to the objection of the wisdom and goodness of God, taken from the present state of the world. It will not always be thus: these things are only permitted for a season by the great Governor of the world that he may draw immense, eternal good out of this temporary evil . . . All unprejudiced persons may see with their eyes that he is already renewing the face of the earth. And we have strong reason to hope that he . . . will never intermit this blessed work of his Spirit until he has fulfilled all his promises; until he hath put a period to sin and misery, and infirmity, and death; and re-established universal holiness and happiness.[64]

It is important to note here that Wesley does not see God acting to renew the earth simply by exerting the power of omnipotence, in an act of divine fiat. Instead, God will work persuasively, not setting aside the human intellect, or freedom of action.[65] It is easy to see in such a context

---

62. Wesley, *Works*, 2:495–99.

63. Bounds, "Wesleyan Eschatological Implications," 10–32.

64. Wesley, *Works*, 2:499.

65. Kenneth J. Collins rejects this idea, however, arguing that while there is a "progressive" and "incremental" pattern to the establishing of Christ's millennial reign (something about which Wesley had rather muddled and idiosyncratic views), the new

how the technology developed by human beings can be the sphere of divine action, operating co-operatively within human industry, insight, and discovery to fulfill God's purposes.

Sermon 64, "The New Creation," is another of Wesley's sermons on the theme of cosmic redemption and gives us further insight into his eschatological views.[66] Written in 1785, it includes many speculations, and reflects his unfaltering optimism of grace. He rejects the historicist view that "the new heaven and the new earth," spoken of in Revelation 21, refers only to the age of Constantine, and asserts that the "line of this prophecy reaches father still. It does not end with the present world but shows us the things that will come to pass when this world is no more."[67] Wesley looks forward instead to remarkable changes in the galaxies above us and in the earth's own atmosphere and elements. The plant and animal kingdoms will also share in this cosmic renewal. Wesley indulged in some rather speculative theories about the end of the old earth, which sound like every apocalyptic disaster film ever made—perhaps the present world will end with a comet, a global lightning storm, or a volcanic eruption. In any case, the old world will be replaced by one that has all the elements of the first, but with the destructive potential removed. There will be fire, but without destruction, air without tempests, water without floods, earth without earthquakes, gardens without thorns, animals elevated to a higher level of consciousness and humans no longer exploiting or harming their fellow creatures. Rather, they will enjoy harmonious companionship with other species, through their constant shared communion with God.[68]

Such a vision of the new creation helps to answer the critique of those, such as Ludwig Feuerbach, who reject the traditional view of heaven as merely a futile projection of human desire, "the present in the mirror of the imagination," a wish fulfillment that guarantees heavenly reward to compensate for this world's suffering.[69] In such a view the idea of a mythical heaven turns us away from the needs of our earthly lives to neglect human concerns in favor of the afterlife. In response to this, some theologians have attempted a theology without eschatology, or collapsed eschatology

creation itself will be the work of God alone, "as an utter gift lavished upon the saints." Collins, *Theology of John Wesley*, 316.

66. Wesley, *Works*, 2:500–10.

67. Wesley, *Works*, 2:501–2.

68. Wesley, *Works*, 2:503–10.

69. Feuerbach, *Essence of Christianity*, 182.

entirely into a "realized eschatology" with an exclusive "this-world" focus. But Feuerbach's critique only holds if we imagine a disembodied ethereal heaven that exists as a purely spiritual reality. The expectation of a renewed material creation, on the other hand, fills our actions in this present world with eschatological significance. Just as the human body matters and is valued because it will participate in the resurrection, so the wider world of matter and all its life forms have significance because they also will participate in the new creation. Human industry, science, culture, technology, and enhancement all matter, because they are participation with divine action and anticipations of the new creation.[70]

Conclusion

Drawing on Andy Miah, Ferrando points out that Posthuman discourse does not simply ask about moving beyond humanness but asks what insights have been missed by relying on the anthropocentric viewpoint.[71] What is absent in the theology shaped by the Enlightenment that posthumanism might recover? In what sense might John Wesley's theological anthropology coupled with his eschatological views contribute to such a move? First, it shows that ideas about the future state of human existence are not bound historically by the period "after Humanism." Wesley's "post-Humanism" (if we may call it that) emerges in the eighteenth century on the cusp of the Industrial Revolution and during a time when the healing capacities of electricity and other forms of technology were just becoming known. Wesley held the traditional view of human beings as uniquely made in the image of God, and thus sitting at the top of creation's pyramid of life forms. Other animals possess certain aspects of the *imago dei*, such as self-motion, and some degree of reason, conscience, and will, but only human beings may enjoy God (at least so he argues). Yet these human beings are set on a teleological trajectory that will see them inhabit a restored universe in which other species share a deeper level of connection with God and with each other than they presently enjoy. He anticipated a time when the rationality, affectivity, and volitional capacities of non-human

70. Kenneth Wilson reflects such an idea when he states that in Methodist theology, "love of God and love of neighbour constitute a seamless activity which must include love of God's world in all its dimensions," so that the public life of Christians in the present is a participation in the new creation. Wilson, *Methodist Theology*, 117.

71. Ferrando, *Philosophical Posthumanism*, 22.

species would be expanded to enable unprecedented non-human enjoyment of God. He did not limit God's saving purposes to the human species but saw other sentient beings (and even things without sentience) as the objects of God's providential action and as participants in the new creation. Without dislodging humanity from its role as a unique image-bearer, he broadened the scope of eschatological expectation well beyond the "salvation of souls" to a restored material universe in which the forces of nature are perfectly balanced, no longer the target of rapacious human exploitation. His eschatology is therefore "Posthuman" in the sense that it is situated *after* the Anthropocene and does not limit God's saving purpose to the fate of human beings alone.

Though this chapter has focused on posthuman elements in Wesley's thought, there are also "transhuman" dimensions in the sense that he enthusiastically embraced cutting-edge technology as a sphere in which divine action is revealed and believed that the application of such technology contributed to human flourishing and human enhancement. He appropriated positively the most advanced scientific theories and technologies of his age to address the problems of human existence while recognizing at the same time the noetic effects of sin upon human industry and endeavor. His recommendation of electrical cures, for example, held great potential for people to take responsibility for their own health and not be taken advantage of by a medical fraternity in its infancy. He argued for access to new technology on an equitable and just economic basis to enhance human wellness. Reaching back to ancient paths of wisdom, he also saw in the blending of theological discourse, scientific experimentation, and technological advances, the anticipation of a future cosmic renewal and a universe guided toward the fulfillment of its divine purpose.

Bibliography

Bounds, Christopher T. "Wesleyan Eschatological Implications for the Church's Engagement with Other Religions." *Aldersgate Papers* 11 (June 2015) 10–32.

Collins, Kenneth J. *The Theology of John Wesley: Holy Love and the Shape of Grace.* Nashville: Abingdon, 2007.

Cortez, Marc. *Theological Anthropology: A Guide for the Perplexed.* London: T. & T. Clark, 2010.

Ferrando, Francesca. *Philosophical Posthumanism.* London: Bloomsbury Academic, 2019.

Frijda, Nico H., et al., eds. *Emotions and Beliefs: How Feelings Influence Thoughts.* Cambridge: Cambridge University Press, 2000.

Feuerbach, Ludwig. *The Essence of Christianity*. Translated by Marian Evans. London: Kegan Paul, Trench, Trubner and Co., 1890.

Green, Joel B. *Body, Soul and Human Life: The Nature of Humanity in the Bible*. Grand Rapids: Baker, 2008.

Maddox, Randy. "Salvation as Flourishing for the Whole Creation." In *Wesleyan Perspectives on Human Flourishing*, edited by Dean G. Smith and Rob A. Fringer, 1–23. Eugene, OR: Wipf and Stock, 2021.

Murray, William. *A Treatise on Emotional Disorders of the Sympathetic System of Nerves*. New York, 1866.

Runyon, Theodore. *The New Creation: John Wesley's Theology for Today*. Nashville: Abingdon, 1998.

Sorgner, Stefan Lorenz. *On Transhumanism*. Translated by Spencer Hawkins. University Park: Pennsylvania State University Press, 2020.

Trotter, Thomas. *A View of the Nervous Temperament: Being a Practical Enquiry into the Increasing Prevalence, Prevention and Treatment of the Disease*. London, 1807.

Wesley, John. *The Works of John Wesley: Volume 2: Sermons II, 34–70*. Edited by Albert C. Outler. Nashville: Abingdon, 1985.

———. *The Works of John Wesley: Volume 3: Sermons III, 71–114*. Edited by Albert C. Outler. Nashville: Abingdon, 1986.

———. *The Works of John Wesley: Volume 4: Sermons IV, 115–151*. Edited by Albert C. Outler. Nashville: Abingdon, 1987.

———. *The Works of John Wesley: Volume 21: Journal and Diaries IV (1755-1765)*. Edited by W. Reginald Ward and Richard P. Heitzenrater. Nashville: Abingdon, 1992.

———. *The Works of John Wesley: Volume 32: Medical and Health Writings*. Edited by James G. Donat and Randy Maddox. Nashville: Abingdon, 2018.

Wilson, Kenneth. *Methodist Theology*. London: Bloomsbury, 2011.

Wolfe, Cary. *What is Posthumanism?* Minneapolis: University of Minnesota Press, 2010.

2

Tracing the Contours of a Biblical Techno-Theology

Genesis 1–11 and the Story of God

ARSENY ERMAKOV

Introduction

A WESLEYAN CONVERSATION ABOUT technology—its social, economic, religious, cultural, and environmental impact and the future it ushers in—is unimaginable without turning to the Scripture. Even in the age of genetic engineering and Artificial Intelligence, Wesleyan hermeneutics draws us to engage with the invaluable trove of inspired wisdom. What does the Bible say about technology? Where does it come from? What is the relationship between technology, humans, God, and the environment? Does it have a role to play in the story and the mission of God? Does the Bible identify any dangers related to technology? Does it have a future in the world to come? Some of those questions arise from modern experiences of technology and its increasing role in today's Western cultures. According to Noreen Herzfeld, in our time, technology ceased to be a mere tool for survival and turned into a worldview shaper. Modern people—for the first time in human history—started to define themselves and the environment through their relationship with technology.[1]

But what is technology? As with many other modern terms, "technology" comes to us from ancient Greek. *Technē* referred to "art," "skill," "craft," "a set of rules," or a "method for doing things," and described the work of artisans, artists, and rhetoricians.[2] This word appears a few times in the New Testament and in the majority of cases refers to "craft" and "trade" (e.g., Acts 19:24, 38; Heb 11:10; Rev 18:22). Acts 18:3 mentions that Paul, Aquila, and Priscilla were tentmakers by trade (*tē technē*). In the Hebrew Bible, the work of artisans is a reflection of their "skill, intelligence, and knowledge" (1 Kgs 7:14). However, modern definitions of technology go beyond the ancient understanding of arts and crafts. Ian McNeil observes that technology lies behind every human-made object which "has passed through the process of conception, testing, design, construction, refinement, to be finally brought to a serviceable state suitable for the market."[3] Yet, in a broad sense, technology is not just about making and using tools for creating certain objects and products; it involves the application of (scientific) knowledge and skills to resolve any practical issue by means of "techniques, processes, and goals."[4] Ultimately, technology could be seen as a way of utilizing and shaping the environment for the purposes arising from the necessities and aspirations of human existence. Thus, we live in a world where "technology is all around us,"[5] and is found in every aspect of modern human life: from the things we use to the food we eat, from where we live to what we wear, from the way we take care of our health to how we entertain ourselves, from how we travel to the way we work. The same is true of the world of Scripture.

It would not be an exaggeration to say that references to technology and its products are mentioned on almost every page of the Bible. The sheer amount of material renders impossible the task of drawing contours of a biblical theology of technology across scriptural narratives and traditions in the space of a single chapter.[6] Thus—in an attempt to capture some key

1. Herzfeld, "Surrogate, Partner or Tool," 123.

2. LSJ 1785.

3. McNeil, "Basic Tools," 1.

4. Herzfeld, "Surrogate, Partner or Tool," 122; Gerstein, *Story of Technology*, 46.

5. McNeil, "Basic Tools," 1.

6. For this paper, I am borrowing the language of contours and some hermeneutical insights from Methodist scholar, Bernard Anderson. Anderson, *Contours*, 3–36.

trajectories of "techno-theology" in the context of the "overarching narrative of Scripture"—I must attend to a less ambitious task.[7] Putting aside, for now, the issues related to history, archeology, and ancient mythologies, this paper will explore different aspects of the narrative representation of technology and its origins in the biblical primeval history and trace theological themes arising from the rest of the story of God.[8]

General Overview

To uncover the roots of technology in the Bible, "it is only logical" to turn to the story of origins, beginnings, and generations—to Genesis. The initial chapters of the prologue to Israel's story touch upon the origins of the cosmos and all the things in it (Gen 1–11) and reveal when certain technologies find their way into the life of the ancients. It does not take long in the Genesis timeline for the first humans to engage in activities that require knowledge, skills, and tools. The second generation, the sons of Adam and Eve, somehow already have knowledge of animal husbandry and crop production; Abel was "a keeper of sheep" and Cain "a tiller of the ground" (Gen 4:2). They are the ancestors of all shepherds and farmers. But the narrator does not provide any explanation of how the knowledge and practice of agriculture and husbandry came about.

The same could be said about the passing comment on Cain being the first city builder (Gen 4:17). Even if the "city" referred to was just a town, to build it was no mean task. It required not only knowledge of construction, sourcing of materials, and skills but also the organizing of people. Yet, no details are provided, suggesting that it is obvious to the implied readers how such things are done. As the story continues, with further generations come new technologies. Genesis 4:20–22 lists the ancestors of certain occupations: Jabal—grazers/ranchers, Jubal—artists, Tubal-cain—craftsmen. The eighth generation of Adam brings with it the practice and knowledge of animal husbandry, tentmaking, music, production of string and wind instruments, and bronze and iron tool crafting. All these technologies assume the existence of other practices such as woodwork, leatherwork, fabric-making, mining, and metalwork. The story of the Ark also implies that Noah is familiar with construction techniques

---

7. Bartholomew and Goheen, *Drama of Scripture*, 17–23.

8. For some historical and archeological insights see Greer et al., *Behind the Scenes*.

(Gen 6:14–16). The origins of viticulture and winemaking are also traced to Noah and his drinking incident (Gen 9:20–21).

Genesis 10 records the appearance of nations and lists Noah's notable descendants; it also notes activities that imply the use of technology. In the postdiluvian world, Nimrod becomes "a mighty warrior" and "a mighty hunter" (10:8–9). Here Genesis hints at the origins of both warfare and hunting which, in the ancient world, were essentially technological endeavors since both required weapons and techniques for their making and use. Nimrod is a morally ambiguous character since this first strongman and builder of an empire does not refrain from using violence—enhanced by technology—against humans and other creatures.[9]

The Tower of Babel story suggests innovation or a different approach to building technology. The builders of the tower decided, "Let us make bricks, and burn them thoroughly" (Gen 11:3). Their technique included burning mud/clay bricks in a kiln to make them stronger and more durable (instead of drying them in the sun) and the use of tar or bitumen (Heb. *homer*) as a bonding agent (e.g., Exod 2:3).[10] This invention allowed them to build more impressive structures—"a tower that reaches to the heavens" (Gen 11:4); perhaps a ziggurat-like temple tower or a defensive structure.[11] Some scholars note that the invention of bricks is one of the most significant building techniques and one that has lasted until today.[12] In the process of storytelling, the narrator also interjects with a technological parenthesis—an explanatory note—on how this technology is different from that employed by Jewish readers who used stone and mortar for their building projects (Gen 11:3).

From early on, the world of primeval history is filled with technology and its products: construction, crafts, tools, arts, warfare, hunting, agriculture, husbandry, developed cities, and kingdoms. Yet, it is quite apparent that Genesis does not provide a comprehensive catalog of technologies/crafts and their origins. Only a few are highlighted—perhaps those that bear importance for an implied Jewish readership—and the existence of others is assumed. This demonstrates the key feature of storytelling regarding technologies, which is a mix of direct references to their origins—etiologies—and reliance on the assumed knowledge of the implied reader.

9. Blenkinsopp, *Creation*, 160–64.
10. Goldingay, *Genesis*, 187; Westerman, *Genesis 1–11*, 546.
11. Blenkinsopp, *Creation*, 166–67; Goldingay, *Genesis*, 188.
12. Westermann, *Genesis 1–11*, 546.

Yet, when direct comments are made, they do not provide any details or extensive explanations. The nature of those passing comments suggests that the narrator is not particularly interested in the history of technology *per se*; the focus lies elsewhere.

A cursory reading of the biblical beginnings might suggest that technology originates with human beings and appears after their banishment from God's garden in Eden. In contrast to some origin stories in other surrounding ancient cultures, no claims are made that craftsmanship directly comes from God or that God reveals technological knowledge to humans.[13] Perhaps this is an invitation to probe the foundational stories of creation and see whether Genesis 1–3 hints at the divine origins of technology.

Creation Narratives

In the first creation story (Gen 1:1–2:4)—told in a rhythmic, formulaic, and somewhat poetic language—the narrator describes the ordering of the primeval chaos by Elohim through the following key verbs: speak (Heb. *amar*), create (Heb. *bara*), make (Heb. *asah*), separate (Heb. *badal*), name/call (Heb. *qara*), see (Heb. *raah*), and bless (Heb. *barak*). Such a word choice does not betray any notion of the technological nature of divine actions. Only two words appear in technological contexts in the Hebrew Bible: *bara* and *asah*. Predominantly used in reference to God's creation, *bara* is also employed to describe cutting down wood (Josh 17:15) or killing with swords (Ezek 23:47); it is hard to see how those technological connotations have any bearing on understanding this Genesis story. *Asah* appears from time to time in technological contexts—Noah makes the Ark (Gen 6:14–16) or Rebekah makes a meal (Gen 27:14)—but it is not necessarily a technical term associated with any particular craft. It is more likely a general word that refers—among other things—to doing something, making something, or working, and in this context does not have strong technical connotations.[14]

The first creation account reveals the apparent absence of substantive technological discourse or any references to technology. The creation of the world takes place through the power of the divine word that calls things into being and commands the earth "to bring forth" living things. Though

---

13. E.g., the artisan gods of Mesopotamia, Canaan, Egypt, and Greece: Enki/Ea, Kothar wa-Hasis, Ptah and Thoth, Hephaestus and Prometheus, etc.

14. BDB 793–95.

divine commands to human beings (Gen 1:28), who are "the image of God," to procreate, fill the earth, subdue, and have dominion over animals, lack clear technological connotations, the latter two imperatives, could be understood as a mandate for animal husbandry but perhaps not for hunting.[15] However, another biblical tradition unapologetically interprets the act of creation in technological terms. Proverbs 8:22–31 recasts the story of creation and points to the role of pre-existent and personified Wisdom as *amon* or "a skilled craftsman," "a master workman," or "an architect" beside God (Prov 8:30).[16] Terry Grey notes:

> . . . Wisdom is understood to operate in synergy with God in the creative enterprise. She, alone with God, is present at creation and thus has knowledge of all its secrets. She "knows" and comprehends the very fabric of the cosmos. Pseudo-Solomon in the end declares that Wisdom is the "fashioner of all things"—πάντων τεχνῖτις—*technitis* (Wisdom 7:22, he uses this phrase again in 8:6; see also 8:5b). This term first arises in inscriptions from Delphi dated in the second century BCE. *Technitis* may be translated craftswoman (feminine substantive), artisan, designer.[17]

Later rabbinic thought also compares God to an architect or an engineer who is guided by Wisdom or Torah in the creation of the cosmos: from design to execution, from aesthetics to functionality.[18] A similar notion of God being an architect (*technitēs*) and a builder (*dēmiourgos*) is found in Heb 11:10.

The second creation narrative (Gen 2–3), however, does not only have a different literary style and theological perspective to the first one; parts of its language, assumptions, and storytelling are based on exposure to ancient technology. A few observations can be made. First, the process of the creation of the first human is described as "to form" (Heb. *yatsar*); as distinct from "make" (*asah*; Gen 1:27) or "create" (*bara*; Gen 1:28) employed in the first story.[19] Elsewhere in the Bible, this language of *forming* or *fashioning* is used to describe the work of an artisan: a potter who shapes objects with clay (e.g., Isa 29:16; 41:25; Jer 18:4, 6), a carver/carpenter giving human form to a piece of wood (Hab 2:18; Isa 44:9–11, 13), or an ironsmith who

---

15. Westermann, *Genesis 1-11*, 159.

16. BDB 54.

17. Grey, "Feminine Face of Wisdom," 164.

18. Blenkinsopp, *Creation*, 50–51.

19. Goldingay, *Genesis*, 57.

shapes metal (Isa 44:12). In Gen 2:7–8, God forms a human (Heb. *adam*) from the dust of the ground (Heb. *adamah*); the process of creation is akin to a potter who fashions a vessel or a figurine out of clay. Here YHWH Elohim is essentially presented as a craftsperson.

Second, Gen 2:8–9 reports that God planted (Heb. *nata*) a garden (Heb. *gan*) with trees that are "pleasant to the sight and good for food" and with an irrigation system in place, "a river flows out of Eden to water the garden" (Gen 2:10). It is hard to miss the technical nature of the discourse used. The ancient Jewish readers would be very familiar with gardens. The Bible mentions a few of them: the king's garden in Jerusalem (2 Kgs 25:4); Qoheleth boasts of planting gardens and parks with "all kinds of fruit trees" (Eccl 2:5); the Song of Songs often uses the garden imagery as background, metaphors, and euphemisms (e.g., Song 4:12–15; 5:1; 6:2–3, 11); Jesus' arrest took place in a garden where, "Jesus often met with his disciples" (John 18:1–2). Gardens were widespread in the ancient world from Egypt to Mesopotamia, and later in the Greek and Roman *oikumene*. They were integral parts of ancient cityscapes and rural landscapes. A variety of gardens existed: sacred/temple gardens, palace gardens, orchards, pleasure gardens, and produce gardens. These played an important role in everyday life, as places of worship, rest, and social interactions, as well as sources of agricultural produce. Often designed with a pond at the center, gardens might have had different trees (e.g., pomegranates, olives, sycamore figs, date palms, vines), vegetables, herbs, and flowers. Gardens were often used as a setting for stories and myths related to gods.[20]

Biblical scholars—drawing on parallels from the ancient world—debate whether God's garden in Eden was envisaged as a temple garden or a palace garden; or whether it was essentially an orchard designed to sustain the first humans.[21] Regardless, the point is that a garden in the ancient world was a product of a variety of technologies. It was often an enclosed/walled space that was designed, constructed, and purposefully planted with carefully selected plants and trees (and sometimes animals). This intentionally designed and built place is set as a background for the drama of the relationship between the first humans and their Creator. YHWH Elohim is presented as a garden designer, builder, and planter.

---

20. Farrar, *Gardens and Gardeners*, chap. 1–4, 6; van Dyk, "In Search of Eden," 651–65.

21. See, for example, Westermann, *Genesis*, 208; Wenham, "Sanctuary Symbolism," 19–25; Alexander, *From Paradise to the Promised Land*, 123–24; Goldingay, *Genesis*, 58.

Third, the garden required ongoing maintenance and God assigned the first human to be a laborer or a gardener with the purpose, "to till (Heb. *abad*) it and keep (Heb. *shamar*) it" (Gen 2:15).[22] There is no description of how this is to be done, which assumes that the implied reader knows what it involves, and that the first human already has the knowledge and skills to do the work. In the ancient mind, the task of cultivating a garden was inseparable from using appropriate tools, agricultural and horticultural knowledge, and irrigation techniques.[23] Here the second creation story implicitly includes technology as defining what it means to be a human. *Adam* is not just a living being who was sculpted by YHWH Elohim from the ground (*adama*) and given the breath of life (Heb. *nishmat hayyim*) but whose purpose is to till the garden and later—"the ground from which he was taken" (Gen 3:23; cf. Gen 2:5).[24] A human is one who wields tools, transforms the natural environment, and takes care of it. Through the notion of *abad*, the narrator introduces technology into the relationship between the three main actors of the story: God, humans, and the land. It becomes an integral part of being a human in interaction with the Creator and cosmos. From the beginning of creation, *adam* is *homo topiaries* (gardener) or *homo technicus*—unimaginable without technology.

Fourth, in Gen 2:10–14, the narrator steps away for a moment from the story world to leave a side note for the implied reader that connects the primeval world with their own. In the description of rivers and geographical locations—that sound familiar to readers—a narrative intrusion is made about the land of Havilah. The narrator comments that this *land of sands* is, "where there is gold; and the gold of that land is good; bdellium and onyx stone are there" (Gen 2:11–12). This short note, perhaps a reference to Egypt or Arabia,[25] not only betrays the knowledge of resource geography but also assumes the existence of technologies of their extraction and use. The extensive gold and precious stone mining industries in ancient Egypt are well-documented; it was a labor-intensive process that involved not only mining (from quartz deposits or river sediment), but also transporting the ore, and metalworking techniques (melting, creating ingots, hammering into sheets

---

22. And enjoy its produce—"freely eat of every tree of the garden" (Gen 2:16).

23. See Borowski, "Seasons, Crops, and Water," 412–14; Farrar, *Gardens and Gardeners*, chap. 1.

24. Note that animals are also formed (*yatsar*) from the ground (*adama*) in Gen 2:19.

25. Goldingay, *Genesis*, 59; Wenham, *Genesis 1–15*, 65.

of metal, etc.) even before it could be used for jewelry crafting.[26] By this digression from the story of creation, the implicit author/readers betray their own world as technologically developed, where the metallurgy of precious metals and gem-cutting are known. Moreover, here we find an example of a blending or an expression of a close relationship between the land, its resources, people, and their technologies. Human work and the products of technology are seen as the fruits of the land. A similar perception is found later in Deut 8:7–9, "For the LORD your God is bringing you into a good land . . . a land of wheat and barley, of vines and fig trees and pomegranates, a land of olive oil and honey . . . a land whose stones are iron and from whose hills you may mine copper." All these resources—though belonging to the land—are in fact the results of the application of agricultural, mining, and metallurgical practices and thus imply human agency.

Fifth, the narrator notes that after eating the fruit from the forbidden tree, the first human experienced something previously unknown (Gen 2:25)—self-consciousness about the nakedness of their bodies and consequent shame. The solution is technological—"they sewed (Heb. *taphar*) fig leaves together and made (*asah*) loincloths (Heb. *hagowr*) for themselves" (Gen 3:7). Here again, the narrator assumes that the first humans already know what sewing is and how it is done (as with tilling in 2:15); this would have been something obvious for narrator and readers who lived in a world where this technology was widespread. *Hagowr* (aprons, girdles or waste-cloths) were fashioned out of the biggest leaves in the garden, but this seemed inadequate, and God had to intervene. Before expelling the first humans from the garden, God makes (*asah*) tunics/robes/coats (Heb. *kethoneth*) from skin/leather and clothes them (3:21). Note that the narrator uses the same word, *asah*, to describe the making of clothes by both humans and God. Here, *asah* is clearly used in a technological context, as distinct from Genesis 1. God improves on design and materials and creates an article of more adequate clothing that will serve them better in life outside of the garden. YHWH Elohim is presented as a dressmaker.[27]

The story clearly had an etiological purpose—here is found the origin of clothes making. But there is more to it. Stephen Lambden argues that the juxtaposition of fig aprons and leather tunics illustrates human folly

---

26. James, "Gold Technology in Ancient Egypt," 38–40.

27. Since fabric production and dress making are normally women's jobs in the Bible (Exod 35:25–26; Prov 31:19–24), is God presented here as a female character?

and "the superior wisdom of God."[28] He notes that despite attaining the knowledge of good and evil (i.e., wisdom), the first humans could not clothe themselves adequately and still had to hide from God. Making such pathetic pieces of clothing—"that serve no real purpose"—demonstrates how human wisdom turns into foolishness. Yet, God's solution reveals superior wisdom and "his awareness of the real needs of his creatures."[29] If Lambden is right, Gen 3:21 suggests that God's wisdom is revealed through technological means (clothes making) and—in this case—is the source of technological knowledge. Moreover, this story starts the conversation about the dialectical relationship between technology and the human psyche as well as its place in human society. Human feelings of shame, nakedness, and desire to hide invited a technological response and solution. But in the wider context of the biblical story, dressmaking exists in the context of social interactions guided by culturally underpinned body politics, values (e.g., honor/shame, decency), and perceptions of the human body. The fashioning and wearing of clothes is never just a technological issue (e.g., Deut 22:5, 11–12; Exod 28:40–43; 1 Cor 11:2–16; 1 Tim 2:9). Perhaps, this episode adds another technological definition; after the garden of Eden, human beings are those who make and wear clothes—*homo vestitus*.

First Techno-Stories: Noah's Ark and the Tower of Babel

Apart from brief references to technology, utilizing technologies-based discourse, or using technology as background, primeval narratives tell two stories where technology is promoted to the center stage. The first is the Flood Story (Gen 6–10), where the biblical narrative—perhaps for the first time—explicitly explores the relationship between God, humans, and technology. In a dramatic act of undoing the corrupted creation, God decides to save Noah's family (and birds, animals, and "creeping things") by technological means. Elohim provides Noah with general instructions about the design and materials for the ark—essentially a huge rectangular wooden box—with a roof (or window?), three decks, rooms, and a door that is covered with pitch (Gen 6:14–16). It reminds the ancient audience more of a building, perhaps a temple, than a ship.[30] God chooses materials and design—"blueprints"—for

28. Lambden, "From Fig Leaves," 77.

29. Lambden, "From Fig Leaves," 77.

30. Westermann, *Genesis 1–11*, 421; Goldingay, *Genesis*, 143; Holloway, "What Ship

what must be made by human hands or by using technology. The execution is left in Noah's hands and assumes that he has the required knowledge and skills of carpentry, construction, and application of pitch, mathematics, and physical properties of materials. In the end, he appears not only to be "a righteous and blameless man" but also a capable craftsman—"he did all that God commanded him" (Gen 6:22). However, this is not a story of shipbuilding or seafaring origins. If anything, it is a story of divine grace and salvation where technology steps in as one of the main actors and means of divine action. The "floating refuge" was built by human hands yet designed and inspired by God. The story makes one thing apparent: divine wisdom contains the knowledge of human technologies.

The infamous Tower of Babel (Gen 11:1–9) is another story that brings technology out of the shadows of the background to the forefront. It starts with introducing a building technology that allowed postdiluvian people to build "a city, and a tower with its top in heavens" (Gen 11:4). Yet the project fails because YHWH sees it as an attempt to usurp the divine place as humans attempt to "force their way into the realm of gods or god,"[31] and perhaps become gods themselves—"nothing that they propose to do will now be impossible for them" (Gen 11:6; cf. Job 42:2). Also, the project is driven by human ambition—"let us make a name for ourselves" (Gen 11:4)—i.e., to assert power, instill fear in surrounding nations, to be remembered, impress with grandeur, draw attention, and seek recognition and fame and not to honor the name of God.[32] In the end, God disrupts their cooperation by targeting communication between the builders and confusing their language (Gen 11:7, 9). Such action would undermine other technological aspects of the undertaking, including logistics, project management, and workforce supervision.

Traditionally, this story is seen as an etiology that explains the origins of different languages, the dispersing of humanity, and where the name "Babel" comes from. But Joseph Blenkinsop in his treatment of "the story of the unfinished tower and abandoned city" concludes that it could be read "as a parable about the ambiguities and dangers of limitless technological progress."[33] It is a warning that human ambition armed with new technol-

Goes There," 349.

31. Westermann, *Genesis 1–11*, 552.

32. Goldingay, *Genesis*, 188; Westermann, *Genesis 1–11*, 548.

33. Blenkinsopp, *Creation*, 170.

ogy could lead to overstepping human limits and disastrous consequences.[34] Andrew Giorgetti, on the other hand, places the story in the context of Mesopotamian building accounts that were "motivated by self-glorification and self-legitimation of kings before the gods, courtiers, ruled peoples and future kings."[35] He then concludes that the story of Babel—by utilizing the key elements of the genre—mocks "name-making ideology and imperialistic endeavors."[36] The biggest offense in the story is an attempt to build "an entirely new city on virgin ground," without divine consent, thus usurping God's prerogative to set nations' boundaries.[37] For Giorgetti, the story opposes royal ambition, imperial propaganda, and the growth of "totalitarian power" exerted against YHWH's plans.[38]

If Giorgetti is right, then technology is not the problem here. It still plays an important role, yet the main critical thrust of the story is aimed at something else. God's action was directed at humans and not technology; building with bricks and bitumen—though it might be seen as inferior or alien[39]—is not forbidden. Nor is the building of a city or tower in general. Technology is not a problem *per se*; it is about human purposes that go against the divine will. Yet, the story clearly shows that human technologies, as advanced as they could be, have limitations.

By juxtaposing the two techno-stories of Noah's Ark and the Tower of Babel, Genesis sets a biblical theological trajectory: technology can serve divine purposes and the synergy between human hands and divine wisdom can lead to salvation and flourishing. At the same time, it could be turned into an instrument of human ambition that goes against God's intentions in which case success could not be guaranteed. Human motives and aspirations play a crucial role in the use of technology.

Emerging Contours

Genesis excels in mapping the generations of "the heavens and the earth" and of "the descendants of Adam." But its take on "the generations" of crafts and technologies might appear confusing and patchy; it highlights the appearance

34. Westermann, *Genesis 1–11*, 552; Blenkinsopp, *Creation*, 170.
35. Giorgetti, "'Mock Building Account' of Genesis 11:1–9," 3.
36. Giorgetti, "'Mock Building Account' of Genesis 11:1–9," 20.
37. Giorgetti, "'Mock Building Account' of Genesis 11:1–9," 16, 20.
38. Giorgetti, "'Mock Building Account' of Genesis 11:1–9," 20.
39. Giorgetti, "'Mock Building Account' of Genesis 11:1–9," 9.

of some (gardening, metal tools, musical instruments, animal husbandry, and clothes production) and assumes the existence of others (stonemasonry and quarrying, woodwork and timber production, metallurgy and mining, agriculture, clothmaking, construction, etc.). There are no detailed or coherent stories related to exploring the history of particular crafts or agricultural practices. References to technology mostly play a supporting role by setting a narrative background or are implied by discourse.

Such an approach to storytelling in relation to technology is dictated by a particular authorial point of view. First of all, the story has a different focus—God, humans, and creation/land are the main characters. After all, it is the story of salvation, not the history of technology. Here, I find myself agreeing with rabbi Schacter and Alan Jacobs: "Technological history and sacred history connect, and sometimes overlap, but are essentially distinct."[40] Moreover, by telling the story of generations, the implied author often assumes knowledge of technologies on the part of their readers. This betrays another vantage point: the narrator and readers belong to a world—outside of the world of the story—that is already technologically developed. Moreover, though the story notes the appearance of new technologies and human innovation as generations of humans arrive on the scene, their rapid acquisition of competencies before and after the Flood creates a narrative world that is not very different from their own—farming, hunting, and animal husbandry are practiced, cities are filled with artisans and artists, kingdoms and empires are established. There are no really significant technological gaps between the ancestors and implied readers; creating the perception that they are almost on the same technological plane. Perhaps here lies a difference between the modern and ancient sense of historicity: one is measured by the succession of generations of humans; another by the evolution of technologies.

When it comes to the origin of technology, the primeval narratives ascribe it to both human and divine sources. Divine wisdom and human ingenuity are equally responsible for the appearance of different crafts. For example, the idea of clothes production comes from God, while burning bricks or making metal tools clearly have human origins. By juxtaposing different stories, Genesis demonstrates that divine wisdom and human ingenuity could work in synergy (like in the construction of Noah's ark) or come to dissonance (like in the Tower of Babel).[41] The technology could

---

40. Jacobs, "What Ancient Texts Can Teach Us."

41. Paula McNutt, on the other hand, believes that the primeval narratives see

be used for divine purposes or against them. Yet, human technological endeavor has its clear limits.

A closer look at the creation narratives reveals that technology from the beginning is part of what it means to be a human. In the second creation story, technological language underpins the portrayal of God and the first human. YHWH Elohim acts like a potter, a gardener, and a tailor; the first human is tasked with "tilling" and "keeping," tasks which are only possible by using tools and possessing knowledge. By juxtaposing two creation stories, Genesis welcomes both visions of humanity as *imago dei* and *homo technicus*; they both reflect the character and wisdom of God. The appearance of technology is rooted in both: creativity/ingenuity and groundedness/the practicalities of life.

According to the primeval biblical narratives, human interactions with God and the created order are mediated/facilitated by technology; tilling (*abad*) ground and serving/worshipping (*abad*) God by offering/sacrificing fruits of that work includes technology. Technological endeavor is a natural part of being in the created world. Thus, there was no time when humans existed without technology, and it does not arrive as a result of the "fall." This breaks an old dualism between "pre-fall harmonious existence with nature" and "post-fall technological humanity." There is no other way for humans to exist in this created world and fulfill their God-given mandate but by technological means.

Tracing Theological Contours in the Rest of the Story of God

The rest of the biblical story also reflects theological trajectories and patterns of narration found in the primeval history. There is evident continuity but also amplification and more attendance to details. A few observations can be made.

First, the notion of human life in connection to technologies and their place in the created world is greatly expanded in the rest of the biblical story. As readers of the Bible emerge from the primeval history, they are plunged into a narrative cosmos that is saturated with technologies and their products. Numerous references highlight their importance—not just for storytelling—but in the lives of biblical writers and their readers/

---

civilization and technology in a negative light (McNutt, *Forging of Israel*, 213–14).

listeners. Almost every aspect of human life in the story worlds is marked by utilizing technology: from using a birthing stool to making a tomb, from making food to using things made by artisans, from taking care of domesticated animals to harvesting wheat, from wearing clothes to living in dwellings, from worship in a temple to travel. Technology is built into the fabric of everyday life. This storied world feels very familiar to the writer and the readers as it is based on shared experiences of ancient living.

Technology in the Bible is always narrated and represented.[42] References to knowledge, techniques, practices, and tools are embedded into stories that are woven into a bigger biblical meta-narrative. Moreover, these narrated technologies and their products never stand by themselves; they are tightly wrapped in social, economic, and religious relations. That is where their use is regulated, their value assigned, and symbolic meanings emerge. It is in that sphere where the issues of morality and technology are being discussed. One thing becomes apparent—that in the rest of the Scripture, the story of God, people, and land continues to be told with references to technology.

Second, biblical narratives continue to use technology as a backdrop for the story of God. A few brief examples can be offered. Building and construction create a background for Exodus and Ezra-Nehemiah. Israelites were used as forced labor in the Egyptian building industry as they were put to "hard service in mortar and brick" (Exod 1:14). Ezra and Nehemiah lead the restoration of the devastated city of Jerusalem, its walls, and the temple. Animal husbandry underlines a few stories from the Patriarchal Cycle starting with a note about Abram who, "had sheep, oxen, male donkeys, male and female slaves, female donkeys, and camels" (Gen 12:16), to the final narrative when Joseph distributes food in Egypt, "in exchange for the horses, the flocks, the herds, and the donkeys" (Gen 47:17). But it sharply comes to the focus in Jacob's story when he profits from Laban's flocks through what could be described as selective breeding (Gen 30:25–43).[43] Biblical warfare, whether it is a cosmic clash or a border skirmish, is always a technological endeavor; it is unimaginable without its instruments—military animals (e.g., 1 Sam 13:5; 2 Kgs 6:14–15), weapons, armor, military engineering, and war machines (2 Chr 26:14-15; 2 Sam 20:15)—their production (Isa 54:16), and methods of use (1 Kgs 25:1,

---

42. This raises questions about technologies omitted in the Bible and the gendered character of existing representations.

43. Hamilton, *Book of Genesis*, 284.

4; Jer 6:6; Ezek 26:9–11). Warfare underpins a vast array of biblical stories—from Genesis to Second Chronicles—and spills into prophetic (e.g.,
Isa 36–37; Jer 21; Ezek 38–39) and apocalyptic traditions (Dan 7–11; Rev
19:11–21). Such technologies as writing, agriculture, textile and clothes
making, fishing, hunting, shipbuilding and seafaring, metallurgy, pottery,
and mining also make an appearance in the background of the biblical narrative. Yet, most surprisingly, things that are normally associated with the
work of artisans appear in the visions of the heavenly realm. For example,
Revelation is imbued with references to different objects: temple furniture
and utensils, clothing, musical instruments, military technology, writing,
and its media (scrolls and books). The background of biblical apocalyptic
drama is filled with what seem to be the fruits of "technological" production; yet their provenance is never explained.

In the majority of biblical narratives, technology might not be taking
a central place in the drama of salvation. Yet, it is such a vital background
that the story of God simply cannot be told without it. The world of the
Bible is unapologetically technological; heaven and earth are filled with
God's glory and things fashioned.[44] God acts in that technological world
and the sacred story is painted on a canvas set by technologies.

Third, the technological discourse continues to be used in the description of God's actions, yet it is taken beyond a mere word choice.
It is quite evident that narrated technology easily lends itself to be used
as figurative language: symbolism, analogies, metaphors, parables, and
similes. Biblical narratives provide a trove of technological metaphors
for God. A few brief examples can be offered. Ezekiel proclaims that the
divine smith, Adonai YHWH, will gather the people of Israel—like a
smith who gathers metals to smelt them in a furnace—and melt them
by the fire of wrath (Ezek 22:17–22). YHWH, the divine potter, shapes
Israel's future like a potter who molds clay into a vessel (Jer 18:1–11).
The divine builder lays the unshakable foundations of Zion (Isa 28:16).
The divine vine grower is displeased with the fruits of his vineyard—the
house of Israel (Isa 5:1–7). The divine shepherd takes care of the flock—
God's people (Ezek 34:11–30; Ps 23; Mic 7:14). The divine warrior draws
a sword to protect (Isa 42:13; Zeph 3:17) or destroy the people of Israel
(Ezek 21:1–17). The language related to harvesting (Isa 41:14–16; Rev
14:14–15), fishing (Ezek 47:9–10), hunting (Ezek 17:20), oil and wine

---

44. Yet the same could not be said about the descriptions of the underworld.

production (Isa 63:2–3; Rev 14:17–20), and metallurgy (Mal 3:3) is also used to describe divine punishment or divine blessing.

Jesus often uses technology examples in his parables to reveal the secrets of the kingdom of God or explain the key aspects of discipleship: farming (Matt 13:3–9; 13:24–30), building (Luke 14:28–29), warfare (Luke 14:31–32), vineyard management (Matt 20:1–16), oil lamps (Matt 25:1–3), and shepherding (Matt 25:31–33). Paul does not shy away either from utilizing a variety of technology metaphors: the armor of God (Eph 6:10–16), building (1 Cor 3:10–17), clothing (2 Cor 5:1–5), sowing (1 Cor 15:36–44), and harvesting (Rom 1:13; 2 Cor 9:10).

Fourth, a few theological ideas and narrative patterns found in the primeval history are exemplified in the story of the Tabernacle construction (Exod 25–40). In the beginning, YHWH gives Moses the instructions for materials and designs for the movable sanctuary, its furniture, and priestly vestments (Exod 25:3–9). This echoes the instructions given to Noah, but here they are greatly amplified. In Exod 25:10—30:38, God does not only prescribe certain materials for every item, where it should be placed and how it should be used, but also how it should be made according to the patterns revealed to Moses on Mount Sinai (e.g., Exod 25:40; 26:30; 27:8). All Israelites were urged to participate in the construction project by offering required building materials (Exod 35:5–9), yet the Exodus narrative highlights the role of the "skillful (*hakam-leb*) among you," in doing construction work in "accordance with all that the Lord has commanded" (Exod 35:10; 36:1). One of the striking differences in the description of "skillful ones" from other stories—including the construction of the Jerusalem Temple (1 Kgs 7:14; 1 Chr 22:15; 2 Chr 26:15; Jer 10:9)—is that the source of their technical knowledge and skills is YHWH. The narrator repeats that every artisan involved in the construction of the sanctuary has been given "skill and understanding" by the Lord (Exod 36:1–2; 31:6). But Exodus goes even further, claiming that the master artisan—Bezazel (and, perhaps his assistant, Oholiab)—was filled "with divine spirit (*ruah elohim*), with skill (or wisdom, Heb. *hokma*), intelligence (or understanding, Heb. *tebuna*), and knowledge (Heb. *daat*) in every kind of craft" (Exod 35:31; 31:3). It is hard to miss the resemblance of the language with the Wisdom tradition.[45] Carol Newsom also notes that in this case the discourse of being filled with *ruah* and its connection with "exceptional abilities" employs "the same container

---

45. Dozeman, *Exodus*, 676.

model also used in accounts of creation."[46] John Durham interprets these key elements in the following way:

> wisdom (חכמה), the gift to understand what is needed to fulfill Yahweh's instructions; discernment (תבונה), the talent for solving the inevitable problems involved in the creation of so complex a series of objects and materials; and skill (דעת), the experienced hand needed to guide and accomplish the labor itself. Bezalel, so gifted, is the ideal combination of theoretical knowledge, problem-solving practicality, and planning capability who can bring artistic ideals to life with his own hands.[47]

The artisans' exceptional abilities are directly connected to technological knowledge and skills in "every kind of craft"—metallurgy, design, wood-carving, textiles, and lapidary. This reveals total divine guidance in the construction of the Tabernacle: from its design to minute details in the process of construction. And like Noah, the Israelites did "all the work just as the Lord had commanded" (Exod 39:43). It is not surprising that later rabbinic traditions saw the direct parallels between the Ark and the Tabernacle.[48] Like the story from the primeval narratives, this one also illustrates the synergy between humans and the divine in the use of technology for the purposes of God. Whether their artisan skills were enhanced or directly given by God, there is a direct link between technology and divine inspiration. Univocally, YHWH is the source of wisdom that embodied all the technical knowledge and skills required for accomplishing the task. It is apparent that divine wisdom is the source of human technologies.[49]

The construction of the movable sanctuary and later the stationary temple in Jerusalem took technology right to the center of the relationship between God and the people of Israel. Technology was always a part of worship in primeval narratives in the construction of altars (Gen 8:20) and bringing sacrifices of animal and agricultural produce (Gen 4:3–4), but now it happened on a different scale. It did not only provide a well-designed, furnished, and highly decorated space for the divine and human encounter but was also interwoven into the fabric of ancient worship. Utensils, priestly vestments, musical instruments, oil, spices, and incense are all key elements (instruments/tools?) of worship and products

46. Newsom, "In Search of Cultural Models," 116.
47. Durham, *Exodus*, 410.
48. Westermann, *Genesis 1–11*, 421.
49. See also Isa 28:24–28.

of human hands. Moreover, the sacrificial system—which is central to worship and covenant keeping—is unimaginable without developed agriculture and husbandry. Technology facilitates and mediates worship of YHWH and directly serves divine purposes in the flourishing of the community of Israel. As with tilling (*abad*) the soil, worshipping/serving God (*abad*) is also work (*abad*). Perhaps this suggests that ancient worship is technological in nature; a way of transforming the work of human hands and the fruit of the land into means of grace.[50]

The narrative of the construction of the Tabernacle is disrupted by the story-within-the-story of the making of the golden calf (Exod 32): Aaron "took the gold from them, formed it in a mold (or fashioned it with a graving tool), and cast an image of a calf . . . " (Exod 32:4). This narrative intrusion clearly demonstrates a point—that technology can be used against divine intentions, i.e., for worshipping other gods. This resonates with the prophetic tradition which utilizes narrated technologies in anti-idol argumentation. One of the great examples is Isaiah 44:9–18. The prophet provides a detailed description of the work of a blacksmith and a carpenter to illustrate their work as idol-makers but also to prove a point: it is foolish to worship idols fashioned by artisans; since they are made by "human hands," they are not gods (e.g., Hos 8:4–6; 1 Kgs 19:18; Is 37:19). In this context, "made by human hands" has negative connotations as something fragile, perishable, and inferior to the divine—the nature of any product of human technology; the phrase often refers to idols or even the Jerusalem temple and the Tabernacle (see Acts 7:48; Heb 9:24). What is made by "human hands"—i.e., using technology—is not worth worshipping. Thus, technology in worship and artistic expression has its limits—one cannot make images of God/gods and worship them. The same conviction underlines the conflict between the silversmiths of Ephesus and Paul in Acts 19:21–41. Artisans who made their living from the local cult by fashioning "silver shrines of Artemis" were not happy with Paul's preaching because he was arguing, "that gods made with hands are not gods" (Acts 19:26). As the primeval narratives juxtaposed Noah's Ark to the Tower of Babel, Exodus juxtaposes the Tabernacle to the Golden Calf, and the former prophets the Jerusalem temple to Baal's shrines; this suggests that technology could be for or against divine purposes.

Apart from idolatry, technologies and their products could also stir up human vices. For example, Ezek 27:1–11 provides a list of materials for

---

50. The same could be said about the Eucharist and Christian worship in general.

the construction of different parts of a ship—from hull to sail—and of the people involved in running them. It also lists the content of their cargoes and notes how sea trade in artisan-crafted goods generated "abundant wealth" for the city of Tyre (Ezek 27:12–24) and brought with it pride, corruption, violence, and injustice (Ezek 28:5, 15–18). Revelation 18 echoes the same sentiments in its judgment over Babylon-Rome where opulence and riches—coming from the trade of luxury goods (Rev 18:1–12)—are connected with corruption and violence. This highlights that technology and its products put in the context of (unfair?) economic relationships could make a negative impact on human society. Here the Scripture joins the chorus of ancient writers expressing similar concerns.[51] John Wesley's attitude also resonates with these biblical traditions. In his reflections on the booming British economy of his time, driven by technologies and access to natural resources, Wesley saw its negative social impact and "the dehumanizing effects" particularly on the poor.[52] His criticisms of the slave trade and distillery industry were underpinned by "a humanitarian concern."[53] Also, as Glen O'Brien notes, "He [John Wesley] did not condemn commercial interests, but self-indulgent luxury came in for sharp criticism, reflecting the personal responsibility and moral demand in all of Wesley's social and political writings."[54]

Fifth, the story of the Tower of Babel demonstrates—among other things—the limits of technology. People can use technology to achieve their purposes, but it does not guarantee success; this depends on God. Similar attitudes could be found in other biblical stories. People can use all the right agricultural knowledge and techniques—but ultimately a plentiful harvest depends on God's favor (Gen 26:12). The blessings of the covenant make it clear that the fruitfulness of the land and abundance of rain at the right time of the agricultural cycle depend on YHWH (Deut 28:11–12). But agriculture turns into a fruitless endeavor without the blessing of God (Deut 28:22, 24, 38–42; Jer 12:13). Building projects could suffer the same fate: "Unless the Lord builds the house, its builders labor in vain" (Ps 127:1). On the battlefield, one cannot trust military technology alone. Ultimately,

---

51. Graf, "Mythical Production," 322, explores examples of such critique from Ovid, Virgil, and Tibullus. The closest to biblical traditions is 1 Enoch 7–8 which ascribes the origin of some technologies to fallen angels and their ability to corrupt humanity.

52. O'Brien, *John Wesley's Political World*, 161, 163.

53. O'Brien, *John Wesley's Political World*, 163.

54. O'Brien, *John Wesley's Political World*, 164.

the victory comes from God: "Woe to those who . . . rely on horses, who trust in chariots because they are many and in horsemen because they are very strong, but do not look to the Holy One of Israel . . . " (Isa 31:1; cf. Hosea 10:13 and Ps 20:7–9). Seafaring stories illustrate the same point. Ships and boats break and sink (Jonah 1:4; Mark 4:37; Acts 27:41), and in times of calamity, putting trust solely in sturdy ship construction and the skills of its crew is foolish; the only hope for salvation is in divine intervention (Jonah 1:6, 13–16; Matt 8:25; Acts 27:24–25). Ancient mariners and fishermen knew it all too well; the best strategy for survival was praying to God and throwing things overboard (Jonah 1:5, 14; Acts 27:18–19, 38). Biblical storytellers were aware that human-made-things could be unreliable and easily destroyed; technology has limits when faced with the forces of nature, human-made disasters, and divine resolve. But technologies work very well if God's favor is secured.

Sixth, creation stories also set an eschatological horizon; Isaiah and Revelation see the ultimate consummation of things as restoration of the created order: "For behold, I create new heavens and a new earth" (Isa 65:17; cf. Rev 21:1 and 2 Pet 3:13). In that "brave new world," the harmony between God, human beings and all of creation does not cancel the existence of technology because, since the creation, it has been a vital part of being human. If anything—in that new yet still physical environment—technology will continue to play its role in the service of humanity: "My chosen shall long enjoy the work of their hands" (Isa 65:22). Yet, I suspect, that not all technologies will make the cut; only those that contribute to the flourishing of creation and humankind and serve divine purposes. Perhaps, Isa 2:4 could provide an insight into technological change in the world to come: "They shall beat their swords into plowshares, and their spears into pruninghooks: nation shall not lift up sword against nation, neither shall they learn war any more." In Isaiah's prophecy, for example, construction and agriculture will still exist (Isa 65:21–22). John's vision of the heavenly Jerusalem—the city built with precious stones (Rev 21) and with an irrigated orchard in the middle (Rev 22:2)—presupposes the same; writing and books will also be retained (Rev 21:27). Will that future include smart devices, robots, AI, and space travel? The Scripture is silent yet provides plenty of room for hopeful speculation.

Conclusion

This brief sketch reveals that the Bible is suffused with technology, from Genesis to Revelation. It mostly plays a supporting yet crucial role; the drama of Scripture unfolds on the canvas set by technology and without it the story simply could not be told. In the narrative worlds of the Bible where there are humans, there is technology, and God acts in a technological world. Moreover, biblical storytellers do not shy away from applying technological metaphors to describe divine actions. The primeval stories also set some contours of a biblical theology of technology. Through the notion of *abad,* technology is introduced into the relationship between God, humans, and the land. From the beginning, *imago dei* is *homo technicus*—the one who wields technology in service to God and the earth.[55] Technology is also an area for divine and human collaboration. It can be invented/developed by humans or given/inspired by God. It particularly works well in a synergy of human ingenuity/skill and divine wisdom/spirit applied for divine purposes. Yet, in general, the cautious optimism about technology in the Bible is not without its concerns; humans are warned against worshipping and completely relying on its products. It has its limits in the face of greater forces of the cosmos. Moreover, technology—wielded against divine purposes—ushers in injustice and corruption.

Historically, Wesleyans (as well as other Christians, including Evangelicals) have mostly been enthusiastic about embracing technology, particularly for worship and spreading the Christian message. The Bible itself is a product of technology; God's story is captured and transmitted with the help of letters, ink, reed pens, quills, papyrus, stone tablets, parchment, scrolls, paper, printing press, books, or electronic devices. This fact alone reveals an intrinsic relationship between technology and Christianity; it is integral to our tradition, worship, and spirituality. As Glen O'Brien points out in chapter 1 of this book, John Wesley was a man of both reason and religion, fascinated by science and technology, especially by new technology as it contributed to human well-being. Such Wesleyan openness, grounded in the notion of prevenient grace, recognizes the salvific work of God in and through technology and resonates with the scriptural theological vision. Yet, biblical wisdom—in our age of AI, robotics, the Internet, Big

---

55. This and other notions related to technology require further probing in the light of the Incarnation. What are the implications of God being incarnate in a technological world? What does the cross—a technology of torture, state terrorism, and humiliating public death—mean in that context?

Data, and genetic engineering—also calls for discernment. How could new technological developments serve divine purposes in our world, be used justly, and promote the flourishing of all?

Bibliography

Alexander, T. Desmond. *From Paradise to the Promised Land: An Introduction to the Pentateuch.* 3rd ed. Grand Rapids: Baker Academic, 2012.

Anderson, Bernard W. *Contours of Old Testament Theology.* Minneapolis: Fortress, 1999.

Bartholomew, Craig G., and Michael W. Goheen. *Drama of Scripture: Finding Our Place in the Biblical Story.* 2nd ed. London: SPCK, 2014.

Blenkinsopp, Joseph. *Creation, Un-Creation, Re-Creation: A Discursive Commentary on Genesis 1–11.* London: Continuum, 2011.

Borowski, Oded. "Seasons, Crops, and Water in the Land of the Bible." In *Behind the Scenes of the Old Testament: Cultural, Social, and Historical Contexts*, edited by Jonathan S. Greer et al., 411–15. Grand Rapids: Baker Academic, 2018.

Brown, Francis, S. R. Driver, and Charles A. Briggs. *Hebrew and English Lexicon of the Old Testament.* Oxford: Clarendon, 1907.

Dozeman, Thomas B. *Commentary on Exodus.* The Eerdmans Critical Commentary. Grand Rapids: Eerdmans, 2009.

Durham, John I. *Exodus.* Word Biblical Commentary Series 3. Waco, TX: Word Books, 1987.

Farrar, Linda. *Gardens and Gardeners of the Ancient World: History, Myth and Archeology.* Oxford: Oxbow, 2016. Kindle.

Gerstein, Daniel M. *The Story of Technology: How We Got Here and What the Future Holds.* Amherst, NY: Prometheus, 2019.

Giorgetti, Andrew. "The 'Mock Building Account' of Genesis 11:1–9: Polemic against Mesopotamian Royal Ideology." *Vetus Testamentum* 64.1 (2014) 1–20.

Goldingay, John. *Genesis.* Baker Commentary on the Old Testament. Pentateuch. Grand Rapids: Baker Academic, 2020.

Graf, Fritz. "Mythical Production: Aspects of Myth and Technology in Antiquity." In *From Myth to Reason? Studies in the Development of Greek Thought*, edited by Richard Buxton, 317–28. Oxford: Oxford University Press, 1999.

Greer, Jonathan S., et al., *Behind the Scenes of the Old Testament: Cultural, Social, and Historical Contexts.* Grand Rapids: Baker Academic, 2018.

Grey, Terrence. "The Feminine Face of Wisdom: A Study of Wisdom in the Sapiential Material of the Biblical Period." PhD diss., University of Sydney, 2000.

Hamilton, Victor P. *The Book of Genesis. Chapters 18–50.* The New International Commentary on the Old Testament. Grand Rapids: Eerdmans, 1995.

Herzfeld, Noreen. "Surrogate, Partner or Tool: How Autonomous Should Technology Be?" In *The Robot Will See You Now: Artificial Intelligence and Christian Faith*, edited by John Wyatt and Stephen N. Williams, 121–34. London: SPCK, 2021.

Holloway, Steven W. "What Ship Goes There: The Flood Narratives in the Gilgamesh Epic and Genesis Considered in Light of Ancient Near Eastern Temple Ideology." *Zeitschrift für die Alttestamentliche Wissenschaft* 103 (1991) 328–55.

Jacobs, Alan. "What Ancient Texts Can Teach Us About Technological Change." *The Atlantic*, June 8, 2012. https://www.theatlantic.com/technology/archive/2012/06/what-ancient-texts-can-teach-us-about-technological-change/258278/.

James, T. G. H. "Gold Technology in Ancient Egypt." *Gold Bull* 5 (1972) 38–42. https://doi.org/10.1007/BF03215160.

Lambden, Stephen N. "From Fig Leaves to Fingernails: Some Notes on the Garments of Adam and Eve in the Hebrew Bible and Select Early Postbiblical Jewish Writings." In *A Walk in the Garden: Biblical, Iconographical and Literary Images of Eden*, edited by Paul Morris and Deborah Sawyer, 74–90. London: Bloomsbury, 1992.

Liddell, Henry George, Robert Scott, and Henry Stuart Jones. *A Greek-English Lexicon*. 9th ed. Oxford: Clarendon, 1996.

McNeil, Ian. "Basic Tools, Devices and Mechanisms." In *An Encyclopedia of the History of Technology*, edited by Ian McNeil, 1–43. London and New York: Routledge, 1990.

McNutt, Paula M. *The Forging of Israel: Iron Technology, Symbolism and Tradition in Ancient Society*. Journal for the Study of the Old Testament Supplement 108. Sheffield: Almond, 1990.

Newsom, Carol A. "In Search of Cultural Models for Divine Spirit and Human Bodies." *Vetus Testamentum* 70.1 (2020) 104–23. https://doi.org/10.1163/15685330-12341425.

O'Brien, Glen. *John Wesley's Political World*. Routledge Methodist Studies Series. London and New York: Routledge, 2023.

van Dyk, Peet J. "In Search of Eden: A Cosmological Interpretation of Genesis 2–3." *Old Testament Essays* 27.2 (2014) 651–65.

Wenham, Gordon J. "Sanctuary Symbolism in the Garden of Eden Story." In *Proceedings of the Ninth World Congress of Jewish Studies, Jerusalem, August 4–12, 1985*, 19–26. Jerusalem: World Union of Jewish Studies, 1986. http://www.jstor.org/stable/23527779.

———. *Genesis 1–15*. Word Biblical Commentary 1. Waco, TX.: Word Books, 1987.

3

Looking Ahead

What Does it Mean to be Human? Examining the Importance of Embodiment for Personal Identity through a Transhumanist and Christian Worldview

Sandra Godde

Introduction[1]

WHAT DOES IT MEAN to be human, in light of the exponential technological growth envisaged for our future? How important is embodiment for our personal identity? What is transhumanism and where is it leading us? How does the biblical understanding of personhood survive in a posthuman future? Transhumanism can be defined as a philosophical movement that advocates for the transformation of the human condition by developing sophisticated technologies to enhance human intellect and physiology. Its goal is to overcome fundamental human limitations such as suffering, decay, and even death. It is humanity improving itself by merging with technology.

Great excitement surrounds the vision of the transhumanists as some seek to immortalize the mind by cheating death and replacing the natural

---

1. This chapter is an adaptation from Godde, *Reaching for Immortality*, 1–7, 41–51.

body with a fabricated one, designed to be immune to death. But how far is too far in some of these aspirations? Do we draw the line at therapy, enhancement, or at engineered immortality? And who gets to make these decisions? Whilst most would agree that goals such as developing cures for diseases, transplants, alleviating suffering, and developing prosthetics are good and uncontroversial, the goal to modify our human species into a technological hybrid is more controversial. Foremost visionary, Ray Kurzweil, along with other proponents of the *Humanity+* movement, plan to do just that.[2] Yuval Harari also describes this as humanity's vision of self-made gods in his book: *Homo Deus: A Brief History of Tomorrow.*[3]

Who does not want to live in a perfect world, where there is no death, aging and suffering, no war, hardship or conflict, and a promise of eventual immortality? This is an ideal that humans have always dreamt of and longed for. Christians believe the promise of a new creation is real. It is not just a utopian dream, but a destination with a guide and a known path. However, the transhumanists are a new breed of fellow travelers who also see a Promised Land. They too are confident that they will arrive in a utopian future. They also have a vision and a strategy, with technology as the path and development as the guide. For many secularists, the ultimate goal of cybernetic immortality is a rival concept to the traditional Christian concept of the resurrection of the body. Notwithstanding there are some core convergences between the transhumanist ideology and Christian orthodoxy in terms of aspirations, there are also some core divergencies at a fundamental level between these two worldviews. In particular, I want to highlight from a Christian perspective how the body is part of the integrity and uniqueness of the human species, and should be preserved and dignified, not eradicated in the service of the future progress of humanity.

It has been argued that much of today's modern (and proposed) technology, such as genetic augmentation, cell regeneration, implantable devices that interact directly with the brain, artificial intelligence, robotics, cybernetics, nanotechnology, cloning, uploading the mind and other technologies, point towards a *transhuman future*; that is, a belief that we are transitional humans on our way to becoming *posthuman*.

Many argue we are already in a symbiotic relationship with technology, with things here or on the horizon such as facial coding, wearables (like Apple watches and goggles), embeddables (chip implants), smart pills

---

2. Kurzweil, *Singularity*, 198–99.

3. Harari, *Homo Deus*, 43.

(ingested technology), replaceables (e.g. artificial eyes), designer babies (through genetic engineering and CRISPR-CAS technology), and computer chips in brains (your very own augmented mind). Scientists are also working on implantable memories (experiments have been done in mice already), mind uploading, and the "brain net" (which is a form of virtual telepathy with every memory recorded and available on a cloud service). With these kinds of technologies developing at exponential speeds, many transhumanists say we are becoming a species that transcends and transforms our human biology into a posthuman existence.

Posthumanism often involves the belief that eventually humans will develop enough, either technologically or biologically, as to be able to transition themselves into beings that can no longer be considered simply human. Transhumanists talk about the technological Singularity and predict that within fifteen years the human species will develop superhuman machine intelligence that will change the fabric of what it means to be human. Some see this as a technological imperative in a progressive evolution of the species; a "human upgrade" as it were. Some even say this is inevitable—that the genie is already out of the bottle. But what are the dangers involved in unfettered technology unleashed upon our world without ethics to guide us, in our future decisions?

The crucial question we must ask is this: Are we merely biological machines, that can upgrade or perfect ourselves through technology, or does our being "made in God's image" involve a more complex and satisfying teleological end, designed for us by a living creator? I submit that God's ethical nature and ways are important, if not crucial, and should not be discarded at will, on this march towards reaching for immortality.

What does it mean to be human from a Christian point of view? Is embodiment necessary?

The Christian and transhumanist views of the nature of humanity differ in fundamental ways. The dominant view of Christian orthodoxy affirms the essential goodness of creation and the physical world and promises a future reality which includes a renewal and a recreation of the physical universe.[4] Although there is a diversity of views of the constituent parts of a human being (body/soul or body/mind etc.), the view shaped by the

4. Simut, "Doctrine of the Resurrection of the Body," 31–45.

Judeo-Christian heritage regards the human being as a psychosomatic unity. A human person can be said to be an embodied soul, and the mental-spiritual and bodily aspects of a human being are a unity, with the body sharing fully in one's personal dignity.[5] On the other hand, many liberal secularists or those subscribing to a transhuman ideology view the body, not as an aspect of the personal reality of the human being, but rather as an extrinsic instrument of the mind or self, which is considered the true person. This dualism, setting the body against the person, results in a demeaning of the body as something inferior that is used for purely pragmatic purposes.[6] Typically, a Christian worldview highlights the honoring of the human body and the psychosomatic unity of individual identity, and thus contrasts sharply with the disregard for, or indifference towards the corporeal nature of humanity that transhumanists often espouse. The question of whether we regard the body as either indispensable or disposable has crucial implications for the way we see the future flourishing of humanity and the ethics that will guide it.[7]

For centuries, Western culture has been shaped by a Christian heritage that regarded nature (including humanity) as God's handiwork, and this undergirded a teleological belief that all living things were structured for a purpose or end goal (Ps 19:1; Rom 1:20). Each organ of a living creature is wonderfully adapted to the other parts to form a coordinated, goal-directed purpose for the creature and this integrated structure is the hallmark of design. Engineers will use phrases such as "good engineering design" or "reverse engineering," geneticists will speak about DNA being a "database" of genetic information, and astrophysicists will talk about the physical universe as being "fine-tuned" for our existence on the planet. From the perspective of faith, these all point to careful and intentional design. From a Christian viewpoint, the human person and the human body, as part of nature, is also teleological, and the two form an integrated psycho-physical unity. Therefore, there is no dichotomy between "person" and "physical body" and both "declare the glory of God" (Gen 2:7; 1 Cor 15:45).[8]

Given that our view of the body corresponds to our view of nature, Christians understand nature as essentially good, a gift from God for which to be grateful, and don't generally view the body as a prison, with

---

5. Mercer, "Resurrection of the Body and Cryonics," 2–3.
6. Kraftchick, "Bodies, Selves, and Human Identity," 61.
7. Labrecque, "Glorified Body," 2–3.
8. Pearcey, *Love Thy Body*, 22–23.

negative limitations to be controlled and conquered. The two-level dualism of personhood theory is akin to the Platonic idea of the primary self as spirit/mind imprisoned by a body, and is among other things, an attack on the body. Personhood theory creates a dichotomy between a person and a biological body. To be biologically human is a scientific fact, but to be a person is an ethical concept, defined by what we value.[9] Therefore, a biblical defense of the body is needed to heal this alienation between body and person.[10]

The moral code espoused in the Bible presupposes human embodiment and therefore respect for the human person is tied to respect for his or her body. Scripture treats body and soul as a unity, with the body being the means by which we interact with God, other persons, and our world (Ps 32:3; 44:25; 63:1; Prov 4:21–22). Our bodies are also the means by which our inner souls (mind, will, and emotions) are made visible to the world. In the words of Meilaender, "the living body is therefore the locus of personal presence."[11] Welton states that the Bible does not separate the body to a lower level of biochemical machine or reduce it to a material object or bio-physical entity. Rather, "the body is intrinsic to the person," and their place in the moral and spiritual universe. On this basis, given the evidence of the resurrection of Jesus Christ, Christians believe that the body will ultimately be redeemed. The New Testament does not reject the body but argues for its redemption and transformation, along with moral and spiritual transformation.[12] Therefore a biblical ethic is based on the concept of the *imago dei*: that we are made in God's image as embodied beings; that there is no ultimate division or alienation between our minds and bodily actions; and despite the corruption of sin, God purposes to restore the psychosomatic unity of a person at the resurrection.

Furthermore, redemption, from a biblical point of view, is cosmic in its ramifications. Paul writes that the whole creation itself groans under sufferance and brokenness but that it will be liberated at the end of time, and this deliverance is connected to the freedom and the glory of the children of God (Rom 8:21). The gospel message is that the whole physical world will

9. Pearcey, *Love Thy Body*, 19–21, 26.

10. Kraftchick, "Bodies, Selves, and Human Identity," 61. Waldstein notes, "The scientific rationalism spearheaded by Descartes is above all an attack on the body. Its first principle is that the human body, together with all matter, shall be seen as an object of power." Waldstein, "Introduction," 85.

11. Meilaender, *Bioethics*, 6.

12. Welton, "Biblical Bodies," 255.

be transformed in the eschaton, and humanity will not be saved out of the material creation but rather saved together with the material creation. This promised "new earth" is a restoration of the physical world into a glorified state where believers will live in their renewed bodies in a renewed creation (Jesus' resurrection being the first fruits); they will not be floating around in the universe as wispy, filmy spiritual ghosts.[13] Thus the Bible presents a very high view of the physical world.

Scripture does however explain why at times we feel estranged from our bodies or feel the disharmony within them, and this relates to the impact of sin on embodied humanity. This alienation within ourselves and ambivalence towards our bodies harkens back to the "fall" in Eden. However, the disharmony one often feels was not our original created state, nor is it the state of our redeemed selves. Paul talks about his struggle with the "body of sin" in Romans 6:6: "knowing this, that our old self was crucified with him, in order that our body of sin might be done away with, so that we would no longer be slaves to sin." The context makes it clear that the problem is not the body, but *sin,* as the body is merely the site where the battle between good and evil takes place. If one offers one's body to sin, it leads to death, however offering oneself to obedience results in righteousness (Rom 6:16). Paul expresses this unwanted alien force of sin within as the "sin which dwells in me," describing his "flesh" or "carnal" nature as at odds with the spirit or "the law of God in the inner man." However, Paul thanks God that "the law of the Spirit of life in Christ Jesus" has set him free from "the law of sin and death" and promises that we too can overcome (Rom 7:17; 7:25—8:17; 12:1; 1 Cor 6:20). Furthermore, the healing narratives in the gospels stress the importance of the physical in the kingdom realm, and Jesus offers us his "body" and "blood" as symbols for partaking of his life, undergirding the dignity of the body. Scripture is replete with bodily images and analogies, symbols, and metaphors for our participation in the spiritual world.[14]

The understanding of the human person as a unity that forms a single entity is deeply ingrained in the church's theology of the body, undergirded by the incarnation, and affirmed in salvation history. The Catholic Catechism teaches that one should not despise nor dispose of one's body, but ought to, "regard the body as good and to hold it in honor

13. Pearcey, *Love Thy Body,* 38–39.
14. Pearcy, *Love Thy Body,* 43–44.

since God has created it and will raise it up on the last day."[15] Therefore one's identity is rooted in the composite of body and soul as a person, and this continuity of personhood goes on even into the afterlife where the body and soul will be reunited after death. Accordingly, in Christian theology, the human body is indispensable.[16] John Paul II encapsulates the Catholic position when he states that the value of the human body is connected to, "what the human person *is*, rather than what the human person *has*."[17] Tertullian refers to the body as "the hinge of salvation," so that the God who chose to dwell among us in the flesh in order to redeem our bodies can be said to be the distinctive sign of the Christian faith.[18] Therefore, Christian theology depends on the corporeal body as the basis of personhood: both now, in the future, and in the hereafter.

So how does this biblical viewpoint of personhood differ from the Transhumanist worldview?

Transhumanists claim that *homo sapiens* will be replaced by some future posthuman species, such as *homo cyberneticus* or *techno sapiens*.[19] In transhumanist ideology, it is often thought that we are merely biological machines. Since the Enlightenment, modern science has increasingly viewed humans essentially as rational beings. In recent history, with the rise of neuroscience, advanced technology, computers, and Artificial Intelligence it has become common to compare our physical brains to hardware and our minds to software, resulting in a conception of the human person as *a biological machine* or a *biological computer*. In this view, humans are understood to be preprogrammed by biological factors to act in certain ways. This understanding raises questions of human freedom and dignity.

The view of humanity as a machine finds its roots in the eighteenth century, in the work of Julien Offray de La Mettrie (1709–1751), a French physician and materialist philosopher who wrote the book *Man a Machine* in 1748.[20] La Mettrie denied the existence of the soul as separate from matter, and extended Descartes' argument that animals were mere automatons

15. Catholic Church, "Catechism of the Catholic Church."
16. Labrecque, "Glorified Body," 5.
17. John Paul II, *Man and Woman*, 681.
18. Catholic Church, "Catechism of the Catholic Church," n. 1015.
19. Peters, "Progress and Provolution," 67; Jackson, "Image of God," 289–302.
20. de La Mettrie, *Machine Man*.

or machines, to human persons. In the Newtonian age, the universe was conceived as being governed by logical and understandable laws and this was the basis for much Enlightenment thought. This was questioned by the rise of Darwinism in the nineteenth century and the emergence of quantum physics in the twentieth century, both of which saw randomness and chance as drivers of change. However, the belief in a more deterministic model had not completely vanished, especially for neuroscientists. In recent decades the human brain has been compared with digital computers as they both contain circuits for input, output, a central processing unit, and memory.[21] Many physicists, biologists, and philosophers today conceive of the human person as simply a biological computer, with no real ontological distinction between the artifact and the living being.[22]

The recent explosion of knowledge in neuroscience regarding brain function has impacted human self-understanding in profound ways, accompanied by claims of absolute biological determinism. Not only is the brain involved in every aspect of human functioning but some would go further and say that our emotions, thoughts, and personalities are "nothing but" what goes on in our brains.[23] Much reporting of recent discoveries in neuroscience seems to suggest that our genes and physiology are controlling us, and that genes are linked with specific behaviors, emotions, or attitudes that are beyond one's conscious control.[24] Hewlett says that human behavior is completely determined by our genes and all behaviors are merely reflections of some survival advantage in a section of our DNA,[25] whilst neuroscientist Critchlow, argues there is no such thing as free will, it is all an illusion.[26] According to this secular worldview, we are "nothing but" a collection of chemicals and electrical impulses that operate in predetermined ways.

As to the nature of consciousness in a human being, there is no agreed theory. Two different notions emerge within the reductive physicalists' view (those who hold the view that the mind is reducible to physics and chemistry alone). One view is that brain science can access consciousness and

21. Luo, "Why is the Human Brain so Efficient?"

22. Burdett, "Image of God and Human Uniqueness," 8–9. See also Dirckx, *Am I Just My Brain?*, 55–74.

23. Watts, "Multifaceted Nature of Human Personhood," 41–63.

24. Alexander, "Genes, Determinism and God," 1.

25. Hewlett, "What Does It Mean to be Human?"

26. Tucker, "Neuroscientist Dr Hannah Critchlow."

explain it in physical terms, and the other is that consciousness is illusory.[27] Therefore, both these naturalist views believe that consciousness is synonymous with brain activity: it *is* the brain. However, Dirckx argues, based on clinical studies of near death and brain death activity, that consciousness is different to brain activity, although the two work closely together. Thus a reductive physicalist approach to consciousness is inadequate. She maintains that consciousness itself cannot be reduced to merely physical processes in the brain: they are not identical.[28]

Harari, an evolutionary materialist, claims that "humans are merely biological organisms driven by instinct to seek pleasure."[29] He concludes that there is no creator endowing us with "human rights" and that the concept of equal rights is a "Christian myth." In his follow-up book, *Homo Deus,* he examines the possible impact of biotechnology and Artificial Intelligence innovation on *homo sapiens,* promoting the beginning of a new bionic or semi-computerized form of human. Most transhumanists, like Harari, adopt this two-level secular ethic that makes a distinction between being human and being a person with rights. However, the question arises: how would this philosophy play out in a future society if not all humans were considered equal? What would be the concept of justice, if any, for those who were poor, vulnerable and oppressed? Following this reasoning, if humans are nothing special and not made in the *imago dei,* then it is fine to use technology to alter them, and/or create a new stage of life beyond humanity. After all, why not take charge of evolution through genetic engineering, if humans are "only currents in the drift of genes"?[30] Therefore, how we conceive of ourselves as human beings matters; it matters significantly and profoundly in issues of ethics and human flourishing in the future.

Transhumanist enthusiasts promote a vision of a bioengineered utopia in which we will be liberated from our human limitations, and wealthy parents will be able to afford genetic improvements so extensive that they will create a new race of *post-humans.* Once the human body has been reduced to a mechanism on the level of a gadget, it is an easier step to normalize experimentation with DNA and gene editing. At this point some may express concern at the return of eugenics and recoil remembering the tragic results of this under Nazi rule. Transhumanists respond by saying the

27. See Dennett, "Explaining the Magic of Consciousness," 7–8.

28. Dirckx, *Am I Just My Brain?,* 39–50.

29. Harari, *Sapiens,* 108–10.

30. Gray, *Straw Dogs,* 6.

new eugenics will be based on choice. Parents can choose their offspring's genetic traits.[31] Nick Bostrom, a leading transhumanist at the University of Oxford, says that "human nature is a work-in-progress, a half-baked beginning that we can learn to remold in desirable ways."[32] But who decides what is desirable, and will changes of such magnitude realistically remain in the hands of parents? If it becomes possible to remold human nature itself, surely this brings up red flags of possible tyranny. Who will control the technology, and who will have access to it?

Another prominent transhumanist advocate is geneticist Lee Silver, who unfolds a utopian scenario for the future that some might deem a coercive dystopia.[33] He speaks of humanity bifurcating into two separate races. There is firstly the ruling cast, who are the controllers of society (genetic *Übermenschen*: super-persons) and then there is the group who become the low-paid laborers and service providers (*Untermenschen*: sub-persons). This scenario should disturb us. Once we deny that humans have unique dignity simply because they are human and made in the image of God, we have opened the door for tyranny and exploitation in "justifiable" terms. As Adler warns, "groups of superior men [will] be able to justify their enslavement, exploitation, or even genocide of inferior human groups, on factual and moral grounds akin to those that we now rely on to justify our treatment of the animals we harness as beasts of burden."[34] These scenarios call to mind the plotline of countless dystopian movies.[35]

At the far end of the spectrum of transhuman ideology are those who hope to transcend the body altogether. Ray Kurzweil believes humanity can achieve a form of immortality through uploading the brain into a computer, making a "digital immortality" possible. Kurzweil states, "We will gain power over our fates. Our mortality will be in our own hands. We will be able to live as long as we want . . . by the end of this century, the non-biological portion of our intelligence will be trillions of trillions of times more powerful than unaided human intelligence."[36] Furthermore, he says

31. Pearcy, *Love Thy Body*, 97–98.

32. Bostrom, "Transhumanist Values."

33. Silver, *Remaking Eden*.

34. Adler, *Difference of Man*, 264.

35. Such blockbuster Hollywood films include: Besson, *Lucy*; Jonze, *Her*; Pfister, *Transcendence*; Burger, *Limitless*; Garland, *Ex Machina*; Phang, *Advantageous*; and Whannell, *Upgrade*.

36. Kurzweil, *Singularity*, 9.

"the whole idea of a 'species' is a biological concept" and "what we are doing is transcending biology."[37] Bostrom states that if we could build a new, superintelligent machine brain that far surpasses the capacity of any human brain, then "as the fate of the gorillas now depends more on us humans than on the gorillas themselves, so the fate of our species would depend on the actions of the machine superintelligence."[38]

Estulin, author of *TransEvolution: The Coming Age of Human Deconstruction*, states that we are on the cusp of the greatest evolutionary change in the history of mankind.[39] In an interview, he claimed, "I can tell you without a doubt that the generations of children who are being born right now are the last truly 100 percent human generation of human beings on the planet. Their children will be transhuman children—posthuman man-machines, cyborgs, and beings who are not totally human as a result of synthetic biology. It's absolutely inevitable—the whole idea of merging man and machine."[40] Estulin believes that what is coming will revolutionize the very definition of humanity.

Another influential futurist, Martine Rothbatt, also promotes a similar anti-body ideology in her book, *Virtually Human*.[41] Rothbatt's book proposes a digital database of one's life to be used to create a "mindclope" (a digital consciousness that will survive the death of one's body). If one prefers a flesh and blood body, according to Rothbatt, they are guilty of "fleshism." Furthermore, transgenic technologies (creating new life forms across species, including human-animal hybrids) are already being used in experiments and open the way for the refashioning of human nature itself. Why not enhance human capabilities and create a post-human race? We will be able to manufacture and design a human being in the laboratory, taking the DNA of anything and creating organisms that never existed before: new life forms. As a result, the nature of humanity would be up for negotiation.

The value of the human body, and its integration into one's personhood, is a central point of contention between the Christian worldview and transhumanist ideology. For the transhumanist, the future leads to a post-human

37. Kurzweil, quoted in Drevitch, "Tinkering with Morality."

38. Bostrom, *Superintelligence*, vii.

39. Estulin, *TransEvolution*.

40. Estulin's interview with Anderson, quoted in McGuire and Anderson, *Babylon Code*, 122.

41. Rothblatt, *Virtually Human*.

species that includes the demeaning and disparaging of the flesh-and-blood body. In this view, we are biological machines that can be tampered with, improved upon, and even surpassed. In contrast, Christianity emphasizes a sanctification of the soul, physical embodiment in the world to come, and a continuity of personal identity into the afterlife. Depending on what view one takes (biological machine or *imago dei*), the ethical implications for the future of humanity are momentous.

Conclusion

In conclusion, there are fundamental differences in these two worldviews. Christians want to be better human persons; transhumanists want to be trans- or post-humans. What it means to be fully human is very different to each group. There are profound and systemic differences in these two worldviews, including radical human enhancement goals that are incompatible with the final eschatological promise that is offered to us by Christ in the resurrection and the world to come (1 Cor 15:54–55). Transhumanists want to move beyond being human as we know it, including shedding the biological body. Both worldviews have deification claims, but they are based on mutually exclusive goals because at the foundation of their visions lay diverse and competing anthropologies. A Christian's theological or ethical contribution to the discussions of the use of future technology will necessarily caution against unbridled technological possibilities on the human body and person, particularly if they seek to change the nature of the human identity given to them by God. Whilst transhumanists hold out cybernetic immortality as the ultimate vision; Christians hold out resurrection from the dead in a corporeal body as the ultimate vision. In the end, the choice will be either upholding superintelligence as the governing ethic of our world or worshipping the living God who made us.

Bibliography

Adler, Mortimer J. *The Difference of Man and the Difference It Makes*. New York: Fordham University Press, 1967.

Alexander, Denis. "Genes, Determinism and God." *Cambridge Papers* 22.4 (December 2013) 1–4.

Besson, Luc, dir. *Lucy*. Saint-Denis: EuropaCorp, 2014. 90 min.

Bostrom, Nick. *Superintelligence: Paths, Dangers, Strategies*. Oxford: Oxford University Press, 2014.

Burdett, Michael. *Eschatology and the Technological Future*. London: Routledge, 2015.

———. "The Image of God and Human Uniqueness: Challenges from the Biological and Information Sciences." *The Expository Times* 127.1 (2015) 3–10.

Burger, Neil, dir. *Limitless*. Universal City, CA: Virgin Produced and Rouge, 2011. 105 min.

Catholic Church. "Catechism of the Catholic Church." https://www.vatican.va/archive/ENG0015/_INDEX.HTM.

de La Mettrie, Julien Offray. *Machine Man and other Writings*. Translated by Ann Thomson. Cambridge: Cambridge University Press, 2003.

Dennett, Daniel. "Explaining the Magic of Consciousness." *Journal of Cultural and Evolutionary Psychology* 1.1 (2003) 7–19.

Dirckx, Sharon. *Am I Just My Brain?* Epsom: The Good Book, 2019.

Estulin, Daniel. *TransEvolution: The Coming Age of Human Deconstruction*. Walterville, OR: Trine Day, 2014.

Garland, Alex, dir. *Ex Machina*. London: Film4 and DNA Films, 2014. 108 min.

Godde, Sandra J. *Reaching for Immortality: Can Science Cheat Death?* Eugene, Oregon: Wipf & Stock, 2022.

Gray, John. *Straw Dogs*. London: Granta, 2002.

Harari, Yuval Noah. *Sapiens: A Brief History of Humankind*. New York: Harper Collins, 2015.

———. *Homo Deus: A Brief History of Tomorrow*. London: Penguin Random House, 2016.

Hewlett, Martinez. "What Does it Mean to be Human? Genetics and Human Identity." https://www.researchgate.net/publication/289164594_What_does_it_mean_to_be_human_Genetics_and_human_identity.

Jackson, Antje. "The Image of God as *Techno Sapiens*." *Zygon* 37.2 (2002) 289–302.

John Paul II. *Man and Woman He Created Them: A Theology of the Body*. Translated by Michael Waldstein. Boston: Pauline, 2006.

Jonze, Spike, dir. *Her*. Los Angeles, CA: Annapurna, 2013. 126 min.

Kraftchick, Steven John. "Bodies, Selves, and Human Identity: A Conversation between Transhumanism and the Apostle Paul." *Theology Today* 72.1 (2015) 47–69. DOI:10.1177/0040573614563530.

Kurzweil, Ray. *The Singularity is Near: When Humans Transcend Biology*. New York: Penguin, 2005.

———. *The Age of Spiritual Machines: When Computers Exceed Human Intelligence*. New York: Penguin, 2000.

Labrecque, Cory Andrew. "The Glorified Body: Corporealities in the Catholic Tradition." *Religions* 8.166 (2017) 1–9. DOI:10.3390/rel8090166.

Luo, Liquin. "Why is the Human Brain So Efficient? How Massive Parallelism Lifts the Brain's Performance above that of AI." *Nautilus,* April 12, 2018. http://nautil.us/issue/59/connections/why-is-the-human-brain-so-efficient.

McGuire, Paul, and Troy Anderson. *The Babylon Code*. New York: FaithWords, 2015.

Meilaender, Gilbert. *Bioethics: A Primer for Christians*. 3rd ed. Grand Rapids, MI: Eerdmans, 2013.

———. *Should We Live Forever? The Ethical Ambiguities of Aging*. Grand Rapids, MI: Eerdmans, 2103.

Mercer, Calvin. "The Resurrection of the Body and Cryonics." *Religions* 8.96 (2017) 1–9. DOI:10.3390/rel8050096.

Pearcey, Nancy R. *Love Thy Body*. Grand Rapids, Michigan: Baker Books, 2018.

Peters, Ted. "Progress and Provolution: Will Transhumanism Leave Sin Behind?" In *Transhumanism and Transcendence: Christian Hope in an Age of Technological Enhancement*, edited by Ronald Cole-Turner, 63–86. Washington: Georgetown University Press, 2011.

———. "Radical Life Extension, Cybernetic Immortality, and Techno-Salvation. Really?" *Dialog* 57 (2018) 250–56. https://doi.org/10.1111/dial.12432.

Pfister, Wally, dir. *Transcendence*. Los Angeles, CA: Alcon Entertainment, 2014. 119 min.

Phang, Jennifer, dir. *Advantageous*. New York: D.K. Entertainment and I Ain't Playin' Films, 2015. 90 min.

Rothblatt, Martine. *Virtually Human: The Promise and The Peril of Digital Immortality*. New York: Picador, 2014.

Silver, Lee. *Remaking Eden: Cloning and Beyond in a Brave New World*. New York: Avon, 1998.

Simut, Ciprian. "The Doctrine of the Resurrection of the Body in the Theological Thought of Thomas Burnet." *Perichoresis* 18.2 (2020) 31–45. DOI:10.2478/perc-2020-0009.

Welton, Donn. "Biblical Bodies." In *Body and Flesh: A Philosophical Reader*, edited by Donn Welton, 229–58. Oxford: Blackwell, 1998.

Whannell, Leigh, dir. *Upgrade*. Los Angeles, CA: Blumhouse Productions, 2018. 95 min.

4

Why Are Christians Reluctant to Embrace Transhumanism?

Jonathan P. Case

Christian Hysteria Over Transhumanism

Over the past couple of decades, the conversation about transhumanism has broadened from a talk amongst futurists, scientists, and other interested intellectuals to the wider public sphere, where increasing numbers of people are joining in on what Max Tegmark has called "the most important conversation of our time."[1] Amongst Christians, this conversation has occasioned mainly negative responses, ranging from caution and condemnation to outright hysteria. A few examples of titles over the past few years from the popular press will serve to make the point: "Can the church resist the lure of transhumanism?"[2] "Becoming godlike?"[3] and "Christians, beware the cult of transhumanism."[4] Not too many years ago there was widespread outcry amongst Christians over the evils of "postmodernism" (whatever that was supposed to have been—more on this below); now the voices have shifted to shout down what most people

1. Tegmark, *Life 3.0*, 22.
2. Crouch, "Bionic Man and the Body of Christ."
3. Curran, "Becoming Godlike?"
4. Chumley, "Christians, Beware the Cult of Transhumanism."

71

consider to be an extension or updating of the project of modernity. In some respects, this is not surprising. Broadly speaking, on account of its rejection of religious authority, criticism of the category of the supernatural, elevation of the human subject, and emphasis on reason, modernity has rarely been kind to traditional Christianity.

Wesley, of course, responded to these criticisms, even while remaining a product of the English Enlightenment, so placing him in the discussion is tricky business. The anthropological dualism undergirding his oft-quoted "curious machine" observation is unhelpful and troubling, as is his lack of appreciation for "theory" that does not appear to have an immediate and practical benefit. So a few ground-clearing comments are in order.

To begin with reference to Wesley's relationship to the science of his day, enough ink has been spilled to demonstrate that he was not "anti-science."[5] Wesley's questions about Newtonian cosmology and interest in John Hutchinson, for example, must be seen in light of recondite discussions British natural philosophers were having about active powers immanent in matter, and not as the result of any animus he held towards science.[6] Also complicating our view of Wesley in this area is our tendency to import a contemporary understanding of science (largely atheistic and deterministic) onto transitions occurring in the eighteenth-century, a move that papers over the way many scientists understood their work in relation to concerns of "natural philosophy" and even "natural theology."[7]

Of course, Wesley was not a scientist, even given the peculiarities of what that meant during his time. He viewed the scientific enterprise, Haas says, primarily "as an *observer* rather than as a *participant*."[8] Schofield's judgment from over fifty years ago for the most part still stands; on balance, "The result of [Wesley's] general emphasis on science was probably good; at least his followers were assured that the subject matter of science was worthy of interest. The result of any specific study of Wesley's science was probably bad."[9] No doubt one could say the same about much of eighteenth-century science.

Given this recognition about the content of Wesley's views, Joel Green's encouragement that "the way forward for Wesleyans is a discerning

5. See Haas, "John Wesley's Views."
6. Haas, "John Wesley's Vision of Science," 49–50.
7. Maddox, "John Wesley's Precedent," 30–44.
8. Haas, "John Wesley's Views," 382. Emphasis original.
9. Schofield, "John Wesley and Science," 338.

ressourcement" has more to do with recovering and maintaining an openness to (rather than fear of) burgeoning scientific discoveries.[10] Michael Lodahl comes to much the same conclusion in his critique of Wesley's view of the body, saying that for all Wesley's shortcomings in this area, we should be encouraged that he appears to have been willing to learn and rethink his assumptions and commitments in light of new evidence.[11]

In terms of commending a Wesleyan perspective when discussing transhumanism, the comments above seem like pretty thin gruel. After all, being "open" and willing to "rethink" assumptions and commitments is hardly the exclusive province of any theological tradition. This may be an example of bragging too much about the riches of one's home turf. But I will add a couple of other considerations into the mix. In terms of how we communicate our work in these chapters in relation to a wider audience—a discerning *ressourcement* should capitalize on Wesley's role as a "cultural mediator" between complex material and both literate and semi-literate audiences of his day, a role highlighted by Deborah Madden in her outstanding study of Wesley's *Primitive Physic*.[12] In terms of our questions (our default attitude, perhaps) to transhumanists and their work, I suggest we bear in mind Wesley's own response when questioned in the 12 December 1760 *London Magazine*: "Why do you meddle with electricity?" He responded, "for the same reason I published *Primitive Physic*—to do as much good as I can."[13] For good reason, Wesley (and many Wesleyans) would reject many philosophical commitments held by transhumanists, but we dare not lose sight of the fact that, in face of the problems confronting the survival of the human race, most transhumanists are trying to do good, and are doing more practical good than theologians who have the luxury of sitting back and accusing them of being drunk on the heady hubris of modernity. We all enjoy advances in medicine and life extension technologies, communication, artificial intelligence, and so on, but to then pose something that looks like a *post*modern critique of modern rationality and science while enjoying their benefits is a little disingenuous.

That Christians should find both modernity and postmodernity unacceptable, for (as Jamie Smith says) both are characterized by a deep

10. Green, "Science, Theology, and Wesleyans," 188.

11. Lodahl, "Was There Room," 26. See also Maddox's comments about Wesley's "epistemic humility" in "John Wesley's Precedent," 44–46.

12. Madden, *Cheap, Safe, and Natural Medicine*, 14.

13. Haas, "John Wesley's views on Science," 382.

naturalism hostile to the Christian faith.[14] However, the dividing line between the modern and the postmodern has never been clear or stable, so while the discontinuities have tempted theorists to reify these periods as discrete, it is probably more accurate to understand *post*modernity as *late* modernity, or the radicalization of ideas latent in modernity.[15] So what Christian Bio-Conservatives (hereafter BCs) are criticizing when they critique the transhumanist movement defies easy categorization.[16] Perhaps it is what they take to be the worst of both worlds (e.g., modern technological hubris on the one hand and alleged postmodern moral relativism on the other), so they shift from one foot to the other, similar to Isaiah Berlin's classic description of western culture's relationship to the European Enlightenment and its problem child, the Romantic movement.[17] In what follows, the criticisms I mention will sometimes sound like they are directed towards characteristically modern attitudes, while at other times the target will seem to be more characteristically postmodern.

But enough with the declensions of modernity. In this chapter, I will examine three common charges laid by CBs against transhumanism: 1) transhumanists (hereafter THs) are guilty of both playing God and at the same time wanting to become gods, and that 2) this idolatrous aspiration can be seen most acutely in THs' critical attitude towards the body (which attracts the charge of Gnosticism) and in 3) THs' revival of late modern dreams of progress and utopia (which appears to be a rival eschatology). I shall attempt to demonstrate that in each case, what sounds like a legitimate criticism is ill-informed and / or insufficiently nuanced, and that Christians should actually be receptive to many transhumanist proposals.

14. Smith, *Who's Afraid of Postmodernism?*, 26.

15. See Pastor and Cuadrado, "Modernity and Postmodernity."

16. I am using the term "Christian Bio-Conservative" as an umbrella descriptor that covers both conservative and liberal Christians who, although disagreeing on many points of theology, find broad agreement in their criticism of transhumanist attempts to radically alter or "upgrade" the human being in such a way that sets the stage for the next steps of technologically-directed evolution that will result in what has been called the *posthuman*. Many Wesleyans would locate themselves in the Christian Bio-Conservative camp.

17. Berlin, *Sense of Reality*, 193.

Transhumanists Want to Play God / Become Gods

Perhaps the most common and least interesting observation of trans-humanism is that it is a secular religion.[18] If one employs a functional definition of religion, then one can find examples of secular religion in everything from politics to sport. The more specific charge that THs are "playing God" deserves a more extended response, although in my view this rhetoric is ill-informed and needlessly inflammatory. If "playing God" means interfering or altering the course of nature through technological means, one could make the argument that modernity (and perhaps human civilization in general) is one protracted attempt to play God.[19] If "play-ing God" includes things like altering the fundamental building blocks of life, developing the ability to destroy the planet, and acquiring knowledge and abilities that previous generations would have considered "godlike," then human beings passed those milestones some time ago. On the last point in particular, some CBs argue that when this idolatrous pursuit takes the form of fiddling with divinely ordained limits on human nature and promises that humans shall become "gods," it apes what the theological tradition has meant by divinization or *theosis*.[20]

Prohibitions against idolatry run throughout the major monotheistic traditions, but in our context I suggest this criticism of playing / becom-ing god(s) is essentially a critique of how *power* is exercised, a concern that has received a great deal of attention in recent decades largely on account of Michel Foucault's work.[21] Pertinent to my concerns here are Foucault's reference to the medical establishment, which he criticizes *not* primarily for its profit making (!) but because "it exercises an *uncontrolled power* over people's bodies, their health, and their life and death"[22] (how very "godlike"). This power is invariably wrapped up with "the privileges of knowledge" (e.g., competence, qualifications, etc.) and the accompa-nying "secrecy, deformation and mystifying representations imposed

18. For example, see Tirosh-Samuelson, "Transhumanism as a Secular Faith."

19. Ramez Naam comments that "'Playing God' is actually the highest expression of human nature. The urges to improve ourselves, to master our environment, and to set our children on the best path possible have been the fundamental driving force of all of human history. Without these urges to 'play God,' the world as we know it wouldn't exist today." Quoted in Kurzweil, *Singularity*, 299.

20. A concept well-known to Wesley from his familiarity with the Orthodox tradition.

21. For what follows, see Foucault, "Why Study Power."

22. Foucault, "Why Study Power," 211. Emphasis added.

on people."[23] Foucault has in his crosshairs not only general economic and ideological power that erodes our individuality, but also the more insidious scientific "inquisition" (typical of the medical establishment) that actively determines who we are. Given THs' interest in life-extension technology, cybernetics, genetic manipulation, etc., it is easy to see how these critiques of the medical establishment can be transferred and directed against the transhumanist movement.

What Critics Get Right

This criticism of playing God is not entirely unjustified. First, THs (most of whom are atheists) sometimes use the rhetoric of playing God when talking about their aims (especially when the topic of the Singularity comes up). For example, when Zoltan Istvar (former Transhumanist Party candidate for US President) was asked by a reporter what he had to say to people who accused him of trying to play God, Istvar responded, "I would agree that we are, in fact, trying to play God."[24] However, both what "God" and "playing God" means varies amongst THs and has to be carefully unpackaged (more on this below).[25] Beyond generalities about playing God, and keeping in mind Foucault's analysis, the following points must be acknowledged: 1) developing the power over life and death is clearly on the agenda for most THs, 2) at this stage, only the technologically elite (or relatively wealthy) have access to this knowledge, while much of it

---

23. Interestingly enough, similar-sounding sentiments can be found in the preface to Wesley's *Primitive Physic*: "Physicians now began to be had in admiration, as persons who were something more than human . . . They filled their writings with abundance of technical terms, utterly unintelligible to plain men. They affected to deliver their rules, and to reason upon them, in an abstruse and philosophical manner . . . They introduced into practice abundance of compound medicines, consisting of so many ingredients that it was scarce possible for common people to know which it was that wrought a cure" (Wesley, *Works*, 32:113–14).

24. The exchange is reported in O'Connell, *To Be a Machine*, 222.

25. At the same time, it must be acknowledged that most transhumanists assume that theists hold to a philosophically naïve notion of God as a "supreme being"—as though believers think of God as one being among other beings. To understand why thinking about God this way is inadequate, see Shortt, *God is No Thing*. My criticism of transhumanists at this point could be extended to any number of other traditional metaphysical topics on which they sometimes pronounce. Even an astute critic of transhumanism like Yuval Harari operates with a crude view of what Christians have meant by a *soul*. See Harari, *Homo Deus*, 101–6.

indeed seems mystifying to the plebs, and 3) most humanists would sub-scribe to a reductionist and determinist view of the human being known as "computationalism," "dataism," etc. When CBs criticize THs on these particular points, it all sounds so very straightforward. But when one ex-amines the issues, matters are more complicated.

What Critics Get Wrong

Before I address the issue of god language in particular (which is the most interesting part of the accusation), a word needs to be said about the political leanings of most THs as it pertains to "playing god" and associated problems with the development of technology and science in general, as both of these concerns implicitly frame the debate. To begin, against a couple of popular dystopian scenarios: 1) No grand transhumanist conspiracy to take over the world and exercise the power of life and death over individuals exists; the majority of THs are, in fact, libertarians sharply critical of government inter-ference in the choices individuals make affecting their health.[26] (If anything, one would think CBs would be criticizing THs for their individualism, not their totalitarian aspirations.) 2) Furthermore, when the discussion turns to AI, leading transhumanist theorists are well aware of the potential dangers in artificially intelligent agents run amok. Indeed, developing safeguards against these dangers is top priority for most people in the transhumanist movement who work in this area.[27]

As far as the Foucauldian critique of the "privileges of knowledge" associated with the elite is concerned, this is hardly a unique problem. Cutting edge technology is always available first to the technologically competent (most often because this class developed it to begin with) and those with means to afford it (think of everything from automobiles to mobile telephones). Similarly, operating with a scientific reductionist perspective such as "dataism" that purports to determine human be-ings' identity is not unique to transhumanism; one can go back at least as far as Laplace's celebrated response to Napoleon's question as to why

26. E.g., Tim Cannon of Grindhouse Wetware went to Germany to have his custom biochips implanted, since a medical professional in the USA would lose his or her license for performing such a procedure. See O'Connell, *To Be a Machine*, 137.

27. "Before the prospect of an intelligence explosion, we humans are like small chil-dren playing with a bomb." Bostrom, *Superintelligence*, 319. See also Muelhauser and Bostrom, "Why We Need Friendly AI."

he (Laplace) failed to mention the human soul in his work on the human body ("Sire, I have no need of that hypothesis"). My point is that both of these problems exist quite independently from transhumanism and constitute no unique or persuasive argument against it.[28]

When god language ("playing God" and "becoming gods") is deployed, CBs are predictably triggered, but THs such as Francis Heylighen are clear that, by employing the traditional language of divine attributes (omniscience, omnipresence, omnipotence, omnibenevolence) in describing the helpful benefits of increasing technological complexity—eventuating in the Singularity (in Heylighen's case, the Global Brain)—one cannot seriously entertain the notion of infinite capabilities (since in analytical perspective such capabilities are intrinsically impossible). So omniscience, for example, is what Heylighen calls a *"practical omniscience*: the knowledge of everything needed to help humanity deal with its challenges."[29]

Further, to compare the kind of human transformation ("becoming gods") envisioned by THs to what Christians have meant by *theosis* or divinization is to compare transhumanist apples to Christian oranges.[30] A good deal of the confusion at this point arises from what exactly THs mean by claiming that humans will become "gods." Harari, who offers sharp criticisms against THs, nevertheless says that when we

28. See Göcke's similar comments regarding the social injustices arising out of the fact that not everyone will be able to pay for new technology, and his response to the charge that technologies can be used for malevolent purposes. Göcke, "Christian Cyborgs," 353–54.

29. Heylighen, "Return to Eden?," 9. In Heylighen's case, the Singularity as Global Brain cannot be likened to a separate, personal being, and he has "no intention whatsoever to suggest that theology or Scripture can offer a guideline for understanding our future," Heylighen, "Return to Eden?," 8. For a convenient chart of what practical omniscience, omnipresence, omnipotence, and omnibenevolence look like in a Global Brain singularity scenario, see Last, "Big Historical Foundations," 70. In this article, Last quotes futurist George Dvorsky on the Singularity: "Being twice as smart as a human doesn't suddenly mean you are infinitely smart." Last, "Big Historical Foundations," 74.

30. For example, when Gallaher (from an Orthodox perspective) claims that transhumanism is a "systematic elaboration of what various Russian religious thinkers following Dostoevsky called the Luciferian 'religion' of 'Mangodhood' . . . which is characterized by self-worship or the self-deification of humanity," he is setting up a false alternative between the technological transformation offered by transhumanists and the moral transformation of life (i.e., Christlikeness) promised to believers who partake in the *energeia* of the triune God. Gallaher, "Godmanhood vs Mangodhood," 200–1. Peters makes a similar error when he comments, from a Lutheran perspective, that "the public theologian should argue that sin-and-grace provides a much more realistic anthropology and a much more reliable soteriology." Peters, "Ebullient Transhumanist," 113.

contemplate the possibility of human beings becoming "gods" we should think more in terms of Greek gods or Hindu devas who possess super-abilities, rather than in terms of conventional monotheistic attributes (e.g., omnipotence).[31] "Superhuman but fallible gods" might be read as (less theologically-threatening) technologically enhanced "superheroes" approximating those featured in popular films.[32]

On what grounds, then, could one argue that a fantastically augment-ed or enhanced human must be disbarred from enjoying the fellowship of God? (Why couldn't *Wolverine* be a Christian?) Clearly there is some overlap here, but this overlap needs to be carefully parsed. On the level of enhanced *physical and mental abilities*, however these abilities might contribute to the consummation of all things, there is no reason why en-hanced abilities available now or in the future preclude one from sanc-tification or disqualify one from a share in the life to come. On the level of *moral transformation*, two points should be made. First, while Andy Crouch rightly argues that transhumanist augmentation won't necessar-ily increase human beings' capacity to love,[33] the matter is not so simple when one considers the relationship between cognitive ability (important to all THs) and living the virtuous life.[34] And second, if acts of compassion such as alleviating suffering are part of Christians' moral responsibility in this world, then—regardless of how we regard THs' sometimes wild predictions for life extension (ranging from hundreds of years to forev-er!)—transhumanist innovations clearly provide us with practical means to enact compassion and alleviate suffering now.[35]

Two convictions underlie CBs' criticism of humans wishing to be-come "gods" (or possess superhuman abilities). The first is a line some CBs believe they need to draw between technologies used or therapy (or heal-ing) and those used for enhancement (or augmentation); the second is the belief that God has given us a stable human nature that shouldn't be altered,

---

31. Harari, *Homo Deus*, 47.

32. Benek makes this point in "Wonder Woman."

33. Crouch, "Bionic Man," 65.

34. Willows, for example, makes a convincing case that transhumanist technologies promising to address impairments affecting areas of cognition that virtue ethicists treat as necessary for prudence, while unable to guarantee moral progress in and of them-selves, can be legitimately understood as "moral supplements." Willows, "Supplementing Virtue," 184.

35. Göcke, "Christian Cyborgs," 359–60.

and to the degree that this nature is related to our biology, transhumanist attempts to transcend our biology is a Gnostic move.

I will deal with this charge of Gnosticism in some detail in the next section, but here let me briefly respond to the therapy/enhancement argument by saying simply that the division between therapy and enhancement cannot be maintained with any clarity or consistency.[36] For example, if I were to be fitted with a bionic limb on account of an injury, is it reasonable to expect that I would request a limb of similar strength, flexibility, and durability to a "normal" sixty-year-old male?[37] CBs frequently waffle on this dividing line when they take the time to think about it, and often wind up in a "Yes . . . but" position of the order: "*Yes*, of course Christians can affirm technologies that heal and promote human flourishing, *but* only so long as they don't cross the line from improving ordinary life to grasping for god-like abilities"—without specifying the criteria for that line.[38]

Transhumanism as Gnosticism *redivivus*

The charge of playing God takes a particular focus when the discussion turns to THs' attitude towards the body. Given their dissatisfaction with biological constraints, that transhumanists are Gnostics in modern dress is taken almost as a truism by some critics.[39] Christians have argued, rightly so, that embodiment is central to both Christology and theological anthropology, so when THs like Cadell Last announce that "the next step for mankind requires a move beyond biology," a defensive reaction is to be expected.[40] This "move beyond" immediately suggests to some people the scenario of

36. Göcke, "Christian Cyborgs," 351. Göcke notes that it is difficult to specify a standard of normality that one could deploy and take as a measure to distinguish between normal and non-normal features of a human subject and its capacities. Göcke restricts his discussion on this point to quantitative enhancements (measurable, known human abilities) and not speculative, qualitative enhancements that would transform *homo sapiens* into a new species.

37. Already in 1991, Donna Haraway claimed in her "Cyborg Manifesto" that "we are all chimeras, theorized and fabricated hybrids of machine and organism; in short, we are cyborgs." Haraway, "Cyborg Manifesto," 150.

38. Blevins, "Living Wesleyan Theology," 166–67, makes this error in his criticisms of "an enhanced view of life."

39. See, for example, O'Connell, *To Be a Machine*, 62–63; Pugh, "Disappearing Human"; Sweet, "Transhumanism and the Metaphysics of the Human Person."

40. Last, "Next Step For Mankind."

"mind-uploading," but—similar to the above caution about not jumping to conclusions about THs wanting to create a new species—transhumanist attitudes towards embodiment need to be carefully nuanced.

Perhaps the most contentious point in this discussion centers on question of how our biology is related to what we call "human nature." Most bioconservatives involved in this discussion claim that God has given human beings a permanent nature that should not be altered. To the degree that human nature is determined by our biology, transhumanist attempts to transcend our biological constraints is interpreted by critics as Gnosticism *redivivus*. THs' dissatisfaction with human nature as it presently stands and their commitment to "upgrading" the human is said to be inimical to having a relationship with God, since our vulnerability, neediness, and limitation are precisely those elements that make our lives suitable for such a relationship.[41] Despite (as we shall see) ambiguity about one of their central concerns, if there is one thing that CBs seem to share when they talk about "human nature," it is that to be human means to be *limited*. Whatever else one might say about us, our vulnerability, which manifests ultimately in suffering and death, is supposed to be essential to human nature.

What critics get right

THs are vocal about their dissatisfaction with current biological constraints and bio-conservatives' resigned acceptance of mortality, sickness, and death (bio-conservatives are frequently referred to as "deathists"). For some, this dissatisfaction takes the shape of outright disgust with the body and the desire to be rid of it.[42] For others, the body remains important enough to warrant research into anti-aging and cryonics.[43] But no matter the position on the spectrum, THs agree that our present biological limitations will not stand. As mentioned above, THs also understand human beings in terms of computationalism or information processing, with the result that the body is viewed more or less as the vehicle for this process.[44] So, to whatever degree what we call human nature is related to

41. McKenny, "Transcendence, Technological Enhancement," 188. See also Crouch, "Bionic Man," 65.

42. See, for example, O'Connell's experience with Grindhouse Wetware, in *To Be a Machine*, 154–59.

43. See, for example, the SENS Research Foundation, ALCOR, and Cryonics Institute.

44. Kurzweil, *Singularity*, 5, for example, describes himself as "a 'patternist,' someone

our biology, it is fair to say that most THs have few reservations when contemplating tinkering with biology.

By contrast, in biblical perspective the human being is a psychosomatic unity. While terms like body (*soma*), soul (*psyche*), mind (*nous*), and spirit (*pneuma*) are not interchangeable, neither are they discrete components that can be isolated and treated in abstraction—rather, in brief, they indicate different ways of viewing the human being.[45] Although many contemporary exegetes and theologians subscribe to a kind of monist anthropology, this way of understanding the human being has not been the dominant perspective for much of the history of theology, and dualism is still the regnant position in some quarters. Even given the importance of the body for the Christian doctrines of the incarnation and resurrection, for much of its history Christian theologians have in fact held a rather ambivalent attitude towards the human body, and one that even smacks of Gnosticism.[46] It is only a slight exaggeration to say that nearly any book on Christian dogmatics from more than fifty years ago will include analyses of immaterial and material parts of the human being.[47]

In fact, on the face of it, Wesley's own view fits much better with some transhumanist dreams of leaving the body behind entirely in favor of mind-uploading.

> Unquestionably I am something distinct from my body. It seems evident that my body is not necessarily included therein. For when my body dies I shall not die; I shall exist as really as I did before. And I cannot but believe this self-moving, thinking principle, with all its passions and affections, will continue to exist although the body be mouldered into dust.[48]

---

who views patterns of information as the fundamental reality."

45. See Wright, "Mind, Spirit, Soul and Body."

46. For the complex history of how the body has been viewed in the Western philosophical tradition, see Collier, *Recovering the Body*.

47. See, for example, Thiessen, *Lectures in Systematic Theology* (1949), 149–69; Wiley, *Christian Theology*, 15–19.

48. Wesley, *Works*, 4:23. Lodahl notes that Wesley's comments in *Explanatory Notes on the New Testament* on Jesus' relationship to his body during his crucifixion veer towards docetism! Lodahl, "John Wesley and the Body," esp. 25–26. Green claims, though (convincingly I think), that Wesley's hierarchical dualism runs against his practical theology and concern for actual human flourishing, which fits better in a monist anthropology. Green, "Science, Theology, and Wesleyans," 182–83.

Classical theological commitments are at work here for Wesley, of course (i.e., God alone is sovereign over any ongoing life after death), but, given the above-mentioned unitive view of the person that seems to be more consistent with the overall testimony of Scripture, this is one area in which Wesleyans who oppose transhumanism would be advised to stand against Wesley's dichotomous view (as well as most of the tradition) and adopt an emergentist perspective instead.[49]

What Critics Get Wrong

At the outset, the majority of THs at this point are probably more concerned with cyborgs—the merger of humans with machines (which does not alter human nature, strictly speaking)—than with the possibility of mind-uploading or even creating a new species. But if one does want to argue about altering human nature, one cannot help but notice the confusion in the literature over what we even mean by human nature (or if such thing actually exists).[50] Is this reducible strictly to biology? Or can one sidestep discussions of biology and talk about human nature in strictly philosophical or theological terms?[51] Or do scientific and non-scientific discourse overlap? (More likely.)

In attempting to sort this out, two important questions must be addressed: 1) What do we mean by human nature? and 2) should it be altered if

49. Be as "kind" and "gentle" as you like with Wesley when rolling out excuses based on his time and place (Lodahl, "John Wesley and the Body," 26), but this dichotomy has dogged us down to the present.

50. Masson, "Turning into Gods," 454, for example, accuses transhumanists of not needing to understand "the nature of humanity" in order to build a transhuman and that transhumanism wants to change "the very nature of our existence," without explaining what he means by this "nature." Joel Thompson, "Transhumanism," 174, creates a similar muddle when he claims that the idea of "mind uploading" is based on the premise that our "human essence" is housed within our minds, not our bodies, but he never reveals what this "essence" might be. Fukuyama, *Our Posthuman Future*, 149, rhetorically throws his hands up in the air when he argues that human dignity is based on an undefinable "Factor X," but he is convinced that disaster is waiting in the wings when promised enhancements threaten the moral status of whatever it is that humans uniquely possess.

51. Jenson, *Systematic Theology*, 149–50, for example, opts for understanding human and divine natures as *communal* concepts. For each of us to "'have human nature' is to play a part in the coherent history of humanity, which is made one and coherent by the one determinant call of God to be his partner . . . I am one with myself by and in the communities that present me with myself; and vice versa these communities are what they are by the actions of the persons bestowed on them."

it could be altered? With reference to the first question, one looks in vain for an agreed-upon definition of human nature, at least as far as biology is concerned, since, as Göcke reminds us, "in the long-run of evolution our genetic constitution is constantly changing due to natural and cultural influences."[52] From an evolutionary point of view, the concept of human nature is merely "a cluster concept that entails biological variations by the members of the species *homo sapiens*."[53] Further, as suggested by Travis Dumsday, one plausibly could argue that human nature should not be restricted to *homo sapiens* but broadened to take account of a higher biological taxon, perhaps the genus *homo*, to which both *homo sapiens* and other extinct hominid species like *homo neanderthalensis* belonged.[54]

The ambiguity here bears directly upon basic dogmatic concerns such as the *imago dei*, incarnation, and atonement.[55] Addressing these doctrines in transhumanist context could easily require a volume for each; here I can only brutally abbreviate recent proposals that might point the way forward. Joshua Moritz has argued that if we cannot understand the *imago dei* as residing in something essential to human nature (whatever that is), we might better think of it in terms of our calling: "the fact that humans were chosen by God from among creatures to accomplish God's particular purpose for creation."[56] But in view of the possibility of advanced extraterrestrial life, I wonder if the *imago dei* could be broadened to include *all* life forms that could be described as (to use Gocke's definition of human

52. Göcke, "Christian Cyborgs," 356.

53. Göcke, "Christian Cyborgs," 357.

54. Dumsday, "Transhumanism," 615.

55. Theological concerns with sin ("original sin," "inherited depravity," etc.) compound the problems here. The biblical writers don't give us sophisticated philosophical analyses of how "nature" can be fallen or corrupted. Robert Jenson comments that the classical attempt to explain sin relies on the notion that "human nature" is given to us by biological generation, which passes down "a deprived and infected version of that nature." The difficulty with this proposal, Jenson says, lies in its assumption that human nature is an "impersonal something that makes us humans and the alteration of which would imply an alteration in the definition of humanity." Jenson, *Systematic Theology*, 149. I would add that we do hermeneutical violence by attempting to ground in ancient religious texts our pet theories about the relationship of sin to our biology. Evolutionary insights into lineal descent and speciation are quite beyond scripture writers' ken and interest. The biblical writers *do* give us a raft of traits that characterize people who live apart from God's covenant, and bundle of traits that characterize people who live according to the Spirit. But it would be a mistake, in Gnostic (and Augustinian) fashion, to locate the seat of sin in in our biology or to restrict salvation to a spiritual dimension.

56. Moritz, "Does Jesus save the Neanderthals?," 56.

subjects) "embodied subjects of a stream of consciousness who experience themselves as autonomous and freely acting moral agents"[57]—subjects who carry out God's purpose in the distant reaches of the universe. This proposal would dovetail nicely with Moritz's view that when we speak of the Word becoming *flesh*, we confess our belief that the Logos of God entered into material solidarity not only with *homo sapiens*, but with all living creatures.[58] It also would bring our ideas of incarnation and atonement into closer contact with the cosmic Christ of Colossians 1:15–20.[59]

With respect to the second question I raised above (should human nature be altered if it could be altered?), Allen Buchanan makes a convincing case that even if enhancing human nature might alter or even destroy it, that in itself is no reason to forego enhancement. Maybe there are characteristics that we *should* try to change.[60] At this juncture, it is worth remembering (as mentioned earlier) that when THs talk about wanting to "escape" biology, most of them are not referring to something as radical as "mind uploading," but rather taking the reins of our evolution into our own hands.[61] Cadell Last describes the transition from abiogenesis to what he calls *atechnogenesis* as follows: the physical universe's code gave rise to the biological universe's chemical code, giving rise to growing structures that could replicate on their own. And then,

> . . . biological code gave rise to the cultural universe through the evolution of the human mind/brain. Now it is the human, imbued with a new agency, and a new unpredictability, to take evolution and direct it with imagination towards the full exploration of what makes the human mind unique: an unbounded canvas of imagination.[62]

57. Göcke, "Christian Cyborgs," 348.

58. Moritz, "Does Jesus Save the Neanderthals?," 57.

59. It is possible, of course, to argue that Jesus saves only *homo sapiens*, but restricting the scope of incarnation and atonement to people on this planet calls into question not only the reach of the above passage (note especially Col 1:19–20), but—by implication—also the relationship of the immanent to economic Trinity, which is enormously problematic (but quite outside the immediate concerns of this chapter).

60. Buchanan, "Human Nature and Enhancement," 150.

61. Although, Mercer reminds us that a posthuman entity, such as disembodied intelligence, could manifest in a virtual or robotic body, so that such an entity could be said to have a body, albeit one "qualitatively different from the familiar flesh and blood body." Mercer, "Bodies and Persons," 27.

62. Last, "Next Step for Mankind." For a detailed account of *atechnogenesis* within the framework of "Big History," see Last, "Big Historical Foundations," 78–80.

To those worried that if we alter human nature we would undermine our ability to make judgments about what is good, Buchanan points out that "we already possess standards of evaluation that are independent of our nature in the sense that we can and do make coherent judgments about the defective aspects of human nature, and if these defects were remedied this need not affect our ability to judge what is good."[63]

In my view, this critical ability we have to assess defective aspects of our own nature, and then attempt to redress such aspects, speaks to the self-transcendence that Karl Rahner argued belongs to the nature of every finite being—a self-transcendence that includes a "transcendence into what is substantially new, i.e., the leap to a higher nature."[64] Interestingly enough, Ray Kurzweil also sees transcendence as referring to all levels of reality, with the coming Singularity ("the inevitable next step in the evolutionary process") exemplifying it.[65] So "we can regard . . . the freeing of our thinking from the severe limitations of its biological form to be an *essentially spiritual* undertaking."[66] Given the reach of Christ's redemption, who would want to argue that even "substantially new beings" (possessing a "higher nature"), if they called upon the name of the Lord, could not be saved? Such beings might have an even more acute sense of their own need and of the cosmic scope of redemption.

In sum, given their stated aims, it is not accurate to accuse THs of practical Gnosticism. When you consider the wide array of transhumanist interests and how the work-a-day world of most people will be affected in the near future, THs are clearly possessed by this-worldly and embodied concerns. If anything, given their additional concerns for the threat of climate change, resource wars, the proliferation of WMDs, etc.—coupled with their enthusiasm for space travel and exploration—THs for the most part embrace an immanent eschatology (more about this in the next section). No doubt there is a clever way to charge THs of being both Gnostic and materialist at the same time, but the way these charges are typically formulated comes across as an incoherent and ill-informed muddle.[67]

63. Buchanan, "Human Nature and Enhancement," 150.

64. Rahner, "Christology," 165.

65. Kurzweil, *Singularity*, 387–88.

66. Kurzweil, *Singularity*, 389.

67. By contrast, Redding is surely right that despite Christians accusing THs of reviving Gnosticism, it is Christians themselves who have "often been lured into accepting, practicing, and proclaiming Gnostic values." Redding, "Can Transhumanism Lead Us Back to Orthodoxy?"

Transhumanists Propose a Rival Eschatology

Despite bioconservative criticisms of THs and their continuation of the modern dream of progress, it would be hard to argue that the quality of life for most people on the planet is not better than it was even a century ago. As Harari points out, while "famine, war, and plague will probably continue to claim millions of victims in the coming decades . . . they are no longer unavoidable tragedies beyond the understanding and control of a helpless humanity. Instead, they have become manageable challenges."[68] And, at least according to many THs, there is a good chance that the future will only get better—providing we make sound decisions now.

Eschatological speculation about the coming Singularity and the changes this will bring fuels further comparison to nineteenth-century utopian hopes and plans. Michael Zimmerman, for example, has compared speculation about the Singularity to Hegel's view of human history, in which *Geist* comes to self-consciousness.[69] Specifically, Zimmerman singles out Ray Kurzweil's upgrade of Hegel: not only has the cosmos brought itself to self-awareness through humankind, eventually we will evolve beyond ourselves by generating modes of consciousness and technology that will make possible a cosmic self-realization bearing comparison with St Paul's promise of the creation's liberation from corruption (cf. Romans 8).[70] "In Kurzweil's universe story, the cosmos is not only life-friendly and even consciousness-friendly, but also God-friendly. Post-human divinity will take charge of its own destiny and 'spiritualize' everything in the universe, including supposedly 'dumb' matter/energy."[71]

What Critics Get Right

Transhumanist visions of the deep future of "Big History" and our place in it, such as Cadell Last (for example) articulates it, pushes the edges of a metanarrative far beyond anything imagined by Hegel.[72] So Zimmerman's

---

68. Harari, *Homo Deus*, 19. See also Heylighen, "Global Brain."

69. Zimmerman, "Singularity."

70. Zimmerman, "Singularity," 363.

71. Zimmerman, "Singularity," 363. Kurzweil, *Singularity*, 375, claims that "once we saturate the matter and energy in the universe with intelligence, it will 'wake up,' be conscious, and sublimely intelligent. That's about as close to God as I can imagine."

72. Last, "Big Historical Foundations."

essential insight in seeing the Singularity as occupying roughly the position of Hegel's *Geist* coming to self-awareness is correct, even though, as Last notes, Hegel was not concerned with the dimension of biological evolution in his vision.

In this vision of the future, the notion of the Singularity (and the modern language of progress associated with it) has been the lightning rod for critics who see THs as proposing a rival and godless eschatology. And indeed, THs (the majority of whom are atheist or agnostic) have little hesitation in using the language of utopia or even a return to "Eden" when describing the future possibilities opened up by the Singularity.[73] Yet even at this stage of the discussion consensus does not exist on what the Singularity will look like. Last says "the original essence of the 'singularity' idea is simple: 1) science and technology drive changes in human civilization, and 2) due to its cumulative nature advancing scientific and technological development will eventually reach a stage where change happens faster than the human mind can comprehend."[74]

What shape this stage takes is debatable. Some theorists think of the Singularity in terms of machine intelligence that has moved beyond human-level intelligence to artificial general intelligence (AGI). This idea of AGI is the version that has probably captured the popular imagination the most, with fears of a super computer making decisions on its own to humanity's detriment (and eventual demise). Of course, the exponential growth in computing complexity *is* astonishing; Last notes that the most advanced supercomputers in 2013 could run a thousand trillion calculations per second.[75] Other theorists, however, argue that it is more likely that we will experience a "global brain" Singularity (GB). Francis Heylighen, one of the leading architects of this vision, explains:

> The "global brain" is the name given to the emerging intelligent network that is formed by all people on this planet together with the computers, knowledge bases and communication links that connect them together. Like a human brain, this network is an immensely complex, self-organizing system, that processes information, makes decisions, solves problems, learns new connections and discovers new ideas. It plays the role of a nervous system for the whole of humanity. No single person, organization

73. See Kostick et al., "Engineering Eden," 209–22; Heylighen, "Return to Eden?"
74. Last, "Big Historical Foundations," 66.
75. Last, "Big Historical Foundations," 66.

or computer is in control of this system: its "thought" processes are distributed over all its components.[76]

But regardless of the version of Singularity one buys into, the phenomenon itself (to hear THs talk about it) will be the most significant event since the emergence of *homo sapiens*—the next great step in our evolution. The road to a utopian future may indeed be arduous, as Heylighen admits, but THs are nothing if not optimistic about the future: "We may experience a true *return to Eden*—an idyllic state of abundance, peace and well-being, in which all serious threats have been tackled and people can fully dedicate themselves to further creative endeavors."[77]

What Critics Get Wrong

The misperceptions and caricatures of the Singularity are manifold. The very term "Singularity" is merely a metaphor employed by THs to describe the coming change on account of exploding technological complexity, and a pliable metaphor like this is bound to be reduced to bumper sticker explanations and become the target of ill-informed criticisms.

In response to the criticism, the following points should be noted: First, THs are well aware of the shortcomings and failures of modern dreams of utopia, ensconced as they were within Hegelian-style metanarratives, and often address these shortcomings in the literature.[78] To accuse them of ignorantly republishing the mistakes of the past is simply inaccurate and unfair. Second, THs acknowledge that, despite technological breakthroughs, a utopian future is not guaranteed or inevitable.[79] Humans may very well destroy the planet by any number of means (e.g. nuclear war, climate change) before the future that THs envision is realized. The Singularity, although

---

76. Heylighen, "Global Brain," 2.

77. Heylighen, "Return to Eden?," 30.

78. Contrary to Le Dévédec's accusation that transhumanists concern themselves only with the technological enhancement of individuals (cf. Le Dévédec, "Unfit for the Future"), Last acknowledges the social, economic, and political failures of the modern project and insists that if we are not to repeat the mistakes of the past, we must address the failures of Neoliberal economic theory and develop new modes of sociopolitical governance. Last, "Big Historical Foundations," 60–61.

79. Potapov judges that, given the various definitions of what the Singularity means and the different scenarios envisioned in which the described event takes place, "it is useless to argue about whether Singularity as a specific event will occur and (if yes) when." Potapov, "Technological Singularity," 7.

predictable (given Moore's Law), is not a *metaphysical* inevitability (contra Hegel). Third, as Ronald Cole-Turner points out, a distinction needs to be drawn between *next things* and *last things*.[80] THs can predict and propose the "next things," but the "last things," as Christians understand the matter, is a future that includes "*all things* in their consummation in God,"[81] and as such remains the prerogative of God alone.[82] Fourth, no transhumanist would argue that, even given the promise of, e.g., life extension technologies, "immortality" can be guaranteed for everyone and that death itself finally will be defeated. People will continue to be killed in numerous ways, and—on the cosmic scale—however long humans may live, our existence will come to an end with the end of the universe.[83] And finally, in response to the accusation that THs are proposing an all-encompassing metanarrative bent on swallowing whole individual freedom and dignity before the next stage in human evolution emerges—the *posthuman*—Nick Bostrom suggests we take a wide-angle historical perspective on this issue. "In the eyes of a hunter-gatherer, we might already appear post-human."[84] Our dignity, Bostrom claims, consists *not only in what we are but what we have the potential to become*—so that what we are is not solely a function of our DNA but also emerges from our technological and social context.[85]

In my view, the transhumanist vision is more accurately understood as an invitation to work towards a better world of human flourishing, by using the best that science and technology have to offer. So, yes, this is Modern Optimism 2.0, but Bostrom reminds us that on account of the modern dream, "the set of individuals accorded full moral status by Western societies has actually increased," and that our continuing role in this process "need not be that of passive bystanders. We can work to create more inclusive social

80. Cole-Turner, "Eschatologies," 27.

81. Cole-Turner, "Eschatologies," 28.

82. In relation to this point, Kostick et al., "Engineering Eden?," 218, plausibly suggest that despite the transhumanist's shiny future and its benefits, "religion's promise of eternal life may always be relevant, forever trumping scientific paradigms in mitigating our terror of nonexistence."

83. Göcke, "Christian Cyborgs," 361.

84. Bostrom, "In Defense of Posthuman Dignity," 213.

85. Bostrom, "In Defense of Posthuman Dignity," 213. In connection with this, it also should be remembered that totalitarian movements such as Nazism and Marxism (and certainly not libertarianism) have been the real enemies of both human dignity and progress. Fascists, for example, regarded the ideals of the Enlightenment as leading to the decline and weakening of the human race. Landa, "Progress, Fascism and the Last Humans," 47.

structures and accord moral recognition and legal rights to all who need them, be they male or female, black or white, flesh or silicon."[86]

Conclusion

I have argued that popular CB criticisms of the transhumanist movement are ill-informed and that Christians should be receptive to many TH proposals. To briefly recap:

1. "Playing god" for THs refers to the ability to use an array of vastly extended practical abilities to alter our world, but this is merely a more sophisticated version of what human have always tried to do. "Becoming gods" refers to becoming enhanced human beings who possess powers that people in previous generations would have thought were reserved for the gods, but I have argued there is no reason why a technologically enhanced human should be disbarred from fellowship with God.

2. THs are said to be guilty of reviving Gnosticism on account of their dissatisfaction with our biological constraints. Given transhumanist attempts to address material issues in human life and commitment to solve pressing problems threatening the survival of the planet, however, it is neither fair nor accurate to charge THs with Gnosticism. In fact, we should welcome and be grateful for THs' concern for our physical health and well-being, and that of the planet.

3. The transhumanist vision of a utopian future brought about by human ingenuity and determination is said to be a godless rival to Christian eschatology. On account of the all-encompassing scope of this vision, THs are said to be guilty of proposing a metanarrative of unquestioned authority and one that will marginalize all who resist it. But, while expansive, the transhumanist vision of a utopian future is not inevitable, nor is a vision of the "next things" equivalent to what Christians have meant by the "last things." Such aspirations for a better world should be seen as a challenge and invitation for Christians to accept.

Many of us already benefit from the work THs have done. Let us not be disingenuous by pretending to possess a superior spiritual attitude or bask in an air of holy detachment towards the transhumanist sea change

86. Bostrom, "In Defense of Posthuman Dignity," 210.

happening around us, while in reality we enjoy the benefits of this changing world as much as our neighbors. Instead, following in the spirit of
Wesley, let us encourage THs to do all the good they can. That world
is the object of final redemption. To what degree can proximate means
contribute towards it?

Bibliography

Benek, Christopher. "Wonder Woman Depicts the Need for Christian Transhumanism."
    Christian Post, June 16, 2017. https://www.christianpost.com/news/wonder-woman-
    depicts-need-for-christian-transhumanism-188088/.
Berlin, Isaiah. *The Sense of Reality: Studies in Ideas and Their History.* New York: Farrar,
    Strauss and Giroux, 1996.
Bishop, Jeffrey P. "Transhumanism, Metaphysics, and the Posthuman God." *Journal of
    Medicine and Philosophy* 35 (2010) 700–720.
Blevins, Dean G. "Living Wesleyan Theology in Today's World." In *Wesleyan Theology and
    Social Science: The Dance of Practical Divinity and Discovery*, edited by M. Kathryn
    Armisted et al., 161–75. Newcastle upon Tyne: Cambridge Scholars, 2010.
Bostrom, Nick. "In Defense of Posthuman Dignity." *Bioethics* 19.3 (2005) 202–14.
———. *Superintelligence: Paths, Dangers, Strategies.* Oxford University Press, 2014.
Buchanan, Alan. "Human Nature and Enhancement." *Bioethics* 23.3 (2009) 141–50.
Childs, James M., Jr. "Beyond the Boundaries of Current Human Nature: Some Theological
    and Ethical Reflections on Transhumanism." *Dialog* 54.1 (Spring 2015) 8–19.
Chumley, Cheryl K. "Christians, Beware the Cult of Transhumanism." *Washington Times*,
    September 7, 2018. https://www.washingtontimes.com/news/2018/sep/7/christians-
    beware-cult-transhumanism/.
Cole-Turner, Ronald. "Eschatology and the Technologies of Human Enhancement."
    Interpretation 70.1 (2016) 21–33.
———. "Going Beyond the Human: Christians and Other Transhumanists." *Dialog* 54.1
    (Spring 2015) 20–26.
Collier, Carol. *Recovering the Body: A Philosophical Story.* Ottawa: The University of
    Ottawa, 2013.
Crouch, Andy. "The Bionic Man and the Body of Christ: Can the Church Resist the Lure
    of Transhumanism?" *Christianity Today* (April 2019) 63–65.
Curran, Ian. "Becoming godlike? The Incarnation and the Challenge of Transhumanism."
    Christian Century 134.24 (November 2017) 22–27.
Dumsday, Travis. "Sergius Bulgakov's Critique of N. F. Fedorov's Technologized
    Resurrection (and Why it Still Matters for the Christian Dialogue with
    Transhumanism)." *Zygon* 55.4 (December 2020) 853–73.
———. "Transhumanism, Theological Anthropology, and Modern Biological Taxonomy."
    Zygon 52.3 (September 2017) 601–22.
Foucault, Michel. "Why Study Power? The Question of the Subject." In *Michel Foucault:
    Beyond Structuralism and Hermeneutics*, edited by Hubert L. Dreyfus and Paul
    Rabinow, 208–26. Chicago: The University of Chicago Press, 1983.

Fukuyama, Francis. *Our Posthuman Future: Consequences of the Biotechnology Revolution*. New York: Farrar, Strauss and Giroux, 2002.

Gallaher, Brandon. "Godmanhood vs Mangodhood: An Eastern Orthodox Response to Transhumanism." *Studies in Christian Ethics* 32.2 (2019) 200–215.

Göcke, Benedikt. "Christian Cyborgs: A Plea for a Moderate Transhumanism." *Faith and Philosophy* 34.3 (2017) 347–64.

Green, Joel B. "Science, Theology, and Wesleyans." In *Wesleyan Theology and Social Science: The Dance of Practical Divinity and Discovery*, edited by M. Kathryn Armisted, et al., 177–92. Newcastle upon Tyne: Cambridge Scholars, 2010.

Haas, Jr. John W. "John Wesley's Vision of Science in the Service of Christ." In *Divine Grace and Emerging Creation: Wesleyan Forays in Science and Theology of Creation*, edited by Thomas Jay Oord, 37–57. Eugene, OR: Pickwick, 2009.

———. "John Wesley's Views on Science and Christianity: An Examination of the Charge of Antiscience." *Church History* 63.3 (Sept 1994) 378–92.

Harari, Yuval Noah. *Homo Deus: A Brief History of Tomorrow*. New York: Harper, 2017.

Haraway, Donna. "A Cyborg Manifesto": Science, Technology, and Socialist-Feminism in the Late Twentieth Century," in *Simians, Cyborgs and Women: The Reinvention of Nature*, 149–81. New York: Routledge, 1991. http://faculty.georgetown.edu/irvinem/theory/Haraway-CyborgManifesto.html.

Heylighen, Francis. "The Global Brain as a New Utopia." In *Zukunftsfiguren*, edited by R. Maresh and F. Rötzer, 1–11. Frankfurt: Suhrkamp Verlag, 2002. http://pespmc1.vub.ac.be/Papers/GB-Utopia.pdf

———. "Return to Eden? Promises and Perils on the Road to a Global Superintelligence." In *The End of the Beginning: Life, Society and Economy on the Brink of the Singularity*, edited by B. Goertzel and T. Goertzel, 243–306. Los Angeles: Humanity+ Press, 2015.

Jenson, Robert W. *Systematic Theology Volume II: The Works of God*. New York: Oxford University Press, 1999.

Kostick, Kristin, Leah Fowler, and Christopher Scott, "Engineering Eden: Does Earthly Pursuit of Eternal Life Threaten the Future of Religion." *Theology and Science* 17.2 (May 2019) 209–22.

Kraftchick, Steven John. "Bodies, Selves, and Human Identity: A Conversation Between Tranhumanism and the Apostle Paul." *Theology Today* 72.1 (2015) 47–69.

Kurzweil, Ray. *The Singularity is Near: When Humans Transcend Biology*. New York: Penguin, 2005.

Landa, Ishay. "Progress, Fascism and the Last Humans." *Journal of Political Ideologies* 22.1 (2017) 30–51.

Last, Cadell. "Big Historical Foundations for Deep Future Speculations: Cosmic Evolution, Atechnogenesis, and Technological Civilization." *Foundations of Science* 22 (2017) 39–124.

———. "The Next Step For Mankind Requires a Move Beyond Biology." *Business Insider*, July 21, 2014. https://www.businessinsider.com/next-step-for-mankind-2014-7.

Le Dévédec, Nicolas. "Unfit for the Future? The Depoliticization of Human Perfectibility, from the Enlightenment to Transhumanism." *European Journal of Social Theory* 21.4 (2018) 488–507.

Lodahl, Michael. "Was There Room in Wesley's Anthropology for *Any*body? Particularly that of the Lowly Jesus?" In *This Is My Body: Philosophical Reflections on Embodiment in a Wesleyan Spirit*, edited by John Thomas Brittingham and Christina M. Smerick, 21–26. Eugene, OR: Pickwick, 2016.

Madden, Deborah. *"A Cheap, Safe and Natural Medicine"*: *Religion, Medicine, and Culture in John Wesley's Primitive Physic*. Leiden: Brill, 2007.

Maddox, Randy L. "John Wesley's Precedent for Theological Engagement with the Natural Sciences." *Wesleyan Theological Journal* 44.1 (Spring 2009) 23–54.

Masson, Olivier. "Turning Into Gods: Transhumanist Insight on Tomorrow's Religiosity." *Implicit Religion* 17.4 (2014) 443–58.

McKenny, Gerald. "Transcendence, Technological Enhancement, and Christian Theology." In *Transhumanism and Transcendence: Christian Hope in an Age of Technological Enhancement*, edited by Ronald Cole-Turner, 177–92. Washington, DC: Georgetown University Press, 2011.

Mercer, Calvin. "Bodies and Persons: Theological Reflections on Transhumanism." *Dialog* 54.1 (Spring 2015) 27–65.

Moritz, Joshua M. "Does Jesus Save the Neanderthals? Theological Perspectives on the Evolutionary Origins and Boundaries of Human Nature?" *Dialog* 54.1 (Spring 2015) 51–60.

Muelhauser, Luke and Nick Bostrom. "Why We Need Friendly AI." *Think* 13.36 (March 2014) 41–47.

O'Connell, Mark. *To Be a Machine: Adventures Among Cyborgs, Utopians, Hackers, and the Futurists Solving the Modest Problem of Death*. New York: Anchor, 2017.

Pastor, Luis Miguel and José Angel Garcia Cuadrado, "Modernity and Postmodernity in the Genesis of Transhumanism-Posthumanism." *Cuadernos de Bioética* 25.3 (2014) 335–50.

Peters, Ted. "The Ebullient Transhumanist and the Sober Theologian." *Scientia et Fides* 7.2 (2019) 97–117.

Potapov, Alexy. "The Technological Singularity: What Do We Really Know?" *Information* 9.4 (2018) 1–9. https://www.mdpi.com/2078-2489/9/4/82.

Pugh, Jeffrey C. "The Disappearing Human: Gnostic Dreams in a Transhumanist World." *Religions* 8 (2017). https://www.mdpi.com/2077-1444/8/5/81.

Rahner, Karl. "Christology within an Evolutionary View of the World." In *Theological Investigations* Vol. 5, 157–92. Baltimore: Helicon, 1966.

Redding, Micah. "Can Transhumanism Lead Us Back to Orthodoxy?" *Christ and Pop Culture*, July 18, 2016. https://christandpopculture.com/can-transhumanism-lead-us-back-to-orthodoxy.

Schofield, Robert E. "John Wesley and Science in 18th Century England." *Isis* 44.4 (December 1953) 331–40.

Shortt, Rupert. *God is No Thing: Coherent Christianity*. London: Hurst & Co., 2016.

Smith, James K. A. *Who's Afraid of Postmodernism?* Grand Rapids: Baker Academic, 2006.

Sweet, William. "Transhumanism and the Metaphysics of the Human Person." *Science et Esprit* 67.3 (2015) 359–71.

Tegmark, Max. *Life 3.0. Being Human in the Age of Artificial Intelligence*. New York: Vintage, 2017.

Thiessen, Henry Clarence. *Lectures in Systematic Theology*. Grand Rapids: Eerdmans, 1949.

Thompson, Joel. "Transhumanism: How Far is Too Far?" *The New Bioethics* 23.2 (2017) 165–82.

Tirosh-Samuelson, Havah. "Transhumanism as a Secular Faith." *Zygon* 47.4 (2012) 710–34.

Wesley, John. *The Works of John Wesley: Volume 4: Sermons IV, 115–151.* Edited by Albert C. Outler. Nashville: Abingdon, 1987.

———. *The Works of John Wesley: Volume 32: Medical and Health Writings.* Edited by James G. Donat and Randy Maddox. Nashville: Abingdon, 2018.

Willows, Adam M. "Supplementing Virtue: The Case for a Limited Theological Transhumanism." *Theology and Science* 15.2 (March 2017) 177–87.

Wright, N. T. "Mind, Spirit, Soul and Body: All for One and One for All—Reflections on Paul's Anthropology in his Complex Contexts." Society of Christian Philosophers Regional Meeting, Fordham University, March 18, 2011. http://ntwrightpage.com/2016/07/12/mind-spirit-soul-and-body/.

Zimmerman, Michael. "The Singularity: A Crucial Phase in Divine Self-Actualization?" *Cosmos and History: The Journal of Natural and Social Philosophy* 4.1–2 (2008) 347–70.

5

"I think, Sebastian, therefore I am" (Pris, *Blade Runner*)

Bodies of Reel Critique for Social Hope

John C. McDowell

Introduction: Posthumanist Post-Futurity Beyond Science Fiction

BASED ON RECENT SCIENTIFIC breakthroughs, Singularity theorist Raymond Kurzweil has good reason to proclaim that during "the future period . . . the pace of technological change will be so rapid, its impact so deep, that human life will be irreversibly transformed."[1] To speak about possibilities for biotechnological change, however, is the least interesting thing to be said about such consequential technologies. What is arguably more important to ask about are the very assumptions involved in certain technocratic narratives of change. Where such tales emerge from improperly indulging in feats of fantasy, it is on the occasions they evince a naïve decontextualization regarding what it means to speak about "the human" in the first place. The crucial question, then, is arguably about subjectivity. The conditioning assumption of certain versions of transhumanist rhetoric

---

1. Kurzweil, *Singularity*, 7.

is this: that there is a formal objectivity, or a politically neutral knowledge, involved that is grounded in a substantive commitment to the difference between fact and value. Yet, this assumption involves claims that are themselves constructed within a particular understanding of the *myth* of fact/value, and the presumption that the knowing subject is a free-floating constructively signifying subject. To even begin to conduct an intelligible conversation (one that does not slip into simple praise for technological expertise and innovation, or that resorts to violently self-assertive name calling) would require a concentrated interrogation, and reorientation, of what Mary Midgley calls "the myths we live by."[2]

Where can such a conversation take place? After all, the late-modern market and its intellectual training arm, the corporate university, may have succumbed to a broad technocratism with its moral driver of expansive options for pure choice. Moreover, as moral philosopher Alasdair MacIntyre laments,

> there is no type of institutional arena in our society in which plain persons—not academic philosophers or academic political theorists—are able to engage together in systematic reasoned debate designed to arrive at a rationally well-founded common mind on these matters, a common mind which might then be given political expression. Indeed the dominant forms of organization of contemporary social life militate against the coming into existence of this type of institutional arena. And so do the dominant modes of what passes for political discourse. We do not have the kinds of reading public necessary to sustain practically effective social thought.[3]

An interesting set of questions in this vein can, nevertheless, be asked from observing prominent popular cinematic engagements with matters of bodies, human identity, and technological change. These matters frequently receive a considerably more hesitant expression than tends to be the case with intellectually shallow forms of rhetorically vigorous human biosocial-exceptionalism. This range of cinematic hesitancies interrogate what they deem to be an inability to ask questions regarding the discursiveness of the human and its flourishing, suggesting that these have been problematically displaced within technical rationality through being manipulatively reduced to objectification; the desocialized thinness of visions of flourishing;

2. Midgley, *Myths.*
3. MacIntyre, *Ethics and Politics*, 185.

and the role of consumption. In this way, cinematic regard for issues of the intensively technicized human can function as something of a cipher for a range of questions, concerns, and cultural anxieties over matters such as agential disposability, labor precarity, environmental wellbeing in the anthropocene, fairness of access to technologies in economically accentuating class structuration, among other matters.[4]

To engage in this critical tracing, the following study begins by reflecting on the metaphysical assumptions of transhumanist technophilism. From there, it exposes these neohumanisms to material suspicion as dangerous fictions. Finally, the chapter exhibits the question of the implications of transhumanist assumptions for political agency through a consideration of the cinematic tendency to locate the issues involved within concerns over the shape of late capitalism. According to Daniel Dinello, "At its best, science fiction projects a dark vision of the Technologist's posthuman future that encourages us to create a better one."[5] Within this interrogative study, however, lurks a further question that can only be negatively gestured towards: what would arrangements of cultural responsibility look like, especially those that contest the reactive conditions of nostalgic longing for humanistic values and the fetishization of progressivist transhumanist craving?

Ecce Post-Homo: Techno-Transcendent Dematerialisation Beyond Despair

Where George Steiner speaks of the dark and dehumanizing recent times of the human subject within an account of the tragic as "absolute tragedy," Nicholas Lash critically observes that not all the voices are despairing, or even expressive of any hesitancy over flights of temperographic futurology.[6] In the vein of the latter observation, the theological ethicist Gerald McKenny recognizes that contemporary technological developments entail that "vast areas of life once subject to natural necessity or fate [are] now susceptible to human intervention."[7] By this he refers to a range of bio-enhancement therapies, whether those be prostheses,

---

4. A focus on the technologies that render work precarious is provided by Paus, *Confronting Dystopia*.

5. Dinello, *Technophobia*, 275.

6. See Steiner, "Tragedy," 534–46; Lash, "Beyond the End," 47–55.

7. McKenny, *To Relieve the Human Condition*, 7.

neuropharmacological psycho-physical rehabilitations, IVF treatments, genetic food modification processes, or even spatial redistribution communications of electronic presence. The processes for the technical redesign of so-called natural order and the reshaping of its means of provision are intensifying at an unparalleled pace. It is this that eventuates in the political act of arguing through the use of a rational bluff. By this is meant the trivializing name-calling (for example, "Luddite") of those who gesture towards offering any rational interrogation.[8] The "can" of technical innovation simply appears to equate to "should" and even "ought" within the techno-fetishist imagination.

Transhumanist technophilia tends to take a distinctly science fictionist turn when it rhetorically masks its ontological assumptions and presents them as a form of techno-factism. These assumptions are formed within a soteriological metanarrative that involves offering technical forecasts for artificed evolution, a prediction of what Kurzweil calls "the Singularity." The techno-produced conditions constitute a liminal space in which the very notion of 'the human' is disassembled by bio-transgressive augmentation. In 1957, Julian Huxley, the president of the British Eugenics Society, imagined this as a new stage of the human. He even used the language of teleological responsibility to enhance his rhetoric's persuasiveness. In a telling phrase, he declared that the new possibilities of transhumanism's "threshold of a new kind of existence" suggests that humanity "will at last be consciously fulfilling its real destiny."[9] Transhumanism, in Huxley's design of it, is a term developed for describing the new form of human existence within evolutionary processes, and the theological rhetoric of "destiny" suggests that this is a necessary and telic outcome encoded or hardwired into existence itself. The new form is an irreducible fate. The discourse here operates as if human agency has been replaced by a pure techno-teleological determinism. While the term "transhumanism" has shifted to near displacement of "the human" itself, since Huxley made this claim the strategically directive techno-determinism has largely remained construed in teleological terms. So the futurist known as FM-2030 (renamed from Fereidoun M. Esfandiary) in considerably bourgeois fashion has argued that the "most urgent problem facing us is not social—economic—political" but rather the constrictions imposed by human biology,

---

8. E.g., see Ronald Green's ridicule of Margaret Atwood's *Oryx and Crake* as scare tactics in Green, *Babies by Design*, 2, 5.

9. Huxley, *New Bottles*, 17.

and in particular mortality.[10] Even though being human is imagined to be an improper limit that presently has to be suffered, its limitations can and will be shed through the reparative conditions provided by innovations in the techno-transformation that come from bioengineering possibilities. Accordingly, he maintains, transhumans or transitional humans are "the earliest manifestations of new evolutionary beings," playing a "bridging role in evolution" toward a new and unrestricted kind.[11] "Humans," Kurzweil confidently and utopianly declares in "Immortality at Last," "will have bodies created with nanotechnology which will let us build devices . . . even fake human organs—at the atomic level."[12] According to him, as the title of another book makes clear, *The Singularity is Near*.

Biographizing the Utopian Tale of the Progressivist Techno-Moment

It is important to put the brakes on the runaway futurist assertions made by transhumanist rhetoric so as appropriately to provide the kinds of interrogative examination that techno-determinists appear largely unwilling to countenance themselves. The question has to do with the eschatological moment, or a utopianism of the moment as described by Michael Hauskeller with reference to the claims made by transhumanist Nick Bostrom:

> The singularity heralds a new era in the history of life and consciousness, a time in which we, or our successors, will finally be able to realise all our dreams, here on earth, in this life, where there is no longer anything that would stand in the way of human, or rather posthuman, self-fulfilment. We will finally be like gods: immortal, all-knowing, all-powerful, and, perhaps most importantly, unimaginably happy. This divine happiness will partly result from the absence of all limitations, from the fact that we can then pursue the project of self-creation without being constricted in any way by conditions imposed on us by either the environment or our own nature (which constitute permanent sources of suffering), and partly because we will have found a way not only to eradicate all suffering, but also to get the utmost pleasure out of everything we do, which is nothing less than the "birth right of

10. Cited in Hughes, *Citizen Cyborg*, 161. See FM-2030, *Are You Transhuman?*

11. Cited in Hughes, *Citizen Cyborg*, 205. "In this new era we will take the direction of our evolution into our own hands" (Green, *Babies by Design*, 2).

12. Kurzweil, "Immortality at Last," 183.

every creature." Once we have passed through the Singularity and become posthuman, we will in fact experience so much pleasure that we can "sprinkle it in our tea."[13]

The suggestion here is that the Singularity will involve the flourishing of humanity itself as a species, and thereby constitute progress for the many and not merely for the few. This is important since, as Theodor Adorno starkly warns, "It would be advisable to think of progress in the crudest, most basic terms: that no one should go hungry anymore, that there should be no more torture, no more Auschwitz. Only then will the idea of progress be free from lies."[14] Among other things, Adorno's critical philosophical therapy counsels attention to a range of social features in the history of material existence that condition the losses that are dehumanizing. By depicting the totalitarian logic of a certain framing of the Enlightenment, his *Dialectic of Enlightenment* (jointly composed with Max Horkheimer) would constitute a therapy of ideology for the sake of socio-political humanizing that asks transhumanists whether their accounts are socially and ethically self-aware. In fact, as I will come to argue, there should be a real concern over the tendency of some transhumanists to construe their utopian imaginings in ways that are less socially responsible. Indeed, their common commitment to a nominalized particular and simple self-as-subject, that can be continually constructed and enhanced, simply cannot do the work that futurist technophilic singularitarianists or bioliberals want it constructively to do. Transhumanistic singularitarianism too easily slips into becoming not that which supports an H+, but rather which produces an "inhumanistic" imagination. Why this is so has to be articulated through the observation that much transhumanism is regulated by a desire for a *technē*-formed Singularity that is driven by a progressivist commitment to individualism.

An important way this is manifested is through the occasional transhuman appearance of an intensive gnostic-like carnophobia. A series of refiguring and defiguring bodily losses is certainly detectable in Kurzweil's account when it involves distinctive displacements of the very conditions of the speakability of the subject. Questions, then, need to be asked about the logic of materiality itself and its significance for subjectivity, the logic of the politics of intersubjectivity, and the logic of instrumentalizing rationality. It is clear for Kurzweil that the configuration of material circumscription

13. Hauskeller, *Sex and the Posthuman Condition*, 2–3.
14. Theodor Adorno, cited by Detlev Claussen, *Theodor W. Adorno*, 338.

is a frustration: "Actually, I often do have a problem with all the limitations and maintenance that my version 1.0 body requires, not to mention all the limitations of my brain."[15] However, just such a post-carnal desire, an erotics of bodilessness, is not necessarily required for transhumanism by the broad position that Kurzweil takes. This is especially so when the connection with the notion of technical *enhancement* is borne in mind. Admittedly, there are a number of points at which Kurzweil appears to be less corporeality-averse than he otherwise appears to be. Accordingly, he admits, "I do appreciate the joys of the human body. My point is that AIs can and will have the equivalent of human bodies in both real and virtual-reality environments."[16] Only the most naïve appeals to "nature," that displace the social histories of developing technical skill and control over "natural" processes, can complain about this way of construing technology and its capacious possibilities. Such a claim cautions the need for considerable attention to be paid to the difficulty of handling a concept such as that of "the natural", when utilised as a critical device in this debate.[17]

Yet there remain two sets of problematic claims embedded within the discourse. The first is one that was the subject of Martin Heidegger's critique: that technologies are only *used* by the human subject rather than construing user and used in more dialectical terms, so that there is a significant sense in which technologies use human beings, refiguring their self-understandings.[18] This critique subverts the notion of a *technē* of pure "use" that depends upon a humanism defined by pure voluntaristic agentialism. A take on this is one that challenges the very perception of reality, of body and machine, as offered by David Cronenberg's *eXistenZ*. What is interesting about Cronenberg's piece is the graphically organic bio-materiality of his technological imagination. There is more of a hybridity between machine and the bio-operations of human beings than one sees in *Farscape* with its living ship Moya, for instance. Cronenberg's integrative portrayal

15. Kurzweil, *Singularity*, 203.

16. Kurzweil, *Singularity*, 203.

17. "Nature . . . seems to function here primarily as the sign of an imaginary regression to the past and to older pre-rational forms of thought." Jameson, *Archaeologies of the Future*, 64.

18. Heidegger's argument that modernity has overemphasized technology's instrumental aspects, thus eliding an earlier perspective that saw *technē* as a generative or creative process or *poiēsis*, suggests the extent to which any notion of posthuman identity must be tied to a redefining of technology that would emphasize its poietic or autopoietic qualities, rather than its instrumentality.

operates somewhat at odds with what Hauskeller detects in a considerable number of transhumanistic visions which are accompanied by something of a "hatred of the flesh-and-blood body, which is usually portrayed as messy, control-defying, limitative, and deadly."[19]

The second comes from the notion of becoming capable of biomechanically digitizing the human consciousness or mind as if it were an information unit, or of producing the *robo-sapiens* or *homo-cyberneticus* for bio-constraining escapological effect. The desire is for the emancipation of the subject from the cave of sensuality and its erotic circumscription.[20] So Kurzweil declares that "My body is temporary. Its particles turn over almost completely every month. Only the patterns of my body and brain have continuity."[21] The loss of the body, then, is not an act of a careless misplacing of it, as much as a highly significant act of theft of ontological unity. It is as if subjectivity is a free-floating and unconditioned consciousness that is the cause of the anxiety in movies such as *The Lawnmower Man, Transcendence*, to a lesser degree the use of the avatars in *Surrogates* and *Avatar*, and more humorously in *The Man With Two Brains*.[22] These features indicate an ontological capture by an unself-reflective Cartesian humanism.[23] It is hardly surprising, given the deep cultural embedding of such a bio-liberalism, that the alien queen in *V* instructs her scientists to discover the location of the "soul" in a human prisoner. She needs to be subjected to a posthumanist philosophy, then, that engages in a form of what Michel Foucault calls "philosophical interrogation" of the modern Western subject.[24] Hauskeller observes that for Kurzweil,

> We might have bodies, but no longer be them. We (i.e. our roving minds) will have a choice which body to use when and where and for which purpose, or not at all. We will be able to wear bodies like garments that can be changed, embellished and also taken off completely. What is important is that we no longer need a body, and as soon as that happens, as soon as we are able to

19. Hauskeller, "Nietzsche," 5, cited in Thweatt-Bates, *Cyborg Selves*, 71.

20. See Kurzweil, *Singularity*, 323; Wolfe, *What Is Posthumanism*, xv.

21. Kurzweil, *Singularity*, 371.

22. The digitizations of consciousness in films like *Tron* and *Tron Legacy* fit into this category as well.

23. According to Young, *Designer Evolution*, 34, "Cartesian duality marks the beginning of human evolution from *Homo sapiens* to *Homo cyberneticus*—man the steersman of his own destiny."

24. Foucault, "What is Enlightenment," 42.

change bodies as we are now able to change our socks, the body ceases to be a threat and can be appreciated for all the things that we can do with it.[25]

It is this sense that is evident in the instrumental envisioning of bodies as clothing-like in *Altered Carbon*. Cortical stacks contain the consciousness and memories of the human subject, and these can be transferred across different bodies. The subject, then, wears a body as what the series of episodes calls a "sleeve." The narrative consequently displays a pronounced chaffing at the notion of finitude, and it has imagined a way of realising a certain kind of technologically facilitated survivalism.

An intelligent response is not to appeal to identity in terms of organic forms of materiality, as if such is an essence performing its own evasion of cultural and even ontological capture, as bio-conservative Francis Fukuyama tends to do in his *Our Posthuman Future*, or Katherine Hayles does with her concern about "the erasure of embodiment," or as do forms of Romantic goddess-feminism that gesture nostalgically and essentialistically to a binarized "feminine natural", or as equally do theologies of creatureliness that imagine that redesigning the embodied form of creatures imperils their very creatureliness.[26] Such an appeal to a metaphysics of embodied substance displaces the irreducible processes of material formations and cultural productions of the very matter of bodies, the encultured subjects they geographically position, and even the socio-political hegemonies that discipline social identities.[27] To parallel Simone de Beauvoir's famous claim about becoming a woman, one is not born an embodied subject, but rather, one becomes one.[28] After all, what constitutes materiality-in-change or the new materialism, including some ways of imagining the self-presentedness of the digitized distributed cyber-self, may well require a more morphologically expansive notion of matter and nature themselves, one that permits the kinds of subject-fluidity in forms of transgressive hybridity that someone like Donna Haraway subversively develops. That entails that there is not one way to be an identifiable body, since even bodies are cultural

25. Hauskeller, *Sex and the Posthuman Condition*, 6.

26. Hayles, *How We Became Posthuman*, XI, "Here, at the inaugural moment of the computer age, the erasure of embodiment is performed so that 'intelligence' becomes a property of the formal manipulation of symbols rather than enaction in the human lifeworld."

27. Butler, *Gender Trouble*, 33, notes how "the notion of an abiding substance is a fictive construction produced through the compulsory ordering of attributes."

28. de Beauvoir, *Second Sex*, 301.

products of discursive practices.[29] Resorting to ridicule, Haraway herself exclaims, "I can't believe the blissed-out techno-idiocy of people who talk about downloading human consciousness onto a chip."[30] Or as Francesca Ferrando recognizes, "The 21st century has ushered in a redefinition of the body by cybernetic and biotechnological developments . . . Physicality no longer represents the primary space for social interaction: the decentralization of the self into virtual bodies and digital identities has turned Baudrillard's simulacra into ultimate hyper-realities, as the growing issue of internet addiction seems to suggest."[31]

What emerges from these critical reflections is the need for transhumanism to provide an account of the subject as *problematic fiction*. It is fictional not because it engages in its imaginative self-construction, as if the subject is subjected only to its own unsituated voluntarism, to its will-to-choose that so sustains the minimal selfhood of capital's market-consumptivism. Rather, it is rendered fictional because it abstracts that self from the conditions that make it actually possible. As Judith Butler maintains, the subject is the production of discursive relations, and the performance of any discourse "has a history that not only precedes but conditions its contemporary usages, and . . . this history effectively decenters the presentist view of the subject as the exclusive origin or owner of what is said."[32] Even "materiality will [need to] be rethought as the effect of power, as power's most productive effect."[33]

We need to say more, however. The transhumanist tendency towards a desire for bio-transcendence is a *dangerous fiction*. This is precisely because its aspiration disorders the self's relations to all that constitutively contributes to the making of that self's generative spontaneity, ultimately constructing an ontological conflictuality between particulars as pure desirous wills. These are Cartesian subjects not subjected to conditions other than their own rational desires, and who are oblivious to the irreducibility of their trans-corporeality and deeply resentful of symbiotic matrices and dependencies. According to Hayles, "What is lethal is not the posthuman

---

29. To adapt Butler's claim for my more expansive consideration of the body within humanist and post-humanist discourse, "the very multiplicity of their construction holds out the possibility of a disruption of their univocal posturing" (Butler, *Gender Trouble*, 44).

30. Gane, "When We Have Never Been Human," 146.

31. Ferrando, "Body," 213.

32. Butler, *Bodies that Matter*, 172.

33. Butler, *Bodies that Matter*, xii.

as such but the grafting of the posthuman onto a liberal humanist view of the self."[34] For instance, the ambiguity of a transhumanist perspective is that, in "enhancing" bio-conditions, its constructivist spirit and progressivist celebration of human fluidity and multiplicity, to use the terms of Frederic Jameson, "replicate the very rhetoric of the late-capitalist market as such."[35] The monadic, self-interested, and acquisitive *homo economicus* eases into the techno-subject of the individuated accumulator of pleasure, and self-survivalist transcendence of the material limitations of finitude. In so doing, transhumanism of this sort fails to resistantly attend to the material forces of production that generate the conditions of alienation of selves at the expense of an articulatable eduamonistic mutuality.

The danger takes a particular shape, and articulating this can occur through asking what it is that qualifies the body within the scope of cultural intelligibility. For Butler, modern hetero-normative humanism demands an "exclusionary matrix by which subjects are formed," thereby requiring "the simultaneous production of a domain of abject beings, those who are not yet 'subjects', but who form the constitutive outside to the domain of the subject," and against whom the subject identifies herself.[36] Consequently, she identifies that "the construction of the human is a differential operation that produces the more and the less 'human', the inhuman, and the humanly unthinkable."[37] That, however, is a rather negative way of framing the relations at issue, and a politically catastrophic one for those whose embodied lives become the spaces of the uninhabitable in the direction taken by the regulation of identificatory practices.

A different rhetorical register is provided by theologian Robert Jenson, which offers (and here I use Butler's terms), "a critical resource in the struggle to rearticulate the very terms of symbolic legitimacy and intelligibility."[38]

---

34. Hayles, *How We Became Posthuman*, 286–87. Kurzweil's technophilism is not entirely naively predicating the soteriological benefits of technology *per se*. As he admits, "As well as its many remarkable accomplishments, the twentieth century saw technology's awesome ability to amplify our destructive nature, from Stalin's tanks to Hitler's trains . . . As technology accelerates toward the full realization of [genetics, nanotechnology, and robotics], we will see the same intertwined potentials: a feast of creativity resulting from human intelligence expanded manifold, combined with many grave new dangers" (Kurzweil, *Singularity*, 397–98).

35. Jameson, "Antimonies of Utopia," 31.

36. Butler, *Bodies that Matter*, xiii.

37. Butler, *Bodies that Matter*, xvii.

38. Butler, *Bodies that Matter*, xiii.

Bodies, he argues, are communicative practices, circumscribed spaces for being bodied-forth-unto-other-communicative-bodies that matter materially within the intersubjective and interdependent matrices of subject-formation."[I]n Paul's language, someone's 'body' is simply the person himself, in so far as this person is *available* to other persons and to himself, in so far as the person is an *object* for other persons and himself."[39]

The conditions for being a self only reflect larger patterns or symbiotic relations of engagement and dependency (or being "companion species") that render the very notion of this "self" a problematic fabrication.[40] If that is the case, then the problem of the performativity of the human is not what is left out corporeally, but rather what the transhumanist drive towards post-human decorporealization does as an operative way of leaving out, and erasing, "the other" and its own relations of citationality or reiteration. It communicates the desire to be free from others and from its own finitude by its intensification of an individuatedly atomized construal of subjectivity.

Reel Bodies of Difference

It is unsurprising that within humanism there is an identifiable inability to think difference differently than from thinking of it within its own hegemonically bourgeois notion of self-as-identity. Consequently, the self-as-subject and other subjects' *différance* from one another is not thought of as a performative social formation. That means that this type of humanism is indifferent to the eventfulness of subjectivity, that "the human" is not an ideological starting point but is, rather, a term depicting an ever-coming and never-ending appearing. This is not an emancipatory individuation of the subject—the realization of the Enlightenment political ideal of free, rational citizens. It is instead the individuation that manifests itself in sheer indifference to otherness, and therefore to any sense of common humanity and its flourishing. The binary remains that of me-versus-all, that is reducible to the *realpolitik* that is appealed to within an ethics of egoistic self-interest. It is for this reason that *District 9*'s hybridization of Wikus van de Merwe, a bureaucrat at the Department of Alien Affairs, constitutes a threat to the stabilizing of binary boundary setting. The very securing of the identifiability of the "us" or the "me" as conflictually related in inverse

39. Jenson, "Church," 209.
40. Haraway, *Manifestly Haraway*, 215.

proportion to the "them," the "other," is what his transmutation destabilizes and thereby threatens the coherence of.

In particular, it is revealing that in a range of movies and television series this construction of the other by the transcendent technological self involves a replacement of women. In *S1Mone*, *Her*, *Ex Machina*, *Westworld*, *Real Humans* and *Humans*, the female other is a construction that displaces women, particularly through sexbot functionality. *I Am Mother* even substitutes a form of artificial fetal production and a robot for the maternal role. This is less the predication of the simulacra of subjects, and the plasticity of the commodity in the democratization of consumer choice than two quite different matters. Firstly, the fetishization of female artifice or machinic women is generated and thereby renders women as containable objects. *Blade Runner*'s pleasure model, Pris, or the *Matrix*'s woman in the red dress manifest a phantasmic eroticism that displaces women by male technologies, as if those technologies are deeply embedded in troublingly exclusive masculinities.[41] This critical observation is offered not with reference to the fluidity of personhood and or the liveliness or agency available in a posthuman context, as if there is an ordering of interchangeability. It is more about the replaceability of women rendered technically superfluous by the phantasmically desirous male gaze in the compensation of an automated relationality with the responsibility of relational commitment. Secondly, women are erased as agents altogether. Sherry Turkle claims that herein "we are alone and imagine ourselves together."[42] In *Tau*, the female protagonist (Julia or Subject 3) will be deleted once the computer system (Tau) has successfully mapped her neural activity. Moreover, as films such as *The Stepford Wives* and *I Am Mother* suggest, "From creating images of women to creating women, it is but a small step."[43] The difficulty, then, is that of the erasure of difference for the regulatory choice by the consumptive self, the self that commodifies and disposes of objects once consumptive satiation of them has been reached.

These reflections suggest that the screened range of posthumanist issues may well be less about the common metaphysically reduced question of whether the constructed humanoid products can be adjudged to have *human life*. After all, that question can well be directed and constrained by a humanist anthropology. For instance, it is suggestive that in *Blade*

41. See Wajcman, *Feminism Confronts Technology*.

42. Turkle, *Alone Together*, 226.

43. Ezra, *Cinema of Things*, 129.

Runner, Pris responds to J. F. Sebastian's question regarding their identity with a recitation of Descartes's *cogito*. Ridley Scott's filming of a scripted re-interpretation of Philip K. Dick's source novel spends considerable time in setting up another issue. That is, the nature of capital as portrayed through the logic of the contrast between the wealthy elites who have managed to escape off-world from anthropocentric disaster and economically squalid conditions of earth, and the pure instrumentality of Tyrell's Nexus-6s. The very ecological devastation, and the subsequently degraded environmental conditions, as well as the instrumentalizing of the lives of what the police in derogatory fashion refer to as "skin jobs," have a common origin. *Moon's* big reveal reduces Sam Bell to the eternal recurrence of the same in pure laboring servitude to Lunar Industries. His very life, and death, are owned as industrial products used for industrial self-interest. *Repo Men* portrays the medical industry's profiteering, and the brutal consequences for those who cannot make their repayments. For one thing, people and objects have become increasingly interchangeable, as the mention of the displacement of women earlier makes clear. In consequence, human, and indeed all, life is commodified. The point, then, is less about some interrogation of a "god complex," if by that is meant the very ability to be technically generative, as numerous uninteresting and naïvely theological readings of Mary Shelley's *Frankenstein* aver, in an intellectually unsophisticated fashion. Instead, it is more about a "god complex" in the sense of determining the value of every-thing, and it does so in a way that is self-aggrandizing and other-disposing. So, Daniel Dinello claims that, "While the machinic replacement of lost body parts enhances the lives of disabled people, the sheer number of mon-strous cyborgs reflects a pervasive anxiety that our technological lust will propagate grotesquely deformed, superhuman techno-creatures that will ultimately extinguish us."[44] While the machines of the *Matrix* maintain hu-man existence as an ongoing source of energy, *Avengers: Age of Ultron's* AI (Ultron) attempts to wipe out humanity to clear the way for the evolution of the machine (although any potential for technophobia is quickly curtailed by the appearance of Vision).

It is not incidental that *Blade Runner's* Eldon Tyrell lives at the summit of what appears to be a Babylonian pyramidic structure. The suggestion is that *Blade Runner*, among other movies, is less a film about the nature of the humanity of constructed products (the Pinocchio effect, perhaps, such as with the Data of *Star Trek Next Generation*) than about displaying a concern

---

44. Dinello, *Technophobia*, 12.

over the self-aggrandisingly hubristic desire of technocrats, and the attendant replaceability of the self in the logic of disposability within the colonial system of neo-capital flows. The backstory of the *Matrix*, particularly as unpacked in a two-part short story, "The Second Renaissance," in the *Animatrix*, is one of the mistreatment of the purely instrumentalized machines who eventually rebel. In the words of Elizabeth Ezra, human beings are "entirely expendable, entirely subject to the needs of those who employ them—available to be exploited as needed, and then ejected, like so much human waste, when their services are no longer required or are somehow deemed intrusive or threatening."[45] They are reduced to their worth in a system of production and consumption, to the market of profitable innovation. It is only when the machines develop consciousness in the *Terminator* franchise, *I, Robot*, *Animatrix*, and *Humans* (including its Swedish source material, *Äkta Människor*), that their independent agency functions to contest and resist the instrumentalization of their lives. What is most terrifying about the Borg of the *Star Trek* franchise is not so much that each member loses his or her individuation, but that each life is reduced within the collective to the singular machinery of colonial conquest and assimilation that means the death of others' agencies.

The reference made earlier to Tyrell's abode in *Blade Runner* indicates a further feature of late capitalist anxiety expressed in many screened features, even if, as Frederic Jameson laments, it remains "easier to imagine the end of the world than the end of capitalism."[46] In an administered society, those with wealth and power capitalize at the expense of the multitude. In *Designer Evolution*, Simon Young, however, does not understand this to be a problem:

> Yes, initially some people more than others will be able to afford bioenhancement beyond the level of 'normal' good health. It's called living in the free world . . . Only the most ideological of extremists could seriously wish to deprive everyone of the benefits of bioenhancement on the grounds that the rich will be the first to benefit.[47]

The defense here in terms of market forces and a rhetorical masking of its ideological function is telling. Yet as Neil Postman admits, with computer technology, for instance, "there are winners and losers . . . It is to

45. Ezra, *Cinema of Things*, 17.
46. Jameson, *Archaeologies of the Future*, 199.
47. Young, *Designer Evolution*, 63.

be expected that the winners will encourage the losers to be enthusiastic about computer technology."[48] Echoing *Blade Runner*, *Elysium* dystopianly portrays the overcrowded and impoverished conditions of the earth as being escapable by those who can afford it. The financial escapology enables their relocated lives to be lived out, in stark contrast, within pristine, lavish, and secure conditions of the space stations. Tyrell lives high above the squalor of the streets below, as do the affluent in the rebooted version of *Total Recall*, or further up the locomotive in *Snowpiercer*. *Gattaca* intensifies the capacity of wealth to enhance the material conditions of the body itself within the available "possibilities for social engineering."[49] Within such a schema, technologies of transhumanism are harnessed not for global enhancement but for the competitive advantage of those already advantaged, thereby intensifying the barrier between haves and have-nots. This evidently leads to new bio-graphical forms of tribalistic discrimination between those deemed "valid" and those who are identified as "in-valid." In *Surrogates*, this binary is between the "enhanced" and the "unenhanced." The dangerous quest in *Prometheus* is undertaken not for the advancement of human knowledge or the aid for earthly material conditions, but rather for the private interests of the corporate tycoon Peter Weyland. More particularly, it is for Weyland's desire to prolong his life. Both *The Island* and *Never Let Me Go* reduce the lives of the on-screen characters to their harvestable parts so as to provide for the hyper-rich's benefit. *Avatar* is premised on the corporate profitability of Pandora's natural resources, and the catastrophic situation requires the compliant or forcibly violent clearing of the natives from their homes.

A further anxiety can be observed from a reference to the bottled lives in the hatchery of the Predestination Center in Aldous Huxley's *Brave New World*. In one momentous scene in George Lucas's *Attack of the Clones*, Jedi Master Obi-Wan Kenobi walks the corridors of the cloning facility on the water-world of Kamino, flanked by the Prime Minister Lama Su. To

---

48. Postman, *Technopoly*, 10–11.

49. Citation from Fukuyama, *Our Posthuman Future*, 15. "If wealthy parents suddenly have open to them the opportunity to increase the intelligence of their children as well as that of all their subsequent descendants, then we have the makings not just of a moral dilemma but of a full-scale class war" (Fukuyama, *Our Posthuman Future*, 16). Fukuyama here seems to have missed the fact that wealth *already* engages in forms of social engineering from the range of options open to parents utilizing costly promises of enhancement technologies (from particular colors of mobiles in cots, to dietary supplements, to expensive tutoring and schooling).

his left is a window onto an array of embryos at varying stages of development, and then, a little further along, two hundred thousand troops ready to fight for the Republic. Lama Su explains that a request for an army had been placed by Jedi Master Sifo Dias a decade earlier. These were the clones specifically bred to be "immensely superior to droids," with an intensified "growth acceleration" ten-year maturation period, and a "modified genetic structure to make them less independent than the original host" and accordingly more "docile." Here is an exemplification of the reduction of lives to the expedient mechanization and disposability within the military-industrial complex, the making of bio-machines or droid-persons of death.[50] This is an image of the manufacture of lives through cloning tanks and the conveyor-belt training in docility, all harnessed in a parallel to the mechanized armies produced in the foundries on the planet Geonosis. The technologies are hitched to the military-industrial complex and the self-aggrandizing machinations of the sovereign system. The clones are biomachines of death constructed solely for the purposes of securing the Galactic Republic against the threats that Chancellor Palpatine identifies as so pressing for the political system's survival.

A similar theme appears in *Alien Resurrection* with the revelation of the horrific experiments for a prototype fusion of human and alien for weapons manufacture.[51] The image is one that echoes the role of the Weyland-Yutani Corporation in *Aliens*, with its hopes of developing a bioweapon from the recently discovered alien species. For every Steve Rogers and the jingoistic celebration of the bio-enhanced national hero there is a clone trooper, or a resurrected Ripley. Accordingly, Haraway worries that the posthuman body can be reduced to the "illegitimate offspring of militarism and patriarchal capitalism."[52] The concern is a commonly voiced one, and Dinello likewise cautions that, "Technologism is a harmful system of propaganda that serves to support military and corporate demand for unbridled and autonomous expansion of dangerous technologies without questions or moral concerns . . . At its most political, science fiction illustrates technology's corruption

50. The term, "military-industrial complex" was popularised by the 1961 farewell address of American president Dwight Eisenhower, who warned that, "in the councils of government, we must guard against the acquisition of unwarranted influence, whether sought or unsought, by the military industrial complex." Quoted in Fellman, "Iron Man," 17.

51. The horror of the discovery of the genetics lab has a partial visual echo in *The Rise of Skywalker*.

52. Haraway, *Simians, Cyborgs and Women*, 151.

and destructiveness, demonstrating that it mirrors the corruption of corporate manipulation and the destructiveness of military agendas."[53]

Conclusion

Towards the end of Elie Wiesel's disturbing *Night*, the author describes looking into a mirror and seeing no human being staring back—instead, what he saw was a corpse. The technologies that served decisions of death mark the end of any recognizably rational humanistic project. While transhumanists appear oblivious of the sufferings of what Frantz Fanon memorably described as "the wretched of the earth," a variety of instances of what may be broadly articulated as posthumanist cinema disturbs this complacent misdirection.

At its best, this filmic performance offers a cinema of the proleptic present rather than of a future *ex nihilo*, and thereby it can function to "defamiliarize and restructure our own experience of our own present."[54] Consequently, Ezra argues, "Cinema is above all a medium that allows us to chart the dehumanization of people triggered by hyperconsumption, which begins as the supplementation of people by objects and results in the supplementation of objects by people, who often become mere "operators" of technologies that determine, rather than reflect, their identities."[55] What emerges are patterns of concern with person-displacement that alienates people and crushes them as disposable waste under the system of commodifiability, with its logic of substitution and replaceability, in the new empire of late capitalism. As Dinello observes, "Science fiction does more than simply reflect cultural despair and technophobia—it wakes us up to a technological world order whose rule is supported by cyborg weapons, corporate greed, macho militarist posturing, governmental warmongering, and techno-religious propaganda."[56]

This critical work functions not to obviate technological progression, especially by nostalgically clinging to some essentialized humanist conception of the human. Rather, it helps by raising the need to interrogate the values that ideologically drive transhumanist visions, and reminding that there should be no evasion of rigorous reflection on the potential

53. Dinello, *Technophobia*, 31, 273–74.

54. Jameson, *Archaeologies of the Future*, 286.

55. Ezra, *Cinema of Things*, 8.

56. Dinello, *Technophobia*, 275.

material consequences of technological "progress." Consequently, and to return to a citation from Dinello, offered early on in this study, "science fiction projects a dark vision of the Technologist's posthuman future that encourages us to create a better one."[57] Reflecting on some importantly provocative texts within this genre of cinema, can help to focus crucial questions on the kinds of discursive transhumanist strategies that circumvent the potential for critically generating and supporting a politics of agential social participation and transformative responsibility for the material flourishing of life together.

Bibliography

Bay, Michael, dir. *The Island*. Universal City, CA: DreamWorks, 2005. 136 min.

Blomkamp, Neill, dir. *District 9*. Los Angeles, CA: QED International and TriStar, 2009. 112 min.

———. *Elysium*. Culver City, CA: TriStar, 2013. 109 min.

Brackley, Jonathan, and Sam Vincent, creat. *Humans*. London: Kudos, 2015–2018.

Branagh, Kenneth, dir. *Mary Shelley's Frankenstein*. Culver City, CA: TriStar, 1994. 123 min.

Butler, Judith. *Bodies that Matter: On the Discursive Limits of "Sex."* London: Routledge, 2011.

———. *Gender Trouble: Feminism and the Subversion of Identity*. London: Routledge, 1990.

Cameron, James, dir. *Aliens*. Los Angeles, CA: 20th Century Fox, 1986. 137 min.

———. *Avatar*. Los Angeles, CA: 20th Century Fox, 2009. 162 min.

———. *The Terminator*. Hollywood, CA: Pacific Western Productions, 1984. 107 min.

Claussen, Detlev. *Theodor W. Adorno: One Last Genius*. Translated by Rodney Livingstone. Cambridge, MA: Harvard University Press, 2008.

D'Alessandro, Federico, dir. *Tau*. Los Gatos, CA: Netflix, 2018. 97 min.

de Beauvoir, Simone. *The Second Sex*. Translated by E. M. Parshley. New York: Vintage, 1973.

Dinello, Daniel. *Technophobia! Science Fiction Visions of Posthuman Technology*. Austin: University of Texas Press, 2005.

Ezra, Elizabeth. *The Cinema of Things: Globalization and the Posthuman Object*. London: Bloomsbury, 2018.

Fellman, Paul. "Iron Man: America's Cold War Champion and Charm against the Communist Menace." *Voces Novae: Chapman University Historical Review* 2.1 (2010) 11–22.

Ferrando, Francesca. "The Body." In *Post- and Transhumanism: An Introduction*, edited by Robert Ranisch and Stefan Lorenz Sorgner, 213–26. Frankfurt am Main: Peter Lang, 2014.

FM-2030. *Are You Transhuman? Monitoring and Stimulating Your Personal Rate of Growth in a Rapidly Changing World*. New York: Warner, 1989.

57. Dinello, *Technophobia*, 275.

Foucault, Michel. "What is Enlightenment?" In *The Foucault Reader*, edited by Paul Rabinow, 32–50. London: Penguin, 1984.

Fukuyama, Francis. *Our Posthuman Future: Consequences of the Biotechnology Revolution*, London: Profile, 2002.

Gane, N. "When We Have Never Been Human, What Is to Be Done? Interview with Donna Haraway." *Theory, Culture & Society* 23.7–8 (2006) 135–58.

Garland, Alex, dir. *Ex Machina*. London: Film4 and DNA Films, 2014. 108 min.

Green, Ronald M. *Babies by Design: The Ethics of Genetic Choice*. New Haven: Yale University Press, 2007.

Hamrell, Harald, and Levan Akin, dir. *Real Humans*. Stockholm: Sveriges Television, 2012–2014.

Haraway, Donna J. *Manifestly Haraway*. Minneapolis: University of Minnesota Press, 2016.

———. *Simians, Cyborgs and Women: The Reinvention of Nature*. New York: Routledge, 1991.

Hauskeller, Michael. "Nietzsche, the Overhuman and the Posthuman: A Reply to Stefan Sorgner." *Journal of Evolution and Technology* 21.1 (2010) 5–8.

———. *Sex and the Posthuman Condition*. London: Palgrave Macmillan, 2014.

Hayles, Katherine. *How We Became Posthuman: Virtual Bodies in Cybernetics, Literature and Informatics*. Chicago: University of Chicago Press, 1999.

Hughes, James. *Citizen Cyborg: Why Democratic Societies Must Respond to the Redesigned Human of the Future*. Boulder: Westview, 2004.

Huxley, Aldous. *Brave New World*. London: Chatto & Windus, 1932.

Huxley, Julian. *New Bottles for New Wine*. London: Chatto & Windus, 1957.

Jameson, Frederic. "The Antinomies of Utopia." In *Imagining the Future: Utopia and Dystopia*, edited by Andrew Milner, Matthew Ryan, and Robert Savage, 15–36. Carlton: Arena, 2006.

———. *Archaeologies of the Future: The Desire Called Utopia and Other Science Fictions*. London and New York: Verso, 2005.

Jenson, Robert W. "The Church and the Sacraments." In *The Cambridge Companion to Christian Doctrine*, edited by Colin E. Gunton, 207–25. Cambridge: Cambridge University Press, 1997.

Jeunet, Jean-Pierre, dir. *Alien: Resurrection*. Los Angeles, CA: 20th Century Fox, 1997. 109 min.

Jones, Andy, et al., dir. *Animatrix*. Los Angeles, CA: Village Roadshow, 2003. 102 min.

Jones, Duncan, dir. *Moon*. Culver City, CA: Sony, 2009. 97 min.

Jonze, Spike, dir. *Her*. Los Angeles, CA: Annapurna, 2013. 126 min.

Joon-ho, Bong, dir. *Snowpiercer*. Seoul: Moho, 2013. 126 min.

Kurzweil, Ray. "Immortality at Last." *Forbes*, November 11, 1998. https://www.forbes.com/global/1998/1130/0118098a.html?sh=5dc97be4631c.

———. *The Singularity is Near: When Humans Transcend Biology*. New York: Penguin, 2006.

Lash, Nicholas. "Beyond the End of History." *Concilium* 5 (1994) 47–55.

Lucas, George, dir. *Star Wars: Episode II—Attack of the Clones*. San Francisco, CA: Lucasfilm, 2002. 142 min.

MacIntyre, Alasdair. *Ethics and Politics: Selected Essays*. Volume 2. Cambridge: Cambridge University Press, 2006.

McKenny, Gerald. *To Relieve the Human Condition: Bioethics, Technology, and the Body.* Albany: State University of New York Press, 1997.
Midgley, Mary. *The Myths We Live By.* London: Routledge, 2003.
Mostow, Jonathan, dir. *Surrogates.* Burbank, CA: Touchstone, 2009. 89 min.
Niccol, Andrew, dir. *Gattaca.* Culver City, CA: Columbia, 1997. 112 min.
———. *S1Mone.* Burbank, CA: New Line Cinema, 2002. 118 min.
Nolan, Jonathan, and Lisa Joy, creat. *Westworld.* New York: HBO, 2016–2022.
Oz, Frank, dir. *The Stepford Wives.* Los Angeles, CA: De Line, 2004. 93 min.
Paus, Eva, ed. *Confronting Dystopia: The New Technological Revolution and the Future of Work.* New York: Cornell University Press, 2018.
Postman, Neil. *Technopoly: The Surrender of Culture to Technology.* New York: Vintage, 1993.
Proyas, Alex, dir. *I, Robot.* Los Angeles, CA: 20th Century Fox, 2004. 115 min.
Roddenberry, Gene, creat. *Star Trek.* Hollywood, CA: Paramount, 1966–1969.
———. *Star Trek: Next Generation.* Hollywood, CA: Paramount, 1987–1994.
Romanek, Mark, dir. *Never Let Me Go.* London: Film4 and DNA Films, 2011. 103 min.
Scott, Ridley, dir. *Blade Runner.* Hollywood, CA: Blade Runner Partnership, 1982. 117 min.
———. *Prometheus.* Los Angeles, CA: 20th Century Fox, 2012. 124 min.
Simon Young, *Designer Evolution: A Transhumanist Manifesto.* Amherst, NY: Prometheus, 2006.
Sputore, Grant, dir. *I Am Mother.* Los Gatos, CA: Netflix, 2019. 113 min.
Steiner, George. "Tragedy, Pure and Simple." In *Tragedy and the Tragic: Greek Theatre and Beyond,* edited by M. S. Silk, 534–46. Oxford: Clarendon, 1996.
Thweatt-Bates, Jeanine. *Cyborg Selves: A Theological Anthropology of the Posthuman.* New York: Routledge, 2016.
Turkle, Sherry. *Alone Together: Why We Expect More from Technology and Less from Each Other.* New York: Basic, 2011.
Verhoeven, Paul, dir. *Total Recall.* Los Angeles, CA: Carolco, 1990. 113 min.
Wachowski, Lana, and Lilly Wachowski, dir. *The Matrix.* Burbank, CA: Warner Bros., 1999. 136 min.
Wajcman, Judy. *Feminism Confronts Technology.* Cambridge: Polity, 1991.
Whedon, Joss, dir. *Avengers: Age of Ultron.* Burbank, CA: Marvel Studios, 2015. 141 min.
Wiesel, Elie. *Night.* Translated by Stella Rodway. New York: Hill and Wang, 1960.
Wolfe, Cary. *What Is Posthumanism?* Minneapolis, MN: University of Minnesota Press, 2010.
Young, Simon. *Designer Evolution: A Transhumanist Manifesto.* Amherst, NY: Prometheus, 2006.

6

Vast, Cool and Unsympathetic

Wells's Martians and Life under the Algorithms

CALEB SMITH

"No one would have believed in the last years of the nineteenth century that this world was being watched keenly and
closely by intelligences greater than man's and yet as mortal
as his own; that as men busied themselves about their various
concerns they were scrutinised and studied, perhaps almost
as narrowly as a man with a microscope might scrutinise the
transient creatures that swarm and multiply in a drop of water
. . . intellects vast and cool and unsympathetic, regarded this
earth with envious eyes . . ."—H.G. Wells, *The War of the Worlds*

Introduction

DESPITE ITS AGE, H.G. Wells's *The War of the Worlds* (1898) remains startlingly
relevant for readers grappling with the role of technology in an increasingly
complicated world. The Martian invaders of *The War of the Worlds* (*War* from
hereon) terrify Britain with their unstoppable war machines and their taste
for human blood. They have long since entered the realm of cliché. Yet today,
these "vast, cool and unsympathetic" minds form an eerie portrait of the algorithms and machine intelligences that underpin so much of our world's
economy and culture. The human imagination requires help in grasping the

extraordinary speed, scale and scope of global "algorithmization;"[1] any tool for analysing life during the Fourth Industrial Revolution—even one that predates Facebook by a century!—is welcome.

This paper will explore the "vast, cool and unsympathetic" Martians of *War*, and how that same description serves as a lens for examining life in a world "scrutinized" by algorithms and machine intelligences. This paper concludes with a discussion of the flaws in Wells's vision of the future, a rather Wesleyan remedy to these flaws, and a short exploration of the Christian's role in an increasingly-online world.

"The Immediate Pressure of Necessity has Brightened their Intellects, Enlarged their Powers, and Hardened their Hearts"

Throughout Wells's long career in fiction and non-fiction, a central question remained: what makes a person? What are the elements that comprise a human being? This theme is prominent in Wells' speculative non-fiction. *Anticipations* (1902) for instance, laments the difficulties of building a civilization on humanity—"a creature urged by such imperious passions . . . and controlled by so feeble a reason."[2] *Anticipations* also predicts the rise of a "New Republic" by the end of the twentieth century, where religious belief shall consist of "some orderly theological system . . . reconciled [to] his scientific beliefs; the emotional and mystical elements in his religion will be subordinate or absent."[3] Elsewhere, as elaborated by Hale, Wells describes human culture as "the padding . . . necessary to keep the round Paleolithic savage in the square hole of the civilized state."[4] Wells explores what humans are, what humans have been, and what we might eventually be. A particularly favorite topic in this context is the importance of education. Civilization, having defeated evolution, requires a *new* force to bring humankind to its full potential.[5]

At this point, it may be worth acknowledging the eugenicist elements of Wells' non-fiction. *Anticipations* argues that an explicitly Utopian

---

1. Beranger, *Algorithmic Ethics*, 4.
2. Wells, *Anticipations*, 132.
3. Wells, *Anticipations*, 104.
4. Hale, *Evolution and Socialist Utopia*, 39.
5. Gearon, *Political Philosophy*, 774.

"New Republic" will have to answer the "riddle" of what is to be done with "the black and brown races."[6] It will be obvious at this point exactly *why* Wells is famous today as a science-fiction author, not as an ethicist and philosopher.

Wells's early science fiction works, including *War* itself, take an extremely literal approach to questioning what makes a human. The eponymous surgeon of *The Island of Doctor Moreau* (1896) attempts to fast-forward evolution by surgically assembling humans from various unfortunate animals. The opposite process is found in the distant future described by *The Time Machine* (1895) wherein evolutionary forces have driven humankind to diverge into species typifying different aspects of our species.

Crucially for this paper, Wells's thoughts on the components of humanity lie at the core of *War*. The novel's characters—human or otherwise—form a kind of Venn diagram of Wells's various ingredients of humanity and their interactions. Much of the drama of the story derives from different elements being stripped away, allowing the reader to see what results.

To summarize this paper's schema of Wells's views: the *Heart* is the animal level of emotion, instinct and passion; the *Head* is the center of rationality and calculation; and the *Hand*, the "teacher and agent of the brain,"[7] serves as a kind of embodiment of a being's power over other beings. A precis of the novel generally, and an illustration of the *Hand's* power to let the *Heart* overwhelm the *Head*, can be found in the character of the Artilleryman. For all his grand dreams, he is powerless in the face of Martian technological superiority. Like the rabbits he scorns, he lives in a small burrow, dreaming of healthy mates and abundant food.

The *Head*, the *Heart*, and the *Hand* are never explicitly described as such in *War*. Still, the general shape of this schema seems a good fit for much of Wells's writing. A familiar theme throughout his non-fiction is the necessity of introducing rationality to the savagery of human instincts and passions in a process shaped and assisted by technology. "Humanity," writes Wells, "is held between education and catastrophe."[8]

The dramatic and aesthetic potential of the *Head*, *Heart* and *Hand* schema is also worth considering. *War* is, after all, primarily intended to entertain. This conflict is epitomized in Wells's short story *The Cone* (1895) in which a steel foundry, with all its ingenious complexity and

---

6. Wells, *Anticipations*, 281.

7. Wells, *War*, 132.

8. Gearon, *Political Philosophy*, 766.

controlled power, serves as a striking backdrop for the crimes of a man driven by marital infidelity to murder.

The three terms, *Head, Heart* and *Hand* will now be explained further: the Head represents rationality, thought and calculation. Wells' writings are always quick to praise what he sees as clear-headed, unsentimental rationality, ranging from a paean to Aristotle,[9] to proposals for a sexually liberated New Republic.[10] Under the schema of this paper, *War*'s Martians are entities that typify the Head. (Indeed, physically they consist of nothing more than a head and hands.) The narrator notes the "amazing subtlety"[11] of Martian calculations, contrasts human panic with the Martians' methodical calm,[12] and praises Martian industry as "swift, complex, and perfect."[13]

Further, the narrator informs the reader that these Martians are entirely unaffected by emotion or sentiment. This is attributed to two causes: firstly, the Martians reproduce non-sexually, by simply "budding off" a parent. Secondly, the Martians have no digestive system, subsisting instead on injections of fresh blood. Conversely, the human "digestive processes . . . sap our strength and colour our minds. Men go happy or miserable as they have healthy or unhealthy livers . . . But the Martians were lifted above all these organic fluctuations of mood and emotion."[14] Martian brains are unaffected by the vagaries of instinctive passions and most biological drives. They are beings of pure "Head." Here lies an obvious correlation with *The Time Machine*'s pitiless, cannibalistic, technological Morlocks.

In Wells' *War*, the Heart represents emotions, instincts and passions— and those same "organic fluctuations" which do not plague the Martians. The novel sees one character, the unfortunate Curate, stripped of his meagre reserves of rationality. This "complete overthrow of his intelligence" results in a descent into grandiose madness.[15] He begins—to quote Wells' description of Palaeolithic Man from a non-fiction work—to act "very much as a child . . . he conjured up images, or images presented themselves to his mind, and

---

9. Wells, *Short History*, 91.

10. Wells, *Anticipations*, 310.

11. Wells, *War*, 5.

12. Wells, *War*, 108.

13. Wells, *War*, 129.

14. Wells, *War*, 131.

15. Wells, *War*, 144.

he acted in accordance with the emotions they aroused."[16] This description also matches the helpless, childlike Eloi of *The Time Machine*.

War's narrator tends to oscillate between calm and panic as his Head gains or loses control over his Heart. He is able drily to inform us that "the planet Mars, I need scarcely remind the reader, revolves around the sun at a mean distance of 140,000,000 miles,"[17] yet is frequently given to overwhelming surges of panic, terror, dread, despair, frustration, and anger.

Finally, imagery of the Hand—particularly the hand that makes planned, purposeful, effective use of tools—is central to *War*. The Martians are explicitly described as consisting of nothing more than heads and tentacle-bunches "named . . . by that distinguished anatomist, Professor Howes, the *hands*."[18] Our first glimpse of a Martian consists of this hand, and the Martian's greatest invention is named the *Handling* machine.

What of the novel's human characters? The narrator's heroic brother keeps his head in dire circumstances and wields fist, pistol, and reins with ease. The narrator himself, however, is frequently overcome with passion and nervous energy: his hands fail. His every use of tools is flawed or harmful in some way: he "attacks" a water pump,[19] strikes the curate with a kitchen cleaver,[20] and kills a horse when he takes the reins.[21]

Thus the Hand becomes a way of "keeping score," of making apparent who has the upper hand (so to speak) within the narrative. The Hand represents civilization and its technological power. *War*'s opening chapters are a kind of diorama of the works of the human Hand. This is typified by repeated references to the speed, power and organization of trains on railways, to the extent that Otjen characterizes *War* as a "coal Utopia."[22] The following chapters take a certain vicious delight in seeing this civilized world upended and shattered by the superior Hand of the Martians. (It is tempting to view these chapters as the daydreams of a certain young, poor, frustrated retail worker named Herbert Wells.)

All throughout *War*, beings possessed of a superior Hand make prey, livestock, or pets of their inferiors. At the risk of "spoiling" a century-old

---

16. Wells, *Short History*, 37.

17. Wells, *War*, 3.

18. Wells, *War*, 130. Original emphasis.

19. Wells, *War*, 148.

20. Wells, *War*, 145.

21. Wells, *War*, 45.

22. Otjen, *Energy Anxiety*.

novel: the Martians subsist on the blood of captured living humans. *War* describes humanity's power over rabbits,[23] humanity's power over ants,[24] and, startlingly, "European immigrants" and their "extermination" of "the Tasmanians."[25] The ultimate expression of the Hand sees the terrified narrator flee to a coal cellar; he bites his own hand to keep from screaming while a Martian hand gropes about exploring its new dominion. The narrator, in desperation, buries himself among the coal and firewood; he has become, after all, just another source of fuel.[26]

"Their Mathematical Learning is Evidently Far in Excess of Ours"

Wells had his own reasons for creating this tale of Heads, Hearts and Hands, not least of which was entertainment. Still, for present-day readers, *War* does an uncannily good job of helping us analyze human life in a networked world: Wells's Martians make an excellent portrait of machine intelligence. *War*'s famous opening words describe the Martian mind as "vast, cool and unsympathetic."[27] This description also applies to the machines of our own data-mined, algorithm-driven, software-saturated world.

This chapter will now examine *vast, cool,* and *unsympathetic* in turn-both as Wells understood the terms, and in the context of twenty-first century information technology. "Vast" refers to the range, subtlety and raw power of Martian calculations and engineering. The advanced age of their home planet has granted the invaders a head-start on humanity. Evolution has honed their minds and sciences to the point where they are capable of launching war machines across space towards Earth—towards middle-class Britain—with unerring precision.

Vast is a description that applies equally well to the computing power at work in our own networked civilization. The scale of this is difficult to overstate: Google, for instance, processes around 40,000 search queries *per second*, or 3.5 billion searches per day.[28] When we ask our phones for directions, or check which of seven billion available videos YouTube has

23. Wells, *War*, 131.
24. Wells, *War*, 161.
25. Wells, *War*, 5.
26. Otjen, *Energy Anxiety*.
27. Wells, *War*, 3.
28. Internet Live Stats, "Google search statistics."

personally recommended for us to watch, a swarm of algorithms of immense power, speed and subtlety set to work.

Crucially, the "vastness" of algorithmic power is not solely a matter of access to ever more entertainment options. "Gradually," writes Hauer, "we have increasingly learned to trust algorithms that tell us where to go, speak for us and order for us, present to us what to talk about and think about."[29] Beranger, writing in the field of digital ethics, describes the process of "algorithmization" of society, across "all fields and areas of activity" wherein "everything becomes data, from objects, our lives, to the human being itself."[30] Beranger presents a list of processes through which we interact (often unknowingly) with "dozens or even hundreds" of algorithmic processes throughout the day. The list is too long to reproduce in full, but ranges from Facebook "likes" through to the tracking of epidemics.[31]

Interestingly, the Hand of *War* comes into play here. Wells speaks in terms of a hierarchy of species, and awareness is part of that hierarchy: the Martians watch humans as humans watch micro-organisms "swarm and multiply" under a microscope.[32] Wells's "lower" levels have imperfect (if any) knowledge of the higher, while the higher species are free to study and analyse the lower. There are obvious similarities here with the perpetual, minutely-detailed gaze of the algorithm combined with the general public's inability to gain understanding or even awareness of that process. Beranger describes this power imbalance as the consequence of "Algorithmic Black Box culture." "Most humans," writes Beranger, "hardly know anything about the computer code, the data used and the choices of values which facilitated the writing of these algorithms by the digital giants."[33]

Continuing with Wells's description, *cool* and *unsympathetic* refer to the Martians' single-minded purity of purpose. The Martians are driven to survive. Evolutionary forces, writes Wells, have stripped everything else away from the Martian mind. The Martians' plans, tactics, inventions, and strategies are discussed at length—but never their emotions. They calculate, but do not hope.

Cool and *unsympathetic* also describe the machines of our own world. Machine-learning algorithms given a specific task tend to do an inhumanly

29. Hauer, *Labyrinth of Algorithms*, 223
30. Beranger, *Algorithmic Ethics*, xlv.
31. Beranger, *Algorithmic Ethics,* xliv.
32. Wells, *War*, 3.
33. Beranger, *Algorithmic Ethics*, 8.

good job of that task; Google's Alpha Zero learning algorithm took less than a day to become the greatest chess player of all time.[34]

Algorithms do what they are designed to do, no more and no less. The programming that steers a self-driving car needs to be instructed that hitting a person is a less desirable outcome than hitting a tree. A search engine does not care if you happen to Google, "how to kill and eat my neighbours;" it will instead give you 42.6 million results in just over half a second (and will helpfully correct your spelling of the word "neighbors.") Meanwhile, researchers in the field of autonomous weapon systems have suggested that a crucial issue facing the use of war-drones is the willingness of frail humans to trust their robot comrades.[35]

As Wells's Martians are shaped by evolution, so software is shaped by humans. Infamously, a former Twitter image-cropping algorithm demonstrated a preference for white faces over black ones.[36] In such cases it is important to remember that algorithms behave only as ethically as they are programmed to. They are machines, essentially, for enacting the worldview of whoever created them—not independent agents that can be blamed for getting things wrong. Rubel et al. have coined the term "agency laundering," to describe "obfuscating one's moral responsibility by enlisting a technology or process to take some action and letting it forestall others from demanding an account for bad outcomes that result."[37] We can blame the Martians' "unsympathetic" behavior on evolutionary forces; but every unsympathetic algorithm has a design team behind it. "Behind these lines of code," writes Beranger, "are hidden numerous mathematicians, computer scientists and engineers responsible for programming [algorithms] and thereby giving them life."[38] It may also be worth mentioning the corporate or governmental structures behind the aforementioned programmers.

"At That Time No One Knew What Food They Needed"

Thus, the "vast, cool and unsympathetic" minds of the Martians form an uncanny portrait of the equally "vast, cool and unsympathetic" networks

34. Strogatz, "One Giant Step."
35. Roff and Danks, "Trust but Verify," 3.
36. Hern, "Twitter Apologises."
37. Rubel et al., *Agency Laundering*, 1018.
38. Beranger, *Algorithmic Ethics*, xlvi.

of algorithms involved in so many aspects of our lives. This is another instance of Wells's famous knack for guessing at the future: this is, after all, the author who wrote about tanks in 1904,[39] and coined the name, if not the theory, of the atomic bomb in 1914.[40] Beyond this, *War* is oddly prescient in another way: it ranks among the earliest of dystopian science fiction apocalypse stories.

Alien invasion stories have been a staple of entertainment for the last century, generally reflecting whichever anxieties are prevalent at the time. Witness the reinterpretations of *War* itself in 1938 (radio), 1953 (film), 1978 (musical), 2005 (film), and 2019 (television, twice). But for the purposes of this paper, it is worth examining Wells's Martians as the forerunners of the "robotic uprising" story.

Chapek's 1920 play *R.U.R.* simultaneously introduced the word robot *and* the concept of the robotic uprising. The following century saw countless novels and short stories featuring computers that conquer or enslave humanity. Over the last few decades, cinema has explored the idea of the computer overlord through hugely popular blockbusters such as *The Matrix, The Terminator, WALL-E, 2001: A Space Odyssey* and many others. These stories—including the various iterations of *War*—are used to explore questions of human identity and, in particular, human hubris. "Yet so vain is man . . ." is a phrase from the opening of *War* that would be right at home in many later works.[41]

Recent years have seen tales of computer overlords gain increasing relevance. "Vast, cool and unsympathetic" machines have an extraordinary impact on our lives and society. And while there are immense benefits associated with (for example) being able to Google virtually anything, the peril posed by these systems is increasingly a subject of mainstream discussion. The film *The Social Dilemma* caused a stir in online communities;[42] YouTube algorithms have been linked to the rise of right-wing extremism;[43] and programmers may need to develop algorithms for self-driving cars that can decide if running over one person is better than running over two

39. Wells, *Land Ironclads.*
40. Wells, *World Set Free*, section 3.
41. Wells, *War*, 4.
42. The Social Dilemma, "Dilemma."
43. Dwoskin, "Youtube Algorithms."

people.[44] A few short decades have seen ethical algorithms go from daring cinematic conceit to uncomfortable reality.

The central conflict of *War* is simple: the Martians, using the Hand of technological superiority, seek to strip away humanity's capacity for rational, organized resistance (the Head). Panicked, scattered humans—creatures of instinct and emotion (the Heart)—are easy prey for the Martians. The invaders, as purely rational entities, survive by stripping rationality from humans. Throughout *War*, the control and calm of the Martians is constantly contrasted with the panic and confusion felt by the humans. For example, the Curate is killed and presumably devoured, having been "robbed . . . of all vestiges of reason or forethought. Practically he had already sunk to the level of an animal."[45]

Just as Wells's "vast, cool and unsympathetic" Martians prey on panicking humans, algorithms can be said to prey on us. Note the internet veteran's truism, "if you're not the consumer, you're the product!" These predatory interactions have been extensively documented. Willis, for example, outlines an extraordinary array of deceptive design features built into online commerce platforms and social networks; this is an inevitable consequence of systems designed to extract profit, rather than promote human wellbeing.[46]

Meanwhile, Facebook reports that its users share one hundred billion messages every day.[47] Driven by corporate evolution to maximize clicks from two billion users, the platform engages users with a steady stream of infinitely scrolling feeds and random notifications. As highly social creatures, humans respond to anger, anxiety, lust, and a gnawing worry that our peers are doing better than we are. Its content algorithms can be thought of as systems to keep human users panicked, outraged, envious, and *feeling* rather than *thinking*.[48]

Misinformation spreads and tribalism flourishes under these circumstances, resulting in a self-reinforcing "echo chamber" effect.[49] Indeed, the very structure of algorithm-mediated social networks allows for

44. Reichman, "Can Engineers Play God?," 82.

45. Wells, *War*, 141.

46. Willis, "Deception by Design," 123.

47. Facebook, "Company info."

48. Haidt and Rose-Stockwell, "Dark Psychology."

49. Del Vicario et al., "Spreading Misinformation," 554.

"emotional contagion"—the spreading of emotional states between users without their awareness or intention.[50]

Further effects of this algorithm-driven space range from the 89 percent of undergraduates who reported "phantom vibrations" from non-existent text messages, through to the one hundred and fifty million Americans exposed to Russian bots on Facebook ahead of the 2016 election.[51] Beyond the monetization of human insecurity, the sheer *scale* of these networks fosters unintentional disaster. YouTube's content algorithms helped propagate videos of the Christchurch Mosque shootings faster than human moderators could pull them down.[52]

These trends have spawned their own neologisms, familiar to many residents of the online world. *Doomscrolling* describes how one relentlessly flicks through social media feeds in search of some crumb of affirmation. The *echo chamber* refers to an online space where a user will only be exposed to information affirming their own worldview. *Lurking* describes those users who passively observe an online community without actually risking any kind of interaction with it. None of these terms suggests much in the way of human flourishing. The net effect of doomscrolling, the "outrage machine"[53] for clickbait, can be a kind of downgrading of the human experience, an unpleasantly numbing and repetitive mash of near-meaningless interactions.

Interestingly, this feeds into a second great theme of Wells's writing: that of escape from the everyday, and of freedom from the tedium of a constrained existence. Edwards writes on the influence Wells's work as a shopkeeper had on his later writing, particularly his rejection of the numbing everyday.[54] We see this theme in the artilleryman's description of the "rabbits" that are "running wild and shining for fear of missing their little season-ticket train . . . in their one little miserable skedaddle through the world."[55] This remains a central theme to much of Wells's later fiction; *The Wheels of Chance* is more or less a hymn to "time off."[56]

50. Kramer et al., "Emotional Contagion."

51. Humane Technology, "Ledger of Harms."

52. Roose, "Youtube Radicalization."

53. Haidt and Rose-Stockwell, "Dark Psychology."

54. Edwards, "Edwardian Escape," 148.

55. Wells, *War*, 162.

56. Wells, *Wheels of Chance*, part IV.

A century of technological progress has, somehow, only made this kind of story more relevant. Wells's Mr Shalford demands "Fishency!" and promises Kipps he will "soon make you fishnet . . . System! System everywhere!"[57] In later non-fiction, Wells cites freedom from "drudgery" as a driving force in history,[58] and his utopian visions are centered on the image of a human race freed from the tedium of the everyday, a narrow existence of scrabbling out of poverty's grasp in various numbing, pointless occupations. Wells, in his own strange way, is a believer in human flourishing and human potential. It is not difficult to imagine Wells's disapproval of the all too familiar image of exhausted retail and office workers seated on a train or bus, endlessly "doomscrolling" their social media feeds in the hunt for the next scrap of serotonin.

"The Extraordinary Intensity of the Immense Eyes . . . at Once Vital, Intense, Inhuman, Crippled and Monstrous"

To return to the original context of *War*, the triumph of the Head (as represented by the Martians) presents a fascinating dilemma for Wells the social theorist. Hale has written extensively on the Fabian socialism that informs Wells's thinking: evolution allowed humans to develop civilization, but through civilization we escaped evolution's grasp. But in freeing ourselves from evolution, Wells believed, we also hobbled those processes that weed out inferior specimens of the species. Humanity's development has stalled, with our species a victim of its own success. Hence, in Wells's view, "the establishment of an administrative 'World State' that might restrain individualism in the common interest was a more tenable political aspiration than waiting on the next stage in human evolution."[59]

Ironically, writes Jonsson, "the spiritualized political theory that [Wells] himself considered the greatest achievement of his life has been largely forgotten or repudiated, overshadowed by the 'playful parables' he wrote to get on as a young man . . . replete with vivid symbolic images that helped make the forces of a changing world comprehensible."[60] Dreams of an all-powerful

57. Wellls, *Kipps*, 41.
58. Wells, *Short History*, 264.
59. Hale, *Evolution and Socialist Utopia*, 38.
60. Jonsson, *Dreams*, 312.

world government with a eugenicist slant were never going to remain popular in a post-war world. It is worth remembering that originally Wells' theories were enthusiastically received. When writing *The Abolition of Man*, for instance, C. S. Lewis found it necessary to argue against what sounds very much like a Wellsian scheme for the future.[61]

Grand plans aside, Jonsson notes that Wells tended to view emotion as a vice to be controlled, rather than an element of a flourishing human life.[62] Wells's *Love and Mr. Lewisham* (1900), for example, depicts a hero led astray by his own hopelessly rigid organizational system *and* by irrational romantic attachment.

Wells can be characterized as a utopian thinker with a dim view of human nature. He grappled with the resulting paradoxes through to the very end of his career. *The Shape of Things to Come* (1933), written a little over a decade before Wells's death, is a future history of humanity's progression from the horrors of the Great War through to a future technological utopia. Wells spends many, many pages detailing the failings of the stunted, ignorant, and bloodthirsty peoples of the early twentieth century—and many more describing the educated, well-adjusted beings that inhabit his utopia. But this world-state requires rulers who possess total authority, perfect judgment, and miraculous benevolence. The crucial few decades linking our world and Wells's utopia are "missing"; Wells was never able to resolve this dilemma. "The human brain released from hunger, fear and the other primary stresses," writes Wells, "is very easily amenable . . . to kindly and helpful impulses."[63] But freeing humans from those stresses becomes a problem precisely on par with opening a crate with the crowbar that is inside it.

The Martians represent a similarly difficult problem for Wells to resolve. The invaders are monsters, yet they represent the very pinnacle of what Wells desired for humanity. Technology has freed them from drudgery, and their rational minds are liberated from the demands of their bodies. The Martians are all Head, no Heart, masters of the Hand: and they are monsters. Wells, it seems, provides us with an uncannily good tool for examining the dangers of life under the algorithms—but he cannot tell us what to do next.

---

61. Lewis, *Abolition*, 424.

62. Jonsson, *Dreams*, 309.

63. Wells, *Shape of Things to Come*, 5–8.

Wesleyan thought provides a fascinating lens for examining Wells's dilemma, and perhaps arriving at answers—or at least questions—that Wells cannot reach. Wesley, notes Maddox, held a life-long interest in "the dynamics of choice and action—what is often called 'moral psychology' . . . What impels or inclines a person to initiate and sustain certain actions? . . . What might enable a person to cease undesirable behaviour, or 'free' that person to engage in more desirable behaviour?"[64]

Intriguingly, this description could also be applied to Wells. But while Wells urges the supremacy of rationality, Wesley explores a very different "topography of the heart." As Collins writes, this emphasizes "the makeup, the structure, of the human heart in terms of its dispositions, tempers and affections as they are transformed from one degree of grace to another in the ongoing process of sanctification."[65]

It is a model of great subtlety; Wesley, in contrast with Wells—and with many thinkers of his own time—believed in the "positive contribution of emotions to truly human life and action."[66] Maddox charts the development of the Wesleyan heart over the centuries, in the context of ongoing developments in psychology, beginning with the Anglicanism of Wesley's day, with its "roots running back to Plato."[67] Leading thinkers had promoted a model of the human mind that sounds not dissimilar to that favored by Wells two centuries later. They "emphasized our ability to reason" and "identified the greatest obstacle to moral rectitude as the passional dimension of human life—those emotional reactions, instincts, and the like that are not a product of rational initiative." Wesley, though, developed a model of the Christian life wherein the "affections" served to "integrate the rational and emotional dimensions of human life into holistic inclinations toward action (like love)."[68] Maddox goes on to chart two centuries of developments in Wesleyan theology, centered on the ongoing battle to value and understand the heart amid changing psychological frameworks.[69] Similarly the heart, writes Clapper, is "the arena . . . where Christian truth is either exhibited or found wanting" and "is crucial for Christianity."[70] In what

64. Maddox, "Wesleyan Theology," 7.

65. Collins, "John Wesley's Topography," 162.

66. Maddox, *Responsible Grace*, 59.

67. Maddox, "Wesleyan Theology," 8.

68. Maddox, "Wesleyan Theology," 10.

69. Maddox, "Wesleyan Theology," 17.

70. Clapper, *Renewal of the Heart*, 18.

would make a splendid counter-argument to Wells, the heart "is not only, or even primarily, the source of irrelevant impulses or merely irrational passions that need to be tamed."[71]

Wells ultimately values the Hand over the Heart. He is a materialist. In both his fiction and non-fiction, we find no God who sees, cares, or judges. The injustices of the present are many; the vindication of history will have to suffice in lieu of justice. Reflecting Wells's concern for those trapped in drudgery, *The Shape of Things to Come* notes the respect and dignity accorded to "barbers and tailors" in the far future.[72] But there is no day of vengeance for the workers of Wells's own time; they are mentioned only to provide a contrast with the perfect specimens bred by his utopia.

War is a similarly materialist work, wherein death is a tragedy unalloyed by the consolations of faith. *War* contains no last stands, no heroic deaths, and no redemptive sacrifices—although later adaptions have found it necessary to rectify this. Crucially, when the navy vessel *Thunder Child* makes a glorious suicidal attack upon the Martians, Wells *makes no mention of the ship's crew whatsoever*. The *Thunder Child* is presented as an autonomous mechanical entity, leaving Wells free to depict every *human* death as a hideous tragedy and nothing more. Even the ship's glorious battle is met with "inarticulate" cries from human spectators, after which Martian machines "rain darkness upon the land." The Head and the Hand win again.

A touching contrast to *War*'s death-imagery may be found in Maddox's collation of letters written by Sarah Wesley (daughter of Charles) upon the deaths of three family members. While acknowledging the shattering grief of death, Wesley takes great care in detailing the physical stages of death, the utterances of the dying, and her own reflections upon the eternal glory that awaits the deceased. Even while grieving, she describes "the delightful privilege of attending his last hours."[73] For Wells, there can be no delight at deathbeds.

Wells and Wesley, at least, agree on the essential *smallness* of humanity. The opening paragraphs of *War* describe humanity's transience and ignorance, while Wesley gives us the verse "Thy frame but dust, thy stature but a span, A moment thy duration, foolish man!"[74] However, this knowledge prompts very different responses from both thinkers. Wells sees a solution

---

71. Clapper, *Renewal of the Heart*, 18.

72. Wells, *Shape,* 5–8.

73. Maddox, "This Distinguished Blessing," 8.

74. Wesley, *What is Man?*

to human failings in further human works, while Wesley reminds us that whatever else we are, God has given his son to die for us.[75]

There is no doubt that Wells possessed a knack for predicting technological trends. Yet he possessed disdain for passion, hopelessness in the face of death, and a seemingly unshakable faith in centralized technocracies: the Heart vs the Head and Hand. Time has rendered his cultural and philosophical musings absurd, if not horrifying; there is good reason for the world to remember Wells as a science fiction author, not as an ethicist. And while Wells' work is an excellent lens for examining "life under the Martians," he cannot tell us what to do next. So, the Martians are coming, the Martians are coming! What are we going to do about it?

"In One Cart Stood a Blind Man in the Uniform of the Salvation Army, Gesticulating with his Crooked Fingers and Bawling, 'Eternity! Eternity!'"

Concern is steadily growing regarding the impact of machine intelligence upon human affairs. A huge proportion of the advertising we witness, the news we consume and the groups we engage with are selected by algorithms optimized not for human flourishing but for commercial purposes.[76] Engagement with these systems has produced such dire neologisms as doom-scrolling, echo-chambers, and outrage machines: programs that discourage rational analysis and incline us to anger, tribalism, and panic. And this downgrading of humanity might just be the beginning of a much larger trend. "We have now transitioned from an explicative science seeking causes," writes Belanger, "to a statistical and mathematical science, whose purpose is to predict paths or trends, and to provide a representation of a possible future."[77] The whole online world now consists of Wells's transient organisms swarming under the microscope lens. When we see a targeted advertisement for something we had thought of an hour ago, it is easy to suspect that the ever-watching algorithms know our hearts better than we do. Nor is this struggle a new one; Maddox's work details how each generation of Wesleyan Christians has had to discover anew the great value of the human heart, even while models of the mind evolve and change.

75. Wesley, *What is Man?*

76. Willis, "Deception by Design," 147.

77. Beranger, *Algorithmic Ethics*, 3.

SMITH—VAST, COOL AND UNSYMPATHETIC

In one of the more infamous resolutions to a narrative, *War*'s humans are saved from the Hand of their Heartless enemy by an accident of biology. A similar solution does not appear forthcoming for *our* problem. What then is to be done?

Reading from a Wesleyan perspective, a first step can be found in the startling realization that *War* contains two references to the Salvation Army. The first is a "squadron of Salvation Army lassies" that helps Wells paint his idyllic, pleasant picture of pre-War Britain. The second is found in the great exodus from the oncoming Martians:

> . . . this was a whole population in movement. It is hard to imagine that host. It had no character of its own. The figures poured out past the corner, and receded with their backs to the group in the lane. Along the margin came those who were on foot threatened by the wheels, stumbling in the ditches, blundering into one another.
>
> The carts and carriages crowded close upon one another . . . sending the people scattering against the fences and gates of the villas . . . In one cart stood a blind man in the uniform of the Salvation Army, gesticulating with his crooked fingers and bawling, "Eternity! Eternity!" His voice was hoarse and very loud so that my brother could hear him long after he was lost to sight in the dust . . . "Eter-nity! Eter-nity!" came echoing down the road.[78]

Can a Christian fix Facebook? Can a Salvationist purify YouTube? Can one individual wipe out tracking algorithms, restore jobs taken by automation, and re-contest elections lost to online propaganda? Almost certainly not. The vast, cool, and unsympathetic forces arrayed against us are simply too strong. Online spaces governed by outrage, anxiety, and tribalism will not disappear any time soon.

We see in Wells's earlier works a creeping dread at the thought of a world lost to drudgery, where freedom is mired in Shalford's drive to become "fishent." This struggle is replicated wherever a parent attempts to regulate how much screen time their children are allowed, and whenever a lonely individual feels a surge of irritation at someone receiving more Facebook Likes than them. Too often the heart feels like the source of "irrelevant impulses" and "irrational passions," rather than Christianity's crucial "arena."[79]

---

78. Wells, *War*, 101.

79. Clapper, *Renewal*, 18.

133

We may not be able to defeat our Martians. But at the very least, we, like Wells's Salvationist, can get amongst the rushing, harried crowd and cry *"Eternity!"* We can, in any number of small steps, set about reminding our world- or at least our family—or at the very least ourselves!—that there is *something* beyond the next click, the next video, the next upvote. God intended the human heart for more than doomscrolling.

Wells's utopias are frequently bizarre or even offensive to today's readers. Still, his insistence on pondering the past and imagining the future is admirable; and his creations remain useful for grappling with life in a very big and complicated world. An author more cynical than Herbert George Wells once stated that, "God has placed eternity in the heart of man" (Eccl 3:11). Let us strive to keep it there.

Bibliography

Beranger, Jerome. *The Algorithmic Code of Ethics: Ethics at the Bedside of the Digital Revolution.* London: Wiley, 2018.

Cameron, James, dir. *The Terminator.* Hollywood, CA: Pacific Western Productions, 1984. 107 min.

Centre for Humane Technology. "Ledger of Harms." https://ledger.humanetech.com/.

Clapper, Gregory. *The Renewal of the Heart is the Mission of the Church: Wesley's Heart Religion in the Twenty First Century Church.* Eugene: Cascade, 2010.

Collins, Kenneth J. "John Wesley's Topography of the Heart: Dispositions, Tempers and Affections." *Methodist History* 36.3 (1998) 162–175.

Cruickshank, Joanna. *Pain, Passion, and Faith: Revisiting the Place of Charles Wesley in Early Methodism.* Lanham: Scarecrow, 2009.

Del Vicario, Michela, et al. "The Spreading of Misinformation Online." *Proceedings of the National Academy of Sciences of the United States of America* 19.113 (2016) 554–59. https://doi.org/10.1073/pnas.1517441113.

Dwoskin, Elizabeth. "YouTube is changing its algorithms to stop recommending conspiracies." *The Washington Post,* January 26, 2019. https://www.washingtonpost.com/technology/2019/01/25/youtube-is-changing-its-algorithms-stop-recommending-conspiracies/.

Edwards, Ryan John. "Edwardian Everyday: the Problem of Escape in H. G. Wells and Arnold Bennett." PhD diss., University of Edinburgh, 2019.

Facebook, "Company Info." https://about.fb.com/company-info/.

Gearon, Liam. "A Very Political Philosophy of Education: Science Fiction, Schooling and Social Engineering in the Life and Work of H. G. Wells." *Journal of Philosophy of Education* 52.4 (2018) 762–77.

Haidt, Jonnathon and Tobias Rose-Stockwell. "The Dark Psychology of Social Networks." *The Atlantic,* December 2019. https://www.theatlantic.com/magazine/archive/2019/12/social-media-democracy/600763/.

Hale, Piers J. "Of Mice and Men: Evolution and the Socialist Utopia. William Morris, H. G. Wells, and George Bernard Shaw." *Journal of the History of Biology* 43.2 (2010) 17–66. DOI 10.1007/s10739-009-9177-0.

Hauer, Tomas. "Society Caught in a Labyrinth of Algorithms: Disputes, Promises, and Limitations of the New Order of Things." *Society* 56 (2019) 222–30. https://doi.org/10.1007/s12115-019-00358-5.

Hern, Alex. "Twitter Apologizes for 'Racist' Image-Cropping Algorithm." *The Guardian*, September 21, 2020. https://www.theguardian.com/technology/2020/sep/21/twitter-apologises-for-racist-image-cropping-algorithm.

Internet Live Stats. "Google Search." https://www.internetlivestats.com/google-search-statistics/.

Jonsson, Emilie. "The Human Species and the Good Gripping Dreams of H. G. Wells." *Style* 47.3 (2013) 296–315.

Kramer, Adam, et al. "Experimental Evidence of Massive-Scale Emotional Contagion through Social Networks." *Proceedings of the National Academy of Sciences of the United States of America* 111.24 (June 2014) 8788–90. https://doi.org/10.1073/pnas.1320040111.

Kubrick, Stanley, dir. *2001: A Space Odyssey*. London: Stanley Kubrick Productions, 1968. 143 min.

Lewis, C. S. "The Abolition of Man" in *Selected Books*. London: HarperCollins, 2002.

Maddox, Randy L. *Responsible Grace: John Wesley's Practical Theology*. Nashville: Abingdon, 1994.

Maddox, Randy L. "'This Distinguished Blessing': Sarah Wesley Jr.'s Witness to a Trio of Faithful Deaths." *Methodist History* 56.1 (2017) 5–13.

———. "Wesleyan Theology and Moral Psychology: Precedents for Continuing Engagement." In *Wesleyan Theology and Social Science: The Dance of Practical Divinity and Discovery*, edited by M. Kathryn Armistead, et al., 7–20. Newcastle upon Tyne: Cambridge Scholars, 2010.

Otjen, Nathaniel. "Energy Anxiety and Fossil Fuel Modernity in H. G. Wells's The War of the Worlds." *Journal of Modern Literature* 43.2 (2020). http://dx.doi.org.divinity.idm.oclc.org/10.2679/jmodelite.43.2.07.

Ott, Phillip W. "John Wesley on Mind and Body: Toward an Understanding of Health as Wholeness." *Methodist History* 27.2 (1989) 61–110.

Price-Linnartz, Jacquelynn. "Warming Hearts and Moving Minds: A Wesleyan Contribution to Theology and the Arts." *The Arts in Religious and Theological Studies* 31.1 (2019) 11–25.

Reichman, Shmuel. "Can Google Engineers Play God? A Jewish Perspective on the Trolley Problem." *Tradition* 52.1 (2020) 80–95.

Roff, Heather M. and David Danks. "Trust but Verify: The Difficulty of Trusting Autonomous Weapon Systems." *Journal of Military Ethics* 17.2 (2018) 2–20. https://doi.org/10.1080/15027570.2018.1481907.

Roose, Kevin. "YouTube's Product Chief on Online Radicalization and Algorithmic Rabbit Holes." *New York Times*, April 2, 2019. link.gale.com/apps/doc/A595675180/STND?u=61_ud&sid=STND&xid=51ee5738.

Rubel, Alan, et al. "Agency Laundering and Information Technologies." *Ethical Theory and Moral Practice* 22 (2019) 1017–41. https://doi.org/10.1007/s10677-019-10030-w.

The Social Dilemma. "The Dilemma." https://www.thesocialdilemma.com/the-dilemma/.

Stanton, Andrew, dir. *WALL-E*. Emeryville, CA: Pixar, 2008. 97 min.

Strogatz, Steven. "One Giant Step for a Chess-Playing Machine." *New York Times,* January 8, 2019. https://www.nytimes.com/2018/12/26/science/chess-artificial-intelligence. html.

Wachowski, Lana, and Lilly Wachowski, dir. *The Matrix.* Burbank, CA: Warner Bros., 1999. 136 min.

Wells, H. G. *Anticipations.* London: Chapman & Hall, 1902. http://www.gutenberg.org/files/19229/19229-h/19229-h.htm.

———. *Kipps.* New York: Scribener, 1906. https://www.gutenberg.org/files/39162/39162-h/39162-h.htm.

———. *The Land Ironclads.* http://gutenberg.net.au/ebooks06/0604041h.html.

———. *The Shape of Things to Come.* http://gutenberg.net.au/ebooks03/0301391h.html#chap1_03.

———. *A Short History of the World, Revised Edition.* London: Penguin, 1965.

———. *The War of the Worlds.* London: Penguin, 2012.

———. *The Wheels of Chance.* https://www.gutenberg.org/files/1264/1264-h/1264-h.htm.

———. *The World Set Free.* http://gutenberg.net.au/ebooks06/0604041h.html.

Wesley, John. *Sermon 103—What is Man?* http://wesley.nnu.edu/john-wesley/the-sermons-of-john-wesley-1872-edition/sermon-103-what-is-man/.

7

Angels and Robots

The Religious Dimensions of Transhumanist
Popular Culture

Stephen Garner

Introduction

Around the midpoint of Mamoru Oshii's now classic 1995 science
fiction film, *Ghost in the Shell*, the protagonist, Major Motoko Kusanagi,
utters the familiar words from Paul's first letter to the Corinthians, "What
we see now is like a dim image in a mirror. Then we shall see face to face"
(1 Cor 13:13). What is striking here is that Kusanagi's words come in the
midst of a conversation with her colleague, Batou, concerning the nature
of human life in an increasingly cybernetic world, offering hints that technology might provide not just a physical trajectory for a different form of
human existence, but also a spiritual one. We later learn that these words
are spoken through Kusanagi's cybernetic body by the film's antagonist,
the Puppet Master, and at the film's conclusion, Kusanagi, who is now in
the process of moving to a new form of posthuman existence, returns to
that text with the words, "When I was a child, my speech, feelings, and
thinking were all those of a child. Now that I am a man, I have no more
use for childish ways" (1 Cor 13:12).

The use of these sacred religious texts in a science fiction context does not privilege them in any particular way, for there are many other religious, spiritual, and philosophical sources drawn on in the film and its sequel. What they do speak to is the role that science fiction plays in exploring the impact of science and technology on human beings and the way science fiction serves as a mirror to examine contemporary societies and cultures. For, by its very nature science fiction is speculative, providing a safe space to ask critical questions about our current world, within imaginative environments used to focus upon those questions. As theologian Stephen May comments, these speculative worlds can be, "a universe as strange as possible (with equally strange creatures inhabiting it), or one like ours—except for one vital difference."[1] Whichever world is narrated, they provide the backdrop for the questions and concerns to be held up and examined.

Often framed as the reconfiguration of human bodies and minds in order to augment human individuals and/or communities, these contemporary narratives highlight what Lelia Green calls, "the widespread fascination with the interface of biology and technology, and the potential for fusion between the two."[2] It is in these types of stories that society explores the boundaries of what it means to be human and tries to distill the essence of humanness, capturing the hopes and fears of people who are increasingly dependent on technology and the cultures it creates.

The latter is particularly apparent in narratives regarding the figure of the trans- or posthuman, where human technological progress and its trajectory are seen to offer ways in which human beings might seize control of their own destinies biologically, and transition to a new and better future. In this future, humanity has been delivered by technology from many of the things seen to plague the human condition, such as illness, mental limitations, bodily limitations, and even death. These narratives exist alongside other, sometimes competing, narratives, such as religious, spiritual, and philosophical understandings of personhood and community, as well as scientific, medical, and psychological perceptions of the same.

This chapter notes a number of science fiction narratives connected to trans- or posthumanism that raise particular questions about being human in the technological world, and uses those to reflect theologically on human technological agency. Its aim is to bring both caution and hope into our reflections on human beings as technological agents.

1. May, *Stardust and Ashes*, 15.
2. Green, *Technoculture*, 167.

Science Fiction, Human, and Transhuman Narratives

This section considers a selection of science fiction narratives as starting points for thinking theologically about being human and human technological agency. These narratives, including *Altered Carbon*, *West World*, *Blade Runner*, and *Ghost in the Shell*, have been selected because they are told across various contemporary media, as well as reflecting aspects of trans- or posthumanism, particularly the application of reason, science and technology to enable human beings to transcend the limitations of their biological condition becoming, perhaps, "angels" comprised of information or "robotic" materiality.[3]

Popular understandings of transhumanism are often associated with the potential impact of particular kinds of emerging technology, such as artificial intelligence, biotechnology, and nanotechnology, upon the human person. Hence, the myriad science fiction narratives which pick up on whichever of these technologies is currently in focus, and which can be used to map societal concerns about technologies and their impact. Thus, as Elaine Graham notes, these science fiction stories form, "an opportunity to think anew about the relationship between humans and their environments, artifacts and tools in a digital and technological age."[4]

Altered Carbon and the Essential Human as Information

The first science fiction narrative world considered is the television series, *Altered Carbon* (2018–2020), which ran for two seasons on Netflix, and is loosely based on the series of cyberpunk novels written by Richard Morgan featuring the protagonist, Takeshi Kovacs.[5] *Altered Carbon* presents the scenario where the informational essence or pattern of a human person—their memories, mind, personality, and identity—can be stored in a memory device or "stack" implanted below the human brain. This information pattern can then be reimplanted in a new cloned human body (known

---

3. Sandberg, "Tranhumanism and the Meaning of Life," 4–8; James Hughes, *Citizen Cyborg*, 164–71, 87–220.

4. Graham, "Bioethics after Posthumanism," 178–79.

5. Morgan, *Altered Carbon*; Morgan, *Woken Furies*; Morgan, *Broken Angels*; Kalogridis, *Altered Carbon*.

as a "sleeve"), can exist as a person in a simulation complete with sensory experience, or just be stored for later use.

This vision of the human future closely matches Katherine Hayles's description as a possible posthuman future.[6] Here, information is privileged over material reality, with the body simply being a biological substrate that human informational essence runs on, and consciousness is seen as a side effect of that biological substrate. Additionally, the body is merely a prosthesis that we learn to manipulate, and that, should we choose, we could extend or replace with other suitable candidates, seen particularly in the seamless melding of biological humanity and intelligent machines.

Altered Carbon takes these ideas and shapes a dystopian world marked by a scarcity of resources and abuse of technological power. Bodies become consumer products to be cloned, manipulated, restructured, replaced as required, and irrelevant in the shaping of personhood. Moreover, the distillation of personhood to gnostic-like information patterns privileges the informational or spiritual over embodiment. Immortality is promised to those who can afford new bodies and ownership of their own information pattern, while for others their bodies and information are possessed by others, becoming indentured sites for dehumanization and oppression. Whether rich or poor, technology for all its promise of immortality, delivers neither spiritual nor moral development for those involved.

Westworld and Liberating Stories

If *Altered Carbon* is concerned with information patterns as the essence of being human, then the series, *Westworld* (2016–current), articulates humanness as the ability to narrate our own stories and those of the world around us.[7] Here *homo informaticus* becomes *homo narrans* as with the life-threatening malfunction of humanoid robots within a theme park. Alongside the repeated science fiction theme of our scientific and technological creations turning on us, these story arcs reflect on human nature and conduct, and on the robots' own quest for narrative meaning.

While most human clients can embed themselves in the mundane aspects of the theme park narratives, for some it is an opportunity to indulge a variety of "pleasures of the flesh," such as murder, genocide, and physical and sexual abuse of the robotic hosts, speaking to how human beings treat those

6. Hayles, *How We Became Posthuman*, 2–3.
7. Nolan and Joy, *Westworld*.

they think are less than human. Moreover, the park company is also recording those events for the purposes of blackmail, leading again to a narrative of technology as a vehicle not for human betterment and transcendence of human vices, but rather a lens for magnifying those vices.

If human beings in *Westworld* are shown to diminish their own and others' humanity, then the robot hosts are attempting to become genuine persons by making sense of the world they are in and what they have to do to escape slavery. Very human questions about the possibilities of genuine freedom, balancing their inherent created nature and the capacity to transcend it, emerge alongside the power of stories to shape hope and destiny. In *Westworld*, it is the power of narrative—that which we are told and that which we create—that is ever present, where the robots' freedom to self-narrate and to reject others' narratives parallels that of human individuals and communities who are marginalized and oppressed. This theme is also picked up in the next science fiction narrative, *Blade Runner*.

Blade Runner and Improving on Humanity

Since its release, *Blade Runner* has spawned an ongoing series of novels, video games, and comic books, each expanding on the original story.[8] Capturing the developing genre of cyberpunk in the 1980s, *Blade Runner* brought the genre into focus for a wider public. Central to the cyberpunk genre is the fusion of high technology with gritty, dark human existence on the margins of society, mixing the information world coined as "cyberspace" with dark urban dystopias.[9] In this particular case, it is a world where humanoid androids, known as replicants, exist with very limited lifespans but superior abilities to humans. These replicants are treated as disposable property who, in their quest to be recognized as persons, turn ultimately on their creators.

Once again, we see recurring themes about the essence of humanness, human technological hubris, and whether our technological creations possess an inherent moral value. The answer to these questions might be, as Norman Spinrad comments, that our creations, such as these replicants, show us what we have lost in our human lives, in this case the ability to empathize

8. Johnson et al., *Blade Runner Origins*; Green and Johnson, *Blade Runner 2019*; Green and Johnson, *Blade Runner 2029*; Jeter, *Blade Runner 4*; Jeter, *Blade Runner 3*; Jeter, *Blade Runner 2*.

9. Bukatman, *Blade Runner*, 47–48.

with others, which the replicants possess.[10] This capacity for empathy in our creations, Elaine Graham asserts, raises the main antagonist, the replicant Roy Batty, to a kind of Christic or savior figure. Rejecting the commonplace science fiction theme of hubris, Graham argues that here human hubris is undermined by Batty's self-sacrifice, complete with theological motifs, in order to save Deckard, the human protagonist.[11]

Thus, the questions raised about true humanness, the moral value of our creations, and our capacity for wise and compassionate use of technology join those from the previously examined narratives including the importance of narratives, the privileging of the spiritual or informational over the material, and whether technology might be a location for spiritual formation or sanctification, all of which are fleshed in more detail in the following discussion of *Ghost in the Shell*.

Ghost in the Shell, Technology, and Transcendence

The Japanese anime films, *Ghost in the Shell (Kōkaku Kidōtai)* (1995), and its sequel, *Ghost in the Shell 2: Innocence* (2004), were directed by Mamoru Oshii, based on Japanese manga created by Masamune Shirow.[12] *Ghost in the Shell* is set in a future post-apocalyptic Japan, but, unlike many post-apocalyptic fictional contexts, the world portrayed has much more of an everyday contemporary setting. Focused on Section 9, a government anti-terrorist unit, led operationally by the cyborg, Major Motoko Kusanagi, the film and subsequent properties stand in contrast to other examples of the *mecha* genre, such as *Neon Genesis Evangelion,* through its focus on philosophical questions around technology and being human.[13]

Robots, cyborgs, and digital networks dominate the stories of *Ghost in the Shell,* but these are less about exploring technological dystopias and more about human stories in a technological world. Moreover, *Ghost in the Shell* serves as a location exploring how technology might be a spiritual vehicle through which a deeper, truer humanity might evolve. The titular 'ghost' from the series title refers to the dualistic notion that the mind and body are separate parts of being human, connected in some way with each other

10. Spinrad, "Transmogrification of Philip K. Dick," 210.

11. Graham, "Final Frontier?," 369.

12. Oshii, *Ghost in the Shell*; Oshii, *Ghost in the Shell 2.*

13. Napier, *Anime from Akira to Howl's Moving Castle,* 104; Anno and Tsurumaki, *Neon Genesis Evangelion.*

while also able to be clearly distinguished. In *Ghost in the Shell,* the "ghost," as distinct from the body or "shell," is "hypothesised to be a somewhat mystical vessel that is in some way connected to [the] brain and that holds and produces . . . free will, adaptability, imagination and intuition."[14]

Ghost in the Shell considers important topics around the ownership of our bodies and the potential for technological enhancement to lock people into unhealthy dependent relationships with the providers of that technology. It also asks, against the classic post-apocalyptic narrative of technology dehumanizing persons, whether technology might uplift our "ghost" to a different plane of existence. It does this, Susan Napier asserts, because it "is a unique text in that it presents the viewer with two kinds of technological futures, artificial intelligence and the cyborg body, as it attempts to reconcile them through a structure that has clearly theological underpinnings."[15]

As such, *Ghost in the Shell* explores being human through the lens of the Major's cybernetic body, which acts both as the vehicle for her transcending the body and becoming information, as well as the site through which the antagonist of the original film speaks the New Testament texts noted earlier, highlighting her spiritual trajectory.[16] This spiritual trajectory sees the Major ultimately leaving her physical body, and her ghost—that soul, mind or source of identity—joining a transcendent informational reality. This, however, does not appear to be a wholesale rejection of the body over the 'ghost' or mind, but rather suggests that technology with its ability to connect both the physical and informational can lead, not to the dehumanizing of persons, but to a hopeful, enhancement of personhood.

Theological Reflections

Information Patterns and Imaging God

One of the dominant themes throughout transhumanism and related science fiction is the idea that information forms the essence of human beings. That information might be encoded biologically, such as in DNA or the neural networks of the brain, or potentially digitally, captured using a simulation of our bodies or another similar substrate that allows the mind not only to be stored but also to continue to exist in a meaningful way complete with

14. Daliot-Bul, "Ghost in the Shell as a Cross-Cultural Franchise," 533.

15. Napier, *Anime from Akira to Howl's Moving Castle,* 105.

16. Napier, *Anime from Akira to Howl's Moving Castle,* 110–11.

personality, emotions, and biology. As *Ghost in the Shell* and *Altered Carbon* highlight, there is a preoccupation with the nature of our "ghost," soul, or consciousness, and to what extent the physical body is necessary.

The question of what exactly makes us human is not new. Human beings have, in different ways, attempted to distill our humanness down into a kind of *locus humanus* shaped by the characteristics we consider unique or distinctive of human beings. Typically, this is a collection of characteristics that human beings alone are said to possess, such as the religious concept of an immortal soul or a collection of psychological attributes such as reason, language, consciousness, and self-consciousness.[17] Any creature or creation that demonstrates these types of characteristics may be seen to transgress some indeterminate boundary and enter into a domain reserved for humans.

The answer that many reach for theologically to define our humanity is the biblical assertion that human beings are made in the image and likeness of God (Gen 1:26–28), a motif which is echoed variously in Scripture (e.g., Gen 5:1–3; Gen 9:6; Ps 8; Jas 3:9). However, as Joel Green notes, the succinctness of the image of God motif does not necessarily lead to clarity around what it embodies.[18] For some, the image is found in the substance of the human person, whether intellectually, physically, or morally, while for others it is found in the ability to enter into relationships with other human beings and with God. Additionally, the image and likeness might be functional, where image-bearers represent God in the world through their presence and agency. In reality, any and all of these interpretations might be in play simultaneously at any given time.

For example, John Wesley in reflecting on the new birth found in Christ, mentions three dimensions to the image of God, though he privileges the moral dimension above the other two:

> "So God created man in his own image, in the image of God created he him:" (Gen. 1:26, 27:)—Not barely in his *natural* image, a picture of his own immortality; a spiritual being, endued with understanding, freedom of will, and various affections;—nor merely in his *political* image, the governor of this lower world, having "dominion over the fishes of the sea, and over all the earth;"—but chiefly in his *moral* image; which, according to the

---

17. Peterson, *Minding God*, 54.

18. Green, "Bodies—That Is, Human Lives," 155.

Apostle, is "righteousness and true holiness." (Eph. 4:24.) In this image of God was man made.[19]

The image of God lends itself to the reasoning that human beings are intentionally embodied creatures, caught up in an intimate web of relationships with God, other humans, and with the natural world that birthed them. However, the image of God is not something that humankind innately grasps through its own devices and effects. It is a designation that is sourced in the Triune God, the one who bestows human identity. Therefore, image-bearing is intimately tied to representing the one who calls humankind into this role, and it is an awareness of this relationship that calls forth a response from those bearing the image and likeness of God. As we will see later, this has implications for human technological agency.

The Significance of Stories

One of the dominant themes that emerges from *Westworld*, and to a lesser degree *Altered Carbon* and *Blade Runner*, is the significance of stories. Not only is the entire *Westworld* theme park shaped around narratives within which the robotic hosts and the human guests interact, but the robots' ability to begin to narrate their own personal stories becomes a dominant metaphor engaging with notions of free will, humanness, and emancipation from oppression.

On the one hand, narratives shape the reality that people live within by explaining where we fit into the world, how things in our world are related to each other, and providing scope for future possibilities. Duncan Forrester comments that stories provide us with a "horizon of meaning within which a society exists, policies are formulated, and actions taken," and lead to the shaping of moral and ethical considerations.[20] Implicit in this is the notion that, if you control the narrative, then you can control the people, something *Westworld's* theme park attempts to do to both human guests and robotic hosts.

On the other hand, *Westworld* and *Blade Runner*, and to a certain extent, *Ghost in the Shell*, highlight how self-narration of one's own life is a key aspect of being human. Not being able to make meaningful decisions, to change one's life or circumstances, to exert purposeful agency, or

19. Wesley, *Works*, 2:88.
20. Forrester, "Scope of Public Theology," 14.

even to aspire to do so at all, reflect a loss of freedom that dehumanizes, disempowers, and ultimately destroys individuals and communities. For the robot hosts in *Westworld*, this means the endless experience and developing trauma of being mistreated and brutalized by the human guests; for the replicants in *Blade Runner*, the loss of freedom is tied to there being no more than four-year of existence and no inherent moral status in persons. In both cases, their limited ability to narrate their own lives limits their personhood.

Theologically, the concern over narratives is witnessed to in the narrative dimensions of much of the biblical text, in creeds and liturgies, and testimonies of individuals and communities. Narratives underpin various covenants (e.g., Gen 17:3–8; Exod 20:1–2), as well as the lament of communities who have lost their narratives or are now unable to indwell them (e.g., Ps 137), highlighting that storytelling is a source of identity, hope, and purpose. Moreover, the Christian story includes the account of God who not only invites individuals and communities freely to join with God's overarching story of creation, history, grace, and love, but the narrative of God who enters into the human story incarnated in the person of Jesus of Nazareth, thus providing both a tangible example of God's story and the means by which human and other stories are reconciled to God.

Engaging theologically with these science fiction stories, and the contemporary anxieties they raise, means attention must be paid to the voices of those around us whose stories have been diminished, lost, disregarded, or suppressed within technoculture. The worlds of *Altered Carbon*, *Westworld*, *Blade Runner*, and *Ghost in the Shell* remind us that while technology may advance, how we use and abuse our technological prowess remains as much a concern of the human heart, as it is of the human mind. Robust theological engagement will look to include the voices of those affected by technology, requiring theological approaches that pay attention to those voices, allow them to be heard and valued, and offer something constructive to be done with and led by those affected.

Therefore, it will be essential to pay attention not only to the traditional theological voices but also to liberationist, feminist, non-white, and non-Western theological approaches to make sure that missing voices and experiences are not only heard but contribute to genuine human flourishing for all people within technoculture.[21] In a very real sense, we are asked not

---

21. Butler, *Black Transhuman Liberation Theology*; Hill, *Black Bodies and Transhuman Realities*; Thweatt-Bates, *Cyborg Selves*.

only what the gospel of Jesus Christ has to say about technology to those in the Christian community, but how something distinctly related to the gospel can be offered into public spaces so as robustly to engage with technology and its effects for all people—in the present and in the future.

Hopeful Visions

While many science fiction narratives, including those surveyed here, are dystopian, others give glimpses of, if not utopian then hopeful, futures such as *Ghost in the Shell*'s notion that technology might be a vehicle for human spiritual development. That said, though, we must be genuinely aware that human technology possesses both our strengths and our weaknesses. Moreover, if we understand sin and ruptured relationships to permeate all human life and activity to some degree, how then do we engage technology faithfully and hopefully? The narratives considered in this chapter, especially *Westworld* and *Blade Runner,* reflect upon human technological hubris, where our technological overreaching and transgressing certain boundaries come back to hurt us. Like Icarus, we fly too near to the sun and fall to our doom, whether because our creations turn upon us or our very nature is dehumanized.

One theological attempt to overcome this problem within the technological context is the metaphor, proposed by Philip Hefner and developed further by others such as Ted Peters, linked to a functional interpretation of the image of God, that describes human beings as created co-creators.[22] The metaphor emphasizes both the immanent and transcendent in human being, with the "created" aspect of the metaphor asserting the creaturehood of the human being as a created, dependent, and finite being, while the "co-creator" aspect speaks of a calling to act as an agent with or for God within the natural world. Both aspects warn against hubris by identifying humans as created and finite, with the "co-" aspect reflecting that the human is never the equal of God in creative agency. The human being as image-bearer is an agent working with and for God's creative activity that embraces both creation from nothing and ongoing creation.

Thus, humans are called to be technological, but to do so in ways that align with God's purposes and never to aspire to be God themselves. Peters, for example, emphasizes that human creaturehood means that while

---

22. Peters, *God—The World's Future*, 155–59; Peters, "Techno-Secularism," 859–60; Hefner, *Human Factor*, 27.

human and divine creativity might be seen in some ways as analogous to each other, the two should never be equated—we are encouraged to create but also warned against utopian hubris. Participation in Christ, through the Holy Spirit, gives human beings and their present agency a futurist trajectory, drawn forward toward the new Adam and new creation that God has in the future.[23] In this trajectory then perhaps a form of Wesleyan sanctification, of becoming more "perfect" in and through technological agency, might be a possibility.

This proleptic vision of human technological agency is then rooted in Christian hope and the anticipation of a new reality, giving adding purposeful, spiritual dynamics to this agency and identifying it as a location for discipleship. We become, as Robert Russell puts it, eschatological companions through the new creation seen in the resurrection of Christ, and the eschatological horizon generated by this event.[24] Not that we usurp God to attempting to create heaven on earth in our own efforts, but we strive to align our human creativity with the vision we see dimly as in a mirror. This adds an ethical dimension to human co-creation that is inspired by the promise of God for a future wherein the world is recreated and humanity and creation flourish.

Conclusion

This chapter opened with noting that the film *Ghost in the Shell* explicitly used parts of 1 Corinthians to explore humanness in relation to technology. Science fiction itself echoes those verses when it looks at the future, as in a mirror dimly, and tells stories that express our hopes and fears about science, technology, and being human in present and future worlds. Each narrative discussed has raised particular questions around identity, freedom and autonomy, human technological agency, and technology as a site for spiritual development and engagement.

In bringing those questions into dialogue with theology this chapter has highlighted that our true human identity is sourced firstly, and above all else, in the triune God. Our grasping to understand that reality, seen particularly in our interpretations of the image of God, is experienced in both the awe and anxiety we feel about human technological ability. Science fiction narratives are a helpful tool for pushing us to think not only

23. Peters, *God—The World's Future*, 155–59; Peters, "Techno-Secularism," 859–60.
24. Russell, "Five Attitudes Toward Nature," 858–61.

about ethical uses of technology, but also how that technology shapes how we think about ourselves and others. This is also framed within an eschatological trajectory, where Christian hope shapes how we are technological and becoming more like the image of Christ every day.

In conclusion, we return to 1 Corinthians and the end of that particular passage of Scripture, where we read, "And now these three remain: faith, hope and love. But the greatest of these is love" (1 Cor 13:13). As we contemplate these science fiction stories and the wider narratives of technology and technoculture, we are reminded that dystopias presented are often because of a lack of those virtues of faith, hope, and love in the application of human agency. Putting those virtues front and center reminds us to create and live with technology in ways that are faithful to God and to others, and which bring hope in all our contexts, particularly as we live in and shape our technological worlds.

Bibliography

Anno, Hideaki, and Kazuya Tsurumaki, dir. *Neon Genesis Evangelion*. Tokyo: TV Tokyo, 1995–1996.

Bukatman, Scott. *Blade Runner*. London: British Film Institute, 1997.

Butler, Philip. *Black Transhuman Liberation Theology: Technology and Spirituality*. New York: Bloomsbury Academic, 2019.

Daliot-Bul, Michal. "Ghost in the Shell as a Cross-Cultural Franchise: From Radical Posthumanism to Human Exceptionalism." *Asian Studies Review* 43.3 (2019) 527–43.

Forrester, Duncan B. "The Scope of Public Theology." *Studies in Christian Ethics* 17.2 (2004) 5–19.

Graham, Elaine. "Bioethics after Posthumanism: Natural Law, Communicative Action and the Problem of Self-Design." *Ecotheology* 9.2 (2004) 178–98.

———. "The Final Frontier? Religion and Posthumanism in Film and Television." In *The Palgrave Handbook of Posthumanism in Film and Television*, edited by Michael Hauskeller, et al., 361–70. Basingstoke, NY: Palgrave Macmillan, 2015.

Green, Joel B. "'Bodies—That Is, Human Lives': A Re-Examination of Human Nature in the Bible." In *Whatever Happened to the Soul? Scientific and Theological Portraits of Human Nature*, edited by Warren S. Brown et al., 149–73. Minneapolis: Fortress, 1998.

Green, Lelia. *Technoculture: From Alphabet to Cybersex*. Crowsnest, NSW: Allen and Unwin, 2002.

Green, Michael, and Mike Johnson. *Blade Runner 2019*. London: Titan Comics, 2019–2020.

———. *Blade Runner 2029*. London: Titan Comics, 2020–.

Hayles, N. Katherine. *How We Became Posthuman: Virtual Bodies in Cybernetics, Literature, and Informatics*. Chicago: University of Chicago Press, 1999.

Hefner, Philip. *The Human Factor: Evolution, Culture and Religion*. Theology and the Sciences. Minneapolis: Fortress, 1993.

Hill, Melvin G., ed. *Black Bodies and Transhuman Realities: Scientifically Modifying the Black Body in Posthuman Literature and Culture*. Lanham: Lexington, 2019.

Hughes, James. *Citizen Cyborg: Why Democratic Societies Must Respond to the Redesigned Human of the Future*. Boulder, CO: Westview Press, 2004.

Jeter, K. W. *Blade Runner 2: The Edge of Human*. New York: Bantam Books, 1995.

———. *Blade Runner 3: Replicant Night*. New York: Bantam Books, 1996.

———. *Blade Runner 4: Eye & Talon*. London: Victor Gollancz, 2000.

Johnson, Mike, K. Perkins, and Mellow Brown. *Blade Runner Origins*. London: Titan Comics, 2021–.

Kalogridis, Laeta, creat. *Altered Carbon*. Los Gatos, CA: Netflix, 2018–2020.

May, Stephen. *Stardust and Ashes: Science Fiction in Christian Perspective*. London: SPCK, 1998.

Morgan, Richard. *Altered Carbon*. London: Gollancz, 2002.

Morgan, Richard K. *Broken Angels*. London: Gollancz, 2003.

———. *Woken Furies*. London: Gollancz, 2005.

Napier, Susan Jolliffe. *Anime from Akira to Howl's Moving Castle: Experiencing Contemporary Japanese Animation*. Updated edition. New York: Palgrave Macmillan, 2005.

Nolan, Jonathan, and Lisa Joy, creat. *Westworld*. New York: HBO, 2016–2020.

Oshii, Mamoru, dir. *Ghost in the Shell 2: Innocence*. Tokyo: Production I.G and Studio Ghibli, 2004. 98 min.

———. *Ghost in the Shell (Kōkaku Kidōtai)*. Tokyo: Production I.G and Bandai Visual, 1995. 82 min.

Peters, Ted. *God—the World's Future: Systematic Theology for a New Era*. Second edition. Minneapolis: Fortress Press, 2000.

———. "Techno-Secularism, Religion, and the Created Co-Creator." *Zygon* 40.4 (December 2005) 845–62.

Peterson, Gregory R. *Minding God: Theology and the Cognitive Sciences*. Minneapolis: Fortress, 2003.

Russell, Robert J. "Five Attitudes toward Nature and Technology from a Christian Perspective." *Theology and Science* 1.2 (October 2003) 149–59.

Sandberg, Anders. "Tranhumanism and the Meaning of Life." In *Religion and Transhumanism: The Unknown Future of Human Enhancement*, edited by Calvin R. Mercer and Tracy J. Trothen, 3–22. Santa Barbara, CA: Praeger, 2015.

Spinrad, Norman. "The Transmogrification of Philip K. Dick." In *Science Fiction in the Real World*, edited by Norman Spinrad, 198–216. Carbondale: Southern Illinois University Press, 1990.

Thweatt-Bates, Jeanine. *Cyborg Selves: A Theological Anthropology of the Posthuman*. Ashgate Science and Religion Series. Farnham: Routledge, 2012.

Wesley, John. *The Works of John Wesley: Volume 2: Sermons II, 34–70*. Edited by Albert C. Outler. Nashville: Abingdon, 1985.

8

Sex Robots and People

GRENVILLE J.R. KENT

> "The eeriness of dolls comes solely from the fact that they are
> modeled on human beings . . . They make us face the fear of be-
> ing made of simple mechanisms and matter. In other words . . .
> that fundamentally all humans belong to the void."—Mamoru
> Oshii, *Ghost in the Shell 2 Innocence*

PAPERS ABOUT SEXBOTS ATTRACT some funny comments at academic
conferences, yet since *Nature* recognized "legitimate scientific questions"
around this topic, researchers in AI, robotics, social science, sexology, law,
and theology are responding.[1] This paper sketches a theological analysis
of sex robots, which can be defined as "machines shaped as humans and
specifically programmed to provide sexual performances."[2]

Fiction

Two millennia before sex dolls, Ovid imagined Pygmalion carving his
ideal woman from ivory and the goddess Aphrodite bringing her to
life. Polybius gave us Apega, which looked like the king's wife but had

---

1. *Nature*, "Let's talk about sex robots," 138.
2. Rigotti, "How to Apply Asimov's First Law," 161–70.

mechanical arms to crush would-be lovers. *The Future Eve* (1886) imagines Thomas Edison inventing a mechanical woman.[3]

Over 200 artificial females or gynoids appear in various media including anime, comics, plays, books, pinball machines, and music, and at least 102 films.[4] *Metropolis* (1927) shows Maria bringing hope to workers until politicians make a *Maschinenmensch* double to deceive them. The replicants in *Blade Runner* (1982) are sexualized, with Pris defined as a "basic pleasure model." *Android* (1982) shows an attempt to develop the perfect female. Austin Powers fights sexy fembots with bullet-firing nipples; the term fembots came from *The Bionic Woman* (1976), another tech-enhanced gynoid. Spielberg's *A.I.* (2001) shows Gigolo Joe and Jane becoming sentient and emotional. *The Stepford Wives* (2004) are murdered women turned into sexy, submissive animatrons. *Lars and the Real Girl* (2007) tenderly depicts a young man's delusion that a RealDoll is real: friends support him, even sitting in church with "her," until she "dies," and he begins a real relationship. *Her* (2013) shows a man falling in love with a virtual assistant with AI, voiced by Scarlett Johansson. Since she has no body, he has phone sex with her and then tries using a sex surrogate, but he cannot sustain this. He discovers she is in thousands of relationships simultaneously. In *Ex Machina* (2014), the humanoid Ava has to convince a young programmer that she is human, so that he will develop empathy for her and not let her be switched off. His tech CEO boss, Nathan, has a robot named Kyoko, who cleans, cooks, and sleeps with him but has no voice. *Westworld* (2016) is a dystopian theme park where people pay to abuse, rape, torture and murder Dolores and the other robots repeatedly. TV series *Humans* and *Black Mirror* both dramatize robotic sexual dilemmas.

These stories are usually gender-asymmetrical.[5] Döring and Poeschl analyzed 710 historic media productions and found most human partners were male and most robots female.[6] Exceptions include *Electric Dreams* (1984), about a man and his PC competing for the love of a musician neighbor, and *Bicentennial Man* (1999), in which Robin Williams' robot upgrades to near-human sentience and emotion and learns to love (rather than being programmed to love), marrying the grown-up grand-daughter

3. de l'Isle-Adam, *Tomorrow's Eve*.

4. Wikimedia Foundation, "List of fictional gynoids"; IMDb, "Artificial Females in Movies and Television."

5. Richardson, "Asymmetrical 'Relationship,'" 290–93.

6. Döring and Poeschl, "Love and Sex with Robots," 665–77.

of his original owners. He can make love (depicted sensitively) and age and die with her. The narrative, co-authored by Isaac Asimov, is rich with questions about humanity, freedom, love, and eternal life.[7]

Gibson argues that "fictional depictions" like these can move the Overton window, the frame of what is socially acceptable.[8] A study found 9 percent of US adults would have sex with robots.[9] Some 2/3 of males were in favor, while 2/3 of females were opposed, however, 86 percent thought robots could satisfy sexual desire. Most viewed robot sex more like masturbation or using a vibrator than having sex with a human.[10] A German study found 9 percent of men and 2 percent of women had already used a sex doll.[11] A Dutch study found 20.2 percent expected sex robots would not have negative consequences while 13.3 percent feared they would change norms and values.[12]

Japan seems most accepting. Its *otaku* subculture, the socially secluded indoor people who enjoy anime and may sleep beside body pillows showing manga characters, feel least eeriness towards sex robots and the highest intention to use them.[13] In Japanese *bishojo* (pretty girl) computer games, wildly popular since the 1980s, male players pursue girls depicted in anime style, with huge eyes and a small nose and mouth, often in school uniform or childlike appearance. These games often involve rape, torture, and incest, as does much Japanese pornography. 70 percent of female Japanese millennials are not in a relationship except with virtual boyfriends on their phones.[14]

Trans-Humanist Fantasy

Many fictional stories assume the meta-narrative of trans-humanism. In *Sex and the Posthuman Condition*, Hauskeller begins with the assumption that, after the Singularity, posthumans will be "super-intelligent" and "capable of experiencing pleasures that go far beyond anything we can experience

7. Cheok and Zhang, *Human–Robot Intimate Relationships*, 4.
8. Gibson, *Desire in the Age of Robots and AI*, 133.
9. HuffPost, "Robot Sex Poll."
10. Scheutz and Arnold, "Are We Ready for Sex Robots?" 351–58.
11. Döring and Poeschl, "Sex Toys, Sex Dolls, Sex Robots," 53.
12. de Graaf and Allouch, "Anticipating Our Future Robot Society."
13. Appel et al., "Otakuism and the Appeal of Sex Robots."
14. Cheok and Zhang, *Human–Robot Intimate Relationships*, 6–7.

now." Hauskeller predicts that by around 2033, silicone evolution will end the human era and "we, or our successors, will finally be able to realize all our dreams, here on earth, in *this* life."[15]

> We will finally be like gods: immortal, all-knowing, all-powerful, and, perhaps most importantly, unimaginably happy. This divine happiness will partly result from the absence of all limitations, from the fact that we can then pursue the project of self-creation without being constricted in any way . . . by either the environment or our own nature.[16]

This begins by enhancing, then replacing, the "deathtrap" or "meatbag" of the human body. You might try "some entirely new sexual organ . . . The possibilities will be endless.[17]

Hauskeller views death as the greatest evil and life as the most valuable thing—but he means one's own life and death, not others'. He predicts immortality by the twenty-second century,[18] and in this non-religious heaven, love would be entirely materialist and reductionist, regulated by neuroenhancers: "it is recommended (even urged as a moral obligation) that we explore these options to enhance our love life." For Hauskeller, the best sex is not "a more complete bodily and spiritual communion with another human being, but . . . the attainment of more intense pleasures and the ability to enjoy those pleasures to the greatest possible extent."[19]

Post-humans will eliminate jealousy and any other emotions left over from pair-bonding, and thus widen their range of sexual pleasures. This will be entirely loveless, since the "logic of transhumanism demands that love be abandoned because it makes us vulnerable."[20] We will reach a stage when "the real person . . . is no longer needed or wanted" and we are free "to think only of ourselves" and "enjoy sex with the person we know best and love most: ourselves."[21] This is in effect the "transformation of the sexual partner into a masturbation device."[22]

---

15. Hauskeller, *Sex and the Posthuman Condition*, 1.
16. Hauskeller, *Sex and the Posthuman Condition*, 3.
17. Hauskeller, *Sex and the Posthuman Condition*, 1, viii, 7.
18. Hauskeller, *Sex and the Posthuman Condition*, 65.
19. Hauskeller, *Sex and the Posthuman Condition*, 5.
20. Hauskeller, *Sex and the Posthuman Condition*, 65.
21. Hauskeller, *Sex and the Posthuman Condition*, 85.
22. Hauskeller, *Sex and the Posthuman Condition*, 1.

Even darker, Hauskeller finds "transhumanist fantasies . . . can be understood as sublimated rape fantasies." Real humans "always resist their complete instrumentalisation and disempowerment" but robots do not. "We can just use them. Humans like to see themselves as ends and tend to resent being treated as a mere means. Sexbots won't object. They *are* means."[23] He claims we will "*all* be happy rapists, which means that there won't be any victims, nobody to complain about it or suffer from it."[24]

Bizarrely, Hauskeller uses the robots' lack of freedom as evidence that they have souls (in quotation marks). They can never abandon us and "will always appear welcoming and loving," and this makes them superior to human lovers and gives them "the 'soul' that we crave for and that we rarely find in humans."[25]

Hauskeller credits the Marquis de Sade for his ethics and worldview, and quotes Dolmancé from Sade's *Philosophy in the Bedroom*, a novel in which a fifteen-year-old girl is sexually corrupted and the mother who tries to protect her is raped, beaten, threatened with murder by her daughter, deliberately infected with syphilis and surgically mutilated. Hauskeller says we have been,

> "tossed reluctantly into this dismal universe" and are forced to lead a miserable existence. There is no God, no afterlife, no hope, no meaning. Religion is a mere superstition and morality has been invented by the weak to . . . hold the strong in shackles. The only thing that matters in such a world is that one does everything in one's power to be happy . . . and happiness consists in nothing other than the satisfaction of one's own passions and desires . . . The pleasure and pain of others is (or should be) nothing to me.[26]

This seems like religion for nerds, and Hauskeller sounds like the serpent who told the first humans, "Ye shall be as gods" (Gen 3:5). Similarly, Ray Kurzweil, pioneer of the singularity, was asked whether there is a God. He replied, "Well, I would say, not yet."[27] Yet humans hoping to be divine should note that it is not we humans who enjoy this future, but the tech-enhanced master-race who will replace us. Logically, the thought

23. Hauskeller, *Sex and the Posthuman Condition*, 23–24.

24. Hauskeller, *Sex and the Posthuman Condition*, 87.

25. Hauskeller, *Sex and the Posthuman Condition*, 11.

26. Hauskeller, *Sex and the Posthuman Condition*, 66.

27. Rennie, "Immortal Ambitions."

of deified silicone replacing our real children should make us about as happy as Neanderthals.

This is scientism on steroids, promising complete mastery of the environment and of ourselves, but will there be no conflict among these self-seeking *Übermenschen*? Can they live with no limitations bar the one "moral obligation" Hauskeller mentions, namely to use chemicals to enhance our entirely chemical romances? Would life with no other people be happy, or tragically lonely, psychologically unhealthy, and solipsistic? Could selfish, instrumental sex hide users from the pleasure of giving pleasure, the empathetic enjoyment of your loved one's enjoyment? Sex with machines could satisfy, "if someone believes humans are things, and if they think instrumental relationships between persons are positive with no resulting impact on social relations between persons."[28] Further, if pair-bonding helps our species survive, why would loveless machines reproduce when their offspring would have needs that impinge on the parents' selfishness? This bleak, atheistic nihilism inspires an ethic of lonely hedonism.

Hauskeller's doubters could say the promised transhumanist utopia has always been a generation away. Floreano and Nosengo predict human-robot marriage by 2071.[29] Yet back in 1986, anthropology professor Arthur Harkins predicted it by 2000.[30] By the time their predictions fail, futurists have had their publicity and made their careers. As Herzfeld says, "the field of AI generally has been one of overpromise and underachievement."[31] In 1999, Ray Kurzweil's *The Age of Spiritual Machines* predicted full touch VR sex by 2019, "the all-enveloping, highly realistic, visual-auditory-tactile virtual environment" which is a "viable competitor to the real thing," offering "sensations that are more intense and pleasurable than conventional sex, as well as physical experiences that currently do not exist."[32] So, how are sexbots progressing?

Current Realities

The Foundation for Responsible Robotics observes that reality is "considerably different," and all we have (even on the drawing boards) are

28. Richardson, "Sex Robot Matters," 52.

29. Floreano and Nosengo, *Tales from a Robotic World*, 87.

30. Cheok and Zhang, *Human–Robot Intimate Relationships*, 189.

31. Danaher, "Regulating Child Sex Robots," 553–75.

32. Kurzweil, *Age of Spiritual Machines*, 185. See Kent, "Cybersex," 24–32.

"essentially mechanized sex dolls with limited expressiveness and minimal conversational capacities."[33]

The market leader is Abyss Creations, USA, whose RealDolls have been in dozens of films and TV shows since 1996. Their Harmony model, starting at US $15,000, has heating and lubrication systems in its vagina.[34] Touch one of its erogenous zones and it will moan and talk dirty.[35] (Think Siri with a different vocabulary.) You can move it into various positions and buy customized faces, nipple sizes, etc. Most developed countries have similar manufacturers, and the majority of dolls look female, though Sinthetics offers a male sex doll with a penis that goes from flaccid to erect. Doll Sweet, from China, speaks, but the servos controlling its body movements are noisy and there is no AI. Dolls can have basic voice interactions, but usually the mouth doesn't match the speech, and the orgasmic moaning doesn't match "the completely immobile silicone form with the fixed expression."[36]

Sex doll brothels are appearing across Europe, the US, Canada, and Japan.[37] David Levy claims they will meet clients' needs,[38] especially those who are without human partners, and will end sex trafficking.[39] Some imagine "perfect sex" for sale by androids (carefully cleaned of "human fluids").[40] But one spokeswoman for a Sex Professional Association said they were no threat: "They do not communicate. They do not listen to you or caress you, they do not comfort you or look at you."[41] Reporter Nick Pritchard found the room he visited investigating his story stank of latex. The doll was glassy-eyed and heavy to move, "more like the horror puppet Chucky than Belle de Jour," and "at one point her wig pops off." He writes, "Can this really be someone's idea of kinky fun? . . . My encounter . . . is as far removed from

33. Sharkey et al., *Our Sexual Future with Robots*, 3.

34. Kleeman, *Sex Robots and Vegan Meat*.

35. Lurie, *Rise of the Sex Machines*, 10.

36. Devlin, "In Defence of Sex Machines," 151.

37. Dickson, "Sex Doll Brothels are Now a Thing." See also "Inside a Robot Sex Brothel" and "Sex Robot Brothels Gaining Popularity in Europe."

38. Levy, *Love and Sex with Robots*.

39. Waddell, "Inside Britain's Sex Robot Brothels."

40. Yeoman and Mars, "Robots, Men and Sex Tourism," 365–71.

41. Devlin, *Turned On*, 236.

real human contact as it is possible to get. Sex has never been further from my mind — so I politely make my excuses and leave."[42]

Current realities include:

Limited physicality

The Centre for Transhumanity predicts

> climaxes thrice as gigantic because they'll be more desirable, patient, eager, and altruistic than their meat-bag competition, plus they'll be uploaded with supreme sex-skills from millennia of erotic manuals, archives, and academic experiments, and their anatomy will feature sexplosive devices . . . [They will] offer us quadruple-tongued cunnilingus, open-throat silky fellatio, deliriously gentle kissing.[43]

Yet anyone expecting that from present technology will be disappointed. Take kissing—or "philematology." The best technology is the Kiss Transmission Device from Kajimoto Laboratory, basically a box with a straw that you swirl with your tongue, and that makes a straw swirl in your faraway lover's mouth. Reviewers admit:

> A problem with this device is the unnatural and rigid user interface. The straw of the device essentially serves as the tongue of a remote kisser, however its shape and texture do not bear any resemblance to a human tongue. The body of the device is also in the form of an unappealing plastic box, making the kissing experience too mechanical and less affective.[44]

Another device called Intimate Mobiles "has a moisture sensor that detects the wetness of the sender's device and the receiver's device will be actuated with the same wetness. Moisture is generated by a membrane over a wet motorized sponge."[45]

Compare that to what a loving, passionate kiss can do. Human lips have vastly superior technology. The mouth and nearby facial tissues have complicated taste receptors plus six types of mechanoreceptors detecting touch, pressure, vibration, stretch, indentation, structure, and texture, as

---

42. Pritchard, "Puppet in a G-String."
43. Pellissier, "Sexbots Will Give Us Longevity Orgasms."
44. Cheok and Zhang, *Human–Robot Intimate Relationships*, 83.
45. Cheok and Zhang, *Human–Robot Intimate Relationships*, 81.

well as thermoreceptors to detect temperature and nociceptors to avoid pain. The lips have more nerves per area than most other body parts, and the brain's cerebral cortex devotes huge data-processing resources to it, making your mouth experiences some of your most vivid and sensitive, with strong phenomenology.[46]

Why would evolution provide that? Cheok and Zhang say it helps in mate selection because kissing gets you close enough to smell chemical signals like pheromones and detect underlying genes, and thus assess compatibility. Yet these require only proximity, not kissing. Cheok and Zhang claim saliva "contains information about one's health and the exchange of saliva during kissing facilitates the detection of genetic diseases,"[47] yet kissing can transmit germs and bacteria so, on balance, it arguably serves no evolutionary purpose. Cheok and Zhang conclude: "With the development of realistic physical communication interfaces between humans and artificial partners, we can expect the aspect of humans having sex, and falling in love with robots . . . to take one more step towards reality."[48] Yet it seems a vast number of steps are needed. The body's technology remains far beyond human designs and is still copied in biomimetics. An argument from design to God's existence could be based here.[49]

What if the pleasures of kissing are not merely for the grim struggle for survival? Mate selection may be part of the story, along with rewarding the important business of eating and allowing articulate speech, but what if a kiss is also for joy and bonding, intended by a generous creator who wanted people to love and enjoy each other and to stay together to care for their children? Levy starts his chapter titled, "Can Robots and Humans Make Babies Together?"[50] by saying "this is not a joke": the fact that he feels a need to say that is telling. He concludes that there could be a genetic robot that uses DNA and reproduces using human cells. Yet this is mind-bogglingly speculative. So far, the only way we can make copies of ourselves is with two human bodies.

46. Haggard and de Boer, "Oral Somatosensory Awareness," 469–84.
47. Cheok and Zhang, *Human–Robot Intimate Relationships*, 78.
48. Cheok and Zhang, *Human–Robot Intimate Relationships*, 95.
49. See Wiker and Witt, *Meaningful World*; Lennox, *God's Undertaker*.
50. Cheok and Zhang, *Human–Robot Intimate Relationships*, ch. 10.

Mind and Personality?

While conversation may not be a priority for a pornified user, it is likely that machine chat will soon progress well past the Siri level thanks to adaptions from the AI developed for ChatGPT, publicly released in December 2022.[51]

Researchers are experimenting on how to classify human emotions and teach machines to recognize them,[52] but this is staggeringly complex: just consider how many subtle variations of smiles exist, expressing how many emotions. Robots can monitor heartbeat and sense arousal, but cannot tell what kind it is. And they can alter their face or voice to simulate emotions of their own,[53] but there is a limited range, and we know their empathy is entirely simulated,[54] and is limited to set circumstances.[55] Levy says the *appearance* of consciousness is just as good in practice and, further, that it is the same thing—that the appearance of consciousness *is* consciousness. He says we should believe a robot that says, "I love you"—as long as its actions back this up.[56] The Federation for Responsible Robotics comments more realistically: "We do not fully understand how human emotion works—chemically, hormonally or neurally—and we have no idea how to create genuine feelings in an artefact. So this is not worth considering for now . . . it remains entirely futuristic and speculative."[57]

And there is the uncanny valley: Professor Masahiro Mori observed that people suspend disbelief as robots look more human, but only to a point—about 80 percent humanlike—and then it seems weird.[58] And studies suggest that the more robots move or talk or feign emotion, the less we are convinced.[59] One journalist trialing the Harmony doll noticed the designer had added bigger eyes and a rounder face than humans really

51. Open AI, "Chat GPT–Release Notes."

52. Calvo and D'Mello, "Affect Detection," 18–37.

53. Becker-Asano and Ishiguro, "Evaluating Facial Displays of Emotion," 1–8.

54. Rosenthal-von der Pütten et al., "Investigations on Empathy," 201–12.

55. Leite et al., "Influence of Empathy," 250–60.

56. Levy, *Love and Sex with Robots*, 11.

57. Sharkey et al., *Our Sexual Future with Robots*, 1, 11, 14.

58. Mori, "Uncanny Valley," 98–100. See also Chu, "I, Stereotype," 76–88 and Burleigh et al., "Does the Uncanny Valley Exist?," 759–71.

59. Pandey, "Lovotics," 1.

have, but still observed, "I was transported to a place I never imagined I'd be: the uncanny valley."[60]

Philosopher Charles Ess says that "since the machines are incapable of real emotions, they are simply *'faking* it,' no matter how persuasively," whereas an ideal sexual encounter is "marked by the full presence and engagement of persons as autonomous, self-aware, emotive, embodied, and unique."[61] Ess argues that mutual desire is crucial—we desire the other, and we desire to be desired, and we desire that our desire be desired, and so on. Kathleen Richardson argues that users of sex robots act like clients who show no empathy, ignoring a prostitute's feelings and human subjectivity, and viewing her as an "object" that feels what they want her to feel.[62] Psychotherapist Federica Facchin and colleagues argue that sex robots are "based on a mechanical view of sexuality," not,

> interactions between physical, psychological, sociocultural, and relational factors. Sexual activity with robots is a masturbatory practice, so someone with sexual dysfunction, which already leads to isolation, might become even more isolated by the illusion of having a substitute satisfaction . . . Robots have no empathy or relational skills: they can only fake them.[63]

Sullins observes: "Fellow humans, on the other hand . . . do not always readily change to accommodate one's every need. They . . . have their own interests and desires that make demands . . . Compromise and accommodation are required."[64]

Many see sex robots associated with de-skilling in empathy, intimacy, social skills and ethics.[65] Other potential problems include guilt, shame, and fear of stigma from friends and family[66] (though some doll-owners tell of "coming out" to accepting friends).[67] This may create social rustiness, fear of reconnecting with people, and thus ultimately deeper loneliness. Hauskeller admits that robot sex means a user has,

60. Trout, "RealDoll's First Sex Robot."

61. Ess, "Love, Sex and Robots." Ess, "What's Love Got to Do with It?," 57–79.

62. Richardson, "Asymmetrical 'Relationship'"; Gee, "Why Female Sex Robots Are More Dangerous"; Farley et al., *Men Who Buy Sex*, 15–17.

63. Facchin et al., "Sex Robots,"

64. Sullins, "Robots, Love, and Sex," 407.

65. Vallor, "Moral Deskilling and Upskilling," 107–124.

66. Knox et al., "Sex Dolls." See also Ray, "Synthetik Love."

67. Döring and Poeschl, "Love and Sex with Robots," 53.

all but given up on the idea that sex can be a true encounter between two persons, as opposed to an act of mutual masturbation
where one uses the other only as a pleasure-generating tool, and
each is essentially alone and only concerned with themselves.[68]

To state the obvious, machines are not conscious. They do not have a mental
state, an inner experience or qualia or personhood.[69] People do, and our
suffering or wellbeing are the basis for much ethical reasoning about our
rights, which does not apply to machines because they do not think or feel. It
is very difficult to explain human consciousness in atheist materialist terms
alone,[70] so difficult in fact that some materialists attempt to deny that humans really have conscious thoughts or free will or identity.[71] This places a
large question-mark over Hauskeller's future scenario: if our hi-tech successors are just material objects or machines, how can they have any pleasure,
qualia, subjectivity, or inner experience at all? Hauskeller recommends we
regulate our function with pills, but what part of "us" would be doing that if
Hauskeller does not allow for any non-physical part of a human? Humans
seem to be made of more than matter, and consciousness and reason support very convincing arguments for the existence of God.[72]

Thoughtful humans know that machines do not think or feel, and
there is no one there behind a sexbot's eyes. Sexbot users can of course
suspend disbelief and choose an illusion (probably not a delusion, as they
are not unaware of it), particularly as technology advances, but reality is
there if they think about it.[73] And this can be unsatisfying.

This problem would not surprise readers of the Bible. If humans were
made in the image of a God who has consciousness, reason, self-determi-
nation, freedom, personality, language, relational ability, objective morality, and intrinsic value, then we should expect to have these characteristics

---

68. Hauskeller, *Sex and the Posthuman Condition*, 13–14.

69. See Smith, "Christian Anthropology," in *Robot Theology*, 62–69.

70. Nagel, *Mind and Cosmos*.

71. Dennett, *Consciousness Explained*; Pinker, *Blank Slate*; Rosenberg, *Atheist's Guide
to Reality*.

72. See Williams, "Mind-Body Problem," "The Mind and Its Creator," and "Freedom
and Responsibility," in *Faithful Guide to Philosophy*. See also Reppert, *C.S. Lewis's Dangerous Idea*; Moreland, "Argument from Consciousness"; Plantinga, *Warranted Christian
Belief*, 227–40; Plantinga, *Where the Conflict Really Lies*. Bos, *Thinking Outside the Brain
Box*.

73. See Graystone, "Sextech."

ourselves.[74] "It is not good for man to be alone," says God, having made both male and female in the image of God.[75] Grenz finds "we do not reflect God's image on our own but in relationship. Thus the *imago dei* is not primarily what we are as individuals. Rather, it is present among humans in relationship."[76] If that is true, we should expect not to be fully satisfied by anything less than a one-flesh relationship with another who is "flesh of our flesh" and whom we "know" wholistically as Adam knew Eve.

Herzfeld sees it as impossible to combine total control with relationship, and that even God makes covenants by mutual consent, assuming human dignity and agency. She cites biblical rebukes of those who made metal idols and prostituted themselves with them (Ezek 16:17) and finds sex dolls "ultimately a form of idolatry," substituting a created thing for the creator and people in God's image.[77]

Abuse

Westworld often depicts clients raping robots, which highlights a problem: robots cannot consent. If they seem to, this may train men to expect that from women. If they refuse, then using them would be rehearsing rape.[78] The concern is not for the machine's feelings (it has none) but for the effect on the user developing a "desire for the real world equivalents of those acts, and/or a disturbing moral insensitivity to the social meaning."[79] Gutiu is concerned about "dehumanization of sex and intimacy" and damage to "men's ability to identify and understand consent in sexual interactions with women."[80] For comparison, much pornography, which many adolescents identify as their primary source of sex education, is found to give direct or indirect support to sexual scripts like these: "Explicit Verbal Consent Isn't Natural," "Sex Can Happen Without Ongoing Communication."[81]

---

74. Moreland, "Image of God," 32–48.

75. See Rana and Samples, "Image of God", ch. 6 in *Humans 2.0*. Also Shatzer, *Transhumanism and the Image of God*.

76. Grenz, "Theological Foundations," 620. See also Westermann, *Genesis*, 1:142–161.

77. Herzfeld, "Religious Perspectives," 122.

78. Sparrow, "Robots, Rape, and Representation," 465–77.

79. Danaher, "Robotic Rape," 1–25. See further Danaher and McArthur, *Robot Sex*.

80. Gutiu, "Roboticization of Consent," 186–212.

81. Willis et al., "Sexual Consent Communication," 52–63.

Some have suggested a "consent-module," which would require the human and robot to "communicate carefully about the kind of interaction that will take place" and "could potentially result in the robot sometimes not consenting and terminating the interaction."[82] Would people buy a robot that sometimes said no? Would some users get angry and reboot, or just go ahead anyway? How does one genuinely communicate with a robot? And if rape is "often about power and control as well as taking pleasure in debasing and humiliating victims," then an "obliging sex robot is unlikely to fulfill these kinds of rapist's desires."[83] Thus it seems unlikely to discourage them from seeking a human who will.

Levy argues that if the robot says it consents and acts like it consents, then it consents. Yet surely thoughtful users would know the consent was given by a machine without consciousness, agency, competence, or "decisional capacity."[84]

Westworld also depicts violence and murder against female dolls. In the real world, Belladolls in Vancouver promises on its very explicit website "an experience like no other, where you are in complete control. Forget the restrictions and limitations that come with a real partner and unleash with Belladolls."[85] Belladolls' PR Director says, "We're not supporting [violence] but we're also not saying that you can't use this service because you're aggressive. At the end of the day they are just dolls."[86] Maras and Shapiro cite factual reports:

> One sex doll repairman indicated that an owner had "ripped the leg off" the female doll and "her calves, from below the knee, had what looked almost like knife puncture wounds. Hundreds of them . . . Some of the dolls or robots were destroyed in grotesque ways, "hacked to pieces," "jaw . . . behind her neck. Her hands ripped off . . . left breast hanging by a thread of skin," "cleavage between her buttocks was torn into a ragged crevasse," "her vagina and anus were a giant gaping hole."[87]

82. Peeters and Haselager, "Designing Virtuous Sex Robots"; Cappuccio et al., "Sympathy for Dolores."

83. Sharkey et al., *Our Sexual Future with Robots*, 29.

84. Frank and Nyholm, "Robot Sex and Consent," 305–23.

85. Woodward, "Posters Advertising Sex Doll Brothel."

86. Woodward, "Posters Advertising Sex Doll Brothel."

87. Maras and Shapiro, "Child Sex Dolls and Robots," 3–21.

Anyone doubting that such violence exists need only read about mainstream pornography. Bridges and colleagues analyzed fifty best-selling pornographic films in the US and found almost 90 percent of scenes depicted physical aggression. "Spanking and gagging with visible obstruction of breathing were the most popular," featuring in some 1/3 of scenes, while 1/7 showed slapping, 1/10 hair-pulling, 1/15 choking hands around the throat. "Almost half of the scenes showed verbal aggression in the form of name-calling, using words such as 'bitch' or 'slut,'" with women the recipients of 94 percent of aggressive acts. So gagging was three times as frequent as "all that quaint old-fashioned stuff such as kissing, laughing, embracing, compliments or caresses put together."[88] Human sexuality seems a long way from Eden now, affected by the Fall of human nature.

Some argue that the use of sex dolls can be cathartic—better a doll than a real woman. But human rights lawyer Kay Firth Butterfield counters that legal prostitution does not prevent abuse and trafficking does not stop child abuse. "In fact, an increase is seen because sex is known to be available in these areas."[89]

Others claim sex dolls may help in sex therapy. Cox-George and Bewley find "major weaknesses in the evidence base" for this claim: while robot sex may allow sexual practice without pressure, it may also "move some further away from human intimacy" and further isolate people by introducing an illusion. Use by a couple may lower the self-esteem of the excluded partner and threaten the integrity of the relationship, resulting in further pain.[90] People with disabilities may experience distress rather than help. Overall, the risks include "commodifying human beings, normalizing sexual deviancy, becoming 'addictive,' acting as a practice ground for violence, and promoting the control of vulnerable individuals."[91]

The catharsis view has been used to argue that sex robots could provide pedophiles a harm-free target for their proclivities.[92] Child sex dolls have been marketed globally by a Japanese company called Trottla, founded by Shin Takagi, a self-confessed pedophile. Takagi said, "We should accept

88. Fina, "Porn Ultimatum," citing Bridges et al., "Aggression and Sexual Behavior." See also Bridges et al., "Sexual Scripts," 1–14.

89. Sharkey et al., *Our Sexual Future with Robots*, 17.

90. Watson et al., "Impact of a Couple's Vibrator," 370–83

91. Cox-George and Bewley, "I, Sex Robot," 153–54.

92. Zhou, "Preventive Strategies," 169–74. See also Rutkin, "Could Sex Robots and Virtual Reality Treat Paedophilia?"

that there is no way to change someone's fetishes. I am helping people express their desires, legally and ethically. It's not worth living if you have to live with repressed desire."[93] Yet catharsis theory treats sexual desire as an appetite like hunger which can be satisfied and then go away,[94] whereas cognitive behavioral therapy predicts that using dolls would have a "reinforcing effect" on pedophilic ideation and would "in many instances, cause it to be acted upon with greater urgency."[95] Using child pornography does not prevent pedophiles from offending, and research suggests it is a "gateway" to real offending because it desensitizes the user, making them want to escalate to the next level through masturbation to images from more extreme child pornography or even acting out with a real child in order to overcome the graduation effect and achieve original levels of stimulation. Social learning theory describes how their chosen media and their pedophile associates can promote twisted thinking that justifies and rationalizes mistreatment of children, allowing denial and reducing fear and shame. Therapists would be trying to stop pairing of pleasure with pedophilic thoughts for fear of reinforcing twisted thinking.[96] Fortunately, law enforcement still provides a line of protection for children: there are regular media news stories of arrests for importing child sex dolls.

Since the vast majority of sex dolls look female and are designed for male users, there are credible concerns regarding sexism and objectification of women.[97] Some see hope in allowing female and Queer designers into the male-dominated industry to produce "better" robots that "refuse fixed identity attributions."[98] Danaher suggests sexbot design could learn from pro-porn feminists and produce feminist sexbots.[99] Some feminist pornography has tried using actors of various ages and body types and replacing money shots with facial close-ups showing emotional connectedness—yet this product reaches only a tiny market share.[100] Further, it tries

93. Morin, "Can Child Dolls Keep Pedophiles from Offending?"

94. Sharkey et al., *Our Sexual Future with Robots*, 26.

95. Morin, "Can Child Dolls Keep Pedophiles from Offending?"

96. Maras and Shapiro, "Child Sex Dolls and Robots," 7–16. See also Danaher, "Regulating Child Sex Robots," 553–75.

97. Gildea and Richardson, "Sex Robots." See also Roper, *Sex Dolls, Robots and Woman Hating.*

98. Kubes, "New Materialist Perspectives," 224.

99. Danaher, "Building Better Sex Robots," 133–47.

100. Royalle, "What's a Nice Girl Like You."

KENT—SEX ROBOTS AND PEOPLE

to avoid "objectification, domination and subordination of women"[101] but some women criticize this, saying they like being objectified,[102] and one should not construct female desire too narrowly.[103]

Conclusion

Buber observed that one could treat others like a "You" or an "It", and that this choice affects who we ourselves become: "The I of the basic word I–You is different from that in the basic word I–It."[104] We might add that an I–I.T. relationship could be equally dehumanizing.

Psychologist Simon Baron-Cohen points out that underlying much human cruelty is a lack of empathy which regards people as objects, and that it is unhealthy to "relate only to things, or to people as if they were just things."[105] The wrong choice here can reduce us to objects or mere sex machines ourselves.[106] Humans can try to be gods and treat others as objects for instrumental use, thus damaging the humanity of both, or can seek love and grace from God and regard others as created in the same image, deserving to be known and loved.

In the Japanese New Wave satire *The Pornographers* (1966),[107] the protagonist is unsatisfied with his life as a pimp and pornography producer and with his voyeuristic, incestuous relationships. He decides to build the perfect robotic woman, but this proves too difficult. He works compulsively for years, neglecting human relationships. He wants to have the doll all to himself on his houseboat, but in the final scene, with an expressionless rubber face hanging near him and a torso with a crude anatomical hole, he is obsessing about hair, not noticing that his mooring ropes have parted, and he has drifted out to sea all alone.[108]

---

101. Danaher, "Building Better Sex Robots," 142.

102. Davies, "Liberal Anti-Porn Feminism?"

103. Devlin "In Defence of Sex Machines."

104. Buber, *I and Thou*, 53; Herzfeld, "Religious Perspectives," 127.

105. Baron-Cohen, *Science of Evil*, 7.

106. Not in the positive sense imagined in James Brown's 1970 song "Sexmachine." See rather Lurie, *Rise of the Sex Machines*, 250.

107. *Pornographers*, 2:08.

108. Sullins, "Robots, Love, and Sex," 401.

Bibliography

Appel, Markus, et al. "Otakuism and the Appeal of Sex Robots." *Frontiers in Psychology* 10 (March 2019). https://doi.org/10.3389/fpsyg.2019.00569.

Barbara, Giussy, et al. "Female Genital Cosmetic Surgery: Beyond a Mechanistic View of Sexual Satisfaction." *Acta Obstetricia et Gynecologica Scandinavica* 94 (2015) 1029.

Baron-Cohen, Simon. *The Science of Evil*. New York: Basic, 2011.

Barron, Steve, dir. *Electric Dreams*. London: Virgin Films, 1984. 94 min.

Becker-Asano, C. and H. Ishiguro. "Evaluating Facial Displays of Emotion for the Android Robot Geminoid F." *2011 IEEE Workshop on Affective Computational Intelligence (WACI)* (July 2011) 1–8. DOI:10.1109/WACI.2011.5953147.

Booker, Charlie, et al., writ. *Black Mirror*. London: Zeppotron and House of Tomorrow, 2011–.

Bos, Arie. *Thinking Outside the Brain Box: Why Humans Are Not Biological Computers*. Translated by Philip Mees. Edinburgh: Floris, 2018.

Bridges, Ana J., et al. "Sexual Scripts and the Sexual Behavior of Men and Women Who Use Pornography." *Sexualization, Media, and Society* 2 (2016) 1–14.

———. "Aggression and Sexual Behavior in Best-Selling Pornography Videos: A Content Analysis Update." *Violence Against Women* 16.10 (October 2010) 1065-85. DOI:10.1177/1077801210382866.

Buber, Martin. *I and Thou*. Translated by Walter Kaufmann. New York: Charles Scribner's Sons, 1970.

Burleigh, Tyler J., et al. "Does the Uncanny Valley Exist? An Empirical Test of the Relationship between Eeriness and the Human Likeness of Digitally Created Faces." *Computers in Human Behavior* 29 (2013) 759–71.

Calvo, R. A., and S. D'Mello. "Affect Detection: An Interdisciplinary Review of Models, Methods, and Their Applications." *IEEE Transactions on Affective Computing* 1.1 (January 2010) 18–37. DOI:10.1109/T-AFFC.2010.1.

Cappuccio, Massimiliano L., et al. "Sympathy for Dolores: Moral Consideration for Robots Based on Virtue and Recognition." *Philosophy and Technology* 33 (2020) 9–31. https://doi.org/10.1007/s13347-019-0341-y.

Cheok, Adrian D., and Emma Yann Zhang. *Human–Robot Intimate Relationships*. Cham: Springer Nature, 2019.

Chu, S.-Y. "I, Stereotype: Detained in the Uncanny Valley." In *Techno Orientalism: Imagining Asia in Speculative Fiction, History, and Media*, edited by D. S. Roh, et al., 76–88. New Brunswick: Rutgers University Press, 2018.

Columbus, Chris, dir. *Bicentennial Man*. Burbank, CA: Touchstone, 1999. 132 min.

Cox-George, Chantal, and Susan Bewley. "I, Sex Robot: The Health Implications of the Sex Robot Industry." *BMJ Sexual and Reproductive Health* 44 (2018) 153–54.

Danaher, John, and Neil McArthur. *Robot Sex: Social and Ethical Implications*. Cambridge, MA: Massachusetts Institute of Technology, 2017.

———. "Building Better Sex Robots: Lessons from Feminist Pornography." In *AI Love You: Developments in Human-Robot Intimate Relationships*, edited by Yuefang Zhou and Martin H. Fischer, 133–47. Cham: Springer, 2019.

———. "Regulating Child Sex Robots, Restriction or Experimentation?" *Medical Law Review* 27.4 (November 2019) 553–75. DOI:10.1093/medlaw/fwz002.

———. "Robotic Rape and Robotic Child Sexual Abuse: Should They be Criminalised?" *Criminal Law and Philosophy* 13 (2014) 1–25.

Davies, Alex. "A *Liberal* Anti-Porn Feminism?" *Social Theory and Practice* (23 November 2017). https://doi.org/10.5840/soctheorpract2017112027.

Dennett, Daniel C. *Consciousness Explained*. Boston: Little, Brown and Company, 1991.

Devlin, Kate. "In Defence of Sex Machines: Why Trying to Ban Sex Robots Is Wrong." *The Conversation* 40 (17 September 2015) 142–53.

———. *Turned On: Science, Sex and Robots*. London: Bloomsbury Sigma, 2018.

Dickson, E. J. "Sex Doll Brothels Are Now a Thing. What Will Happen to Real-life Sex Workers?" *Vox*, November 26, 2018. https://www.vox.com/the-goods/2018/11/26/18113019/sex-doll-brothels-legal-sex-work.

Döring, Nicola, and Sandra Poeschl. "Love and Sex with Robots: A Content Analysis of Media Representations." *International Journal of Social Robotics* 11 (2019) 665–77.

———. "Sex Toys, Sex Dolls, Sex Robots: Our Under-Researched Bed-Fellows." *Sexologies* 27.3 (2018) 51–55. DOI:10.1016/j.sexol.2018.05.009.

Ess, Charles. "Love, Sex and Robots: from The Song of Songs to Ex Machina." *Religion Going Public*, January 22, 2017. http://religiongoingpublic.com/archive/2017/sexbot.

———. "What's Love Got to Do with It? Robots, Sexuality, and the Arts of Being Human." In *Social Robots: Boundaries, Potential, Challenges*, edited by Marco Norskov, 57–79. London: Routledge, 2021.

Facchin, Federica, et al. "Sex Robots: The Irreplaceable Value of Humanity." *The BMJ* (15 August 2017). DOI:10.1136/bmj.j3790.

Farley, M., et al. *Men Who Buy Sex: Who They Buy and What They Know*. London: Eaves, 2009.

Fine, Cordelia. "The Porn Ultimatum: The Dehumanising Effects of Smut." *The Monthly*, September 2011. www.themonthly.com.au/issue/2011/september/1365560803/cordelia-fine/porn-ultimatum.

Floreano, Dario, and Nicola Nosengo. *Tales from a Robotic World: How Intelligent Machines Will Shape Our Future*. Cambridge, MA: MIT Press, 2022.

Forbes, Bryan, dir. *The Stepford Wives*. Los Angeles, CA: Palomar, 1975. 115 min.

Frank, Lily, and Sven Nyholm. "Robot Sex and Consent: Is Consent to Sex between a Robot and a Human Conceivable, Possible, and Desirable?" *Artificial Intelligence Law* 25 (2017) 305–23. https://doi.org/10.1007/s10506-017-9212-y.

Garland, Alex, dir. *Ex Machina*. London: Film4 and DNA Films, 2014. 108 min.

Gee, Tabi J. "Why Female Sex Robots Are More Dangerous Than You Think." *The Telegraph*, July 5, 2018. https://www.telegraph.co.uk/women/life/female-robots-why-this-scarlett-johansson-bot-is-more-dangerous/.

Gibson, Rebecca. *Desire in the Age of Robots and AI: An Investigation in Science Fiction and Fact*. Cham: Palgrave Macmillan, 2020.

Gildea, Florence, and Kathleen Richardson. "Sex Robots—Why We Should Be Concerned." *Campaign Against Sex Robots*, May 12, 2017. https://spsc.pt/index.php/2017/05/05/sex-robots-why-we-should-be-concerned/.

Gillespie, Craig, dir. *Lars and the Real Girl*. Culver City, CA: Metro-Goldwyn-Mayer, 2007. 106 min.

Graaf, Maartje M.A., de, and Soumaya Ben Allouch. "Anticipating Our Future Robot Society: The Evaluation of Future Robot Applications from a User's Perspective." *2016 25th IEEE International Symposium on Robot and Human Interactive Communication (RO-MAN)* (August 2016) 755–62. DOI:10.1109/ROMAN.2016.7745204.

Graystone, Andrew. "Sextech: Simulated Relationships with Machines." In *The Robot Will See You Now: Artificial intelligence and the Christian Faith*, edited by John Wyatt and Stephen N. Williams, 177–92. London: SPCK, 2021.

Grenz, Stanley J. "Theological Foundations for Male-Female Relationships." *Journal of the Evangelical Theological Society* 41.4 (December 1998) 615–30.

Gutiu, Sinziana M. "The Roboticization of Consent." In *Robot Law*, edited by Ryan Calo et al., 186–212. Cheltenham: Edward Elgar, 2016.

Haggard, Patrick, and Lieke de Boer, "Oral Somatosensory Awareness." *Neuroscience and Biobehavioral Reviews* 47 (November 2014) 469–84. DOI:10.1016/j.neubio rev.2014.09.015.

Hauskeller, Michael. *Sex and the Posthuman Condition*. Basingstoke: Palgrave Macmillan, 2014.

Imamura, Shohei, dir. *The Pornographers*. Japan: Imamura Productions, 1966. 128 min.

IMDb, "Artificial Females in Movies and Television." https://www.imdb.com/list/ ls063279126/.

Jacob Shatzer, *Transhumanism and the Image of God: Today's Technology and the Future of Christian Discipleship*. Downers Grove: IVP Academic, 2019.

Johnson, Kenneth, prod. *Six Million Dollar Man*. Season 4, episode 6, "Kill Oscar: Part 2." Aired October 31, 1976, on ABC.

———. *The Bionic Woman*. Season 2, episode 5, "Kill Oscar: Part 1." Aired October 27, 1976, on ABC.

———. *The Bionic Woman*. Season 2, episode 6, "Kill Oscar: Part 1." Aired November 3, 1976, on ABC.

Jonze, Spike, dir. *Her*. Los Angeles, CA: Annapurna Pictures, 2013. 126 min.

Kent, Grenville J. R. "Cybersex, Solipsism, and Paul's Notion of the Body." *Spectrum,* 35.1 (Winter 2007) 24–32.

Kleeman, Jenny. *Sex Robots and Vegan Meat: Adventures at the Frontier of Birth, Food, Sex, and Death*. London: Pegasus, 2020.

Knox, D., et al. "Sex Dolls—Creepy or Healthy? Attitudes of Undergraduates." *Journal of Positive Sexuality* 3.2 (2017) 32–37. DOI:10.1108/JOSM-05-2020-0145.

Kubes, Tanja. "New Materialist Perspectives on Sex Robots. A Feminist Dystopia/Utopia?" *Social Sciences* 8.8 (2019). https://doi.org/10.3390/socsci8080224.

Kurzweil, Ray. *The Age of Spiritual Machines: How We Will Live, Work and Think in the New Age of Intelligent Machines*. London: Phoenix, 1999.

l'Isle-Adam, Auguste Villiers, de. *Tomorrow's Eve*. Translated by Robert Martin Adams. Chicago: University of Illinois Press, 2001.

Lang, Fritz, dir. *Metropolis*. Berlin: UFA, 1927. 153 min.

Leite, Iolanda, et al. "The Influence of Empathy in Human–Robot Relations", *International Journal of Human-Computer Studies* 71.3 (March 2013) 250–60.

Lennox, John C. *God's Undertaker: Has Science Buried God?* Oxford: Lion, 2009.

"Let's Talk about Sex Robots." *Nature* 547 (2017) 138. https://doi.org/10.1038/547138a.

Levy, David. *Love and Sex with Robots: The Evolution of Human-Robot Relationships*. New York: Harper Perennial, 2008.

Lipstadt, Aaron, dir. *Android*. Los Angeles, CA: Sho Films, 1982. 80 min.

Lurie, Barak. *The Rise of the Sex Machines: How Culture and Technology Are Changing Relationships Forever—and Who Will Resist*. Los Angeles: CT3Media, 2019.

Maras, Marie-Helen, and Lauren R. Shapiro. "Child Sex Dolls and Robots. More Than Just an Uncanny Valley." *Journal of Internet Law* 21.5 (December 2017) 3–21.

Moreland, J. P. "The Argument from Consciousness." In *Debating Christian Theism*, edited by J. P. Moreland et al., 119–30. Oxford: Oxford University Press, 2013.

———. "The Image of God and the Failure of Scientific Atheism." In *God is Great, God is Good*, edited by William Lane Craig and Chad Meister, 32–48. Nottingham: InterVarsity, 2009.

Mori, Masahiro. "The Uncanny Valley." *IEEE Robotics Automation Magazine* 19.2 (2012) 98–100.

Morin, Roc. "Can Child Dolls Keep Pedophiles from Offending?" *The Atlantic*, January 11, 2016. https://www.theatlantic.com/health/archive/2016/01/can-child- dolls-keep-pedophiles-from-offending/423324/.

Nagel, Thomas. *Mind and Cosmos: Why the Materialist Neo-Darwinian Conception of Nature is Almost Certainly False*. Oxford: Oxford University Press, 2012.

Nash, Charlie. "Sex Robot Brothels Gaining Popularity in Europe." *Breitbart*, July 31, 2017. https://www.breitbart.com/tech/2017/07/31/worlds-first-sex-robot-brothel-talks-expand/.

Nolan, Jonathan, and Lisa Joy, creat. *Westworld*. New York: HBO, 2016–2022.

Open AI. "Chat GPT—Release Notes." https://help.openai.com/en/articles/6825453-chatgpt-release-notes.

Oshii, Mamoru, dir. *Ghost in the Shell 2: Innocence*. Tokyo: Production I.G and Studio Ghibli, 2004. 98 min.

Oz, Frank, dir. *The Stepford Wives*. Los Angeles, CA: De Line Pictures, 2004. 93 min.

Pandey, Amit K. "Lovotics, the Uncanny Valley and the Grand Challenges." *Lovotics* 1.1 (2014). DOI:10.4172/2090-9888.10000105.

Peeters, Anco, and Pim Haselager. "Designing Virtuous Sex Robots." *International Journal of Social Robotics* 13 (2021) 55–66. https://doi.org/10.1007/s12369-019-00592-1.

Pellissier, Hank. "Sexbots Will Give Us Longevity Orgasms." *Humanity Plus Magazine*, December 11, 2009. http://hplusmagazine.com/2009/12/11/sexbots-will-give-us-longevity-orgasm.

Pinker, Stephen. *The Blank Slate: The Modern Denial of Human Nature*. London: Penguin Putman, 2002.

Plantinga, Alvin. *Warranted Christian Belief*. Oxford: Oxford University Press, 2000.

———. *Where the Conflict Really Lies: Science, Religion, and Naturalism*. Oxford: Oxford University Press, 2011.

Pritchard, Nick. "Puppet in a G-String." *The Sun*, March 6, 2018. https://www.thesun.ie/news/uk-news/2272387/we-go-inside-uks-first-sex-doll-brothel-to-see-the-future-of-sex/.

Rana, Fazale and Kenneth R. Samples. *Humans 2.0: Scientific, Philosophical, and Theological Perspectives on Transhumanism*. Covina: Reasons to Believe, 2019.

Ray, Prayag. "'Synthetik Love Lasts Forever': Sex Dolls and the (Post?)human Condition." In *Critical Posthumanism and Planetary Futures*, edited by Makarand Paranjape and Debashish Banerjee, 91–112. New Delhi: Springer, 2016.

Rennie, John. "The Immortal Ambitions of Ray Kurzweil: A Review of *Transcendent Man*." *Scientific American*, February 15, 2011. https://www.scientificamerican.com/article/the-immortal-ambitions-of-ray-kurzweil/.

Reppert, Victor. *C.S. Lewis's Dangerous Idea: In Defense of the Argument from Reason*. Downers Grove: InterVarsity, 2003.

Richardson, Kathleen. "Sex Robot Matters: Slavery, the Prostituted, and the Rights of Machines." *IEEE Technology and Society Magazine* 35.2 (June 2016) 46–53. DOI: 10.1109/MTS.2016.2554421.

———. "The Asymmetrical 'Relationship': Parallels between Prostitution and the Development of Sex Robots." *ACM SIGCAS Computers and Society* 45.3 (January 2016) 290–93.

Rigotti, Carlotta. "How to Apply Asimov's First Law to Sex Robots." *Paladyn Journal of Behavioral Robotics* 11 (2020) 161–70.

Roach, Jay, dir. *Austin Powers in Goldmember.* Burbank, CA: New Line Cinema, 2002. 93 min.

———. *Austin Powers: International Man of Mystery.* Burbank, CA: New Line Cinema, 1997. 89 min.

———. *Austin Powers: The Spy Who Shagged Me.* Burbank, CA: New Line Cinema, 1999. 95 min.

"Robot Sex Poll Reveals Americans' Attitudes About Robotic Lovers, Servants, Soldiers." *HuffPost*, April 10, 2013. www.huffingtonpost.com/2013/04/10/robot-sex-poll-americans- robotic-lovers-servants-soldiers_n_3037918.html.

Roper, Caitlin. *Sex Dolls, Robots and Woman Hating: The Case for Resistance.* Geelong: Spinifex, 2022.

Rosenberg, Alex. *The Atheist's Guide to Reality: Enjoying Life without Illusions.* London: Norton, 2011.

Rosenthal-von der Pütten, Astrid M., et al. "Investigations on Empathy towards Humans and Robots Using fMRI." *Computers in Human Behavior* 33 (2014) 201–12.

Royalle, Candida. "What's a Nice Girl Like You . . . " In *The Feminist Porn Book: The Politics of Producing Pleasure*, edited by T. Taormino et al., 58–69. New York: The Feminist Press at the City University of New York, 2013.

Rutkin, Aviva. "Could Sex Robots and Virtual Reality Treat Paedophilia?" *New Scientist*, August 2, 2016. www.newscientist. com/article/2099607-could-sex- robots-and-virtual-reality- treat-paedophilia.

Scheutz, Matthias, and Thomas Arnold. "Are We Ready for Sex Robots?" *2016 11th ACM/ IEEE International Conference on Human-Robot Interaction (HRI)* (April 2016) 351–358. DOI:10.1109/HRI.2016.7451772.

Scott, Ridley, dir. *Blade Runner.* Hollywood, CA: Blade Runner Partnership, 1982. 117 min.

Sharkey, Noel, et al. *Our Sexual Future with Robots: A Report by the Foundation for Responsible Robotics.* The Hague: Foundation for Responsible Robotics, 2017.

Smith, Joshua K. *Robot Theology: Old Questions through New Media.* Eugene, OR: Resource Publications, 2022.

Sparrow, Robert. "Robots, Rape, and Representation." *International Journal of Social Robotics* 9.4 (2017) 465–77.

Spielberg, Steven, dir. *A.I. Artificial Intelligence.* Universal City, CA: Amblin Entertainment and Stanley Kubrick Productions, 2001. 146 min.

Sullins, John P. "Robots, Love, and Sex: The Ethics of Building a Love Machine." *IEEE Transactions on Affective Computing* 3.4 (2012) 398–409.

Trout, Christopher. "RealDoll's First Sex Robot Took Me to the Uncanny Valley." *Engadget*, April 17, 2017. www.engadget.com/2017-04-11-realdolls-first-sex-robot-took-me-to-the-uncanny-valley.html.

Vallor, Shannon. "Moral Deskilling and Upskilling in a New Machine Age: Reflections on the Ambiguous Future of Character." *Philosophy of Technology* 28 (2015) 107–124.

"Video from Inside a Robot Sex Doll Brothel." *Vice,* December 12, 2018. www.vice.com/en_au/article/yw7xkb/video-from-inside-a-robot-sex-doll-brothel.

Vincent, Sam, and Jonathan Brackley, creat. *Humans.* London: Channel 4 and AMC, 2015-2018.

Waddell, L. "Inside Britain's Sex Robot Brothels—and 'It IS Legal.'" *Daily Star*, September 10, 2019. https://www.dailystar.co.uk/news/latest-news/sex-robot-brothels-britain-prostitution-17108779.

Watson, E.D., et al. "The Impact of a Couple's Vibrator on Men's Perceptions of Their Own and Their Partner's Sexual Pleasure and Satisfaction." *Men Masculinities* 19.4 (2016) 370–83.

Westermann, Claus. *Genesis.* Biblischer Kommentar Altes Testament. Band 1. Neukirchen-Vluyn: NeukirchenerVerlag, 1974.

Wiker, Benjamin, and Jonathan Witt. *A Meaningful World: How the Arts and Sciences Reveal the Genius of Nature.* Grand Rapids: IVP Academic, 2006.

Wikimedia Foundation, "List of Fictional Gynoids." https://en.wikipedia.org/wiki/List_of_fictional_gynoids.

Williams, Peter S. *A Faithful Guide to Philosophy: A Christian Introduction to the Love of Wisdom.* Milton Keynes: Paternoster, 2013.

Willis, Malachi, et al. "Sexual Consent Communication in Best-Selling Pornography Films: A Content Analysis." *The Journal of Sex Research* 57.1 (2020) 52–63.

Woodward, Jon. "Posters Advertising Sex Doll Brothel Plastered in Downtown Vancouver." *CTV News*, 25 September 2018. https://bc.ctvnews.ca/posters-advertising-sex-doll-brothel-plastered-in-downtown-vancouver-1.4108757.

Yeoman, Ian, and Michelle Mars. "Robots, Men and Sex Tourism." *Futures* 44 (2012) 365–71.

Zhou, Yuefang. "Preventive Strategies for Pedophilia and the Potential Role of Robots: Open Workshop Discussion." In *AI Love You: Developments in Human-Robot Intimate Relationships*, edited by Yuefang Zhou and Martin H. Fischer, 169–74. Cham: Springer, 2019.

9

Wesleyans in Conversation with a Posthumanist Philosopher

ARSENY ERMAKOV, FRANCESCA FERRANDO,
AND GLEN O'BRIEN

THE EDITORS OF THIS volume teach a course at Eva Burrows College, University of Divinity on *Futurism and Theology*. In preparing resources for their students, they came across the online videos of Francesca Ferrando, who effectively communicates posthumanist ideas to a general audience, and teaches Philosophy at NYU-Liberal Studies. Francesca consented to an invitation to participate in a conversation via Zoom as a resource for use in the course. What follows is an edited transcript of that conversation. It is offered here as a model of dialogue between theologians and a posthumanist thinker that shows the value of the mutually enriching exchange of ideas over shared concerns.

Glen O'Brien: Dr Francesca Ferrando (they/them/theirs) is an Adjunct Professor of Philosophy at New York University and an award-winning public intellectual who has been named by *Origin* magazine as one of the one-hundred top creatives making change in the world. Their book, *Philosophical Posthumanism* was published by Bloomsbury in 2019. In the Preface, Rosi Braidotti describes the book as "a rapturous departure—the line of flight of a queen bee." We are delighted, Francesca, that you have accepted our invitation to participate in this conversation.

Francesca Ferrando: Thanks, dear Glen, for this invitation, it is a great joy to be here.

Glen O'Brien: Perhaps we could begin by talking about posthumanism and its appeal to you personally. There are (at least) three philosophical approaches to the place of human beings in possible futures—transhumanism, posthumanism, and antihumanism. You identify as a posthumanist philosopher, but you know a good deal about all the other perspectives so, could you say a little bit about: "Why posthumanism?"

Francesca Ferrando: This is a very relevant question, because the term "posthuman" is becoming truly fashionable, but a lot of people are confused about what "posthuman" means. The reason is that posthumanism is not one but many. There is critical posthumanism, philosophical posthumanism, and cultural posthumanism. There is also transhumanism, extropianism, antihumanism, metahumanism, object-oriented ontology, new materialism . . . you name it. All of this can cause confusion, but it is also very exciting because it means that it is a conversation that is happening. The idea of "the posthuman" can be simplified by asking this question: "What does it mean to be human in the twenty-first century?" No one before us was living in our specific condition. No one before us was living during the late Anthropocene. No one before us was living in a techno-centered society, in which AI has already taken over, on some level. Many people on planet Earth are spending their days in front of the computer. This is an unprecedented situation. People living a thousand years ago were also living within their own unique situation and they brought their insights and wisdom. We, in turn, have a responsibility towards the people who are coming after us. We have response-ability towards our planet. We are not just living on a planet; we *are* the planet. In this sense, posthumanism is really asking an existential question, which is also theological, scientific, and philosophical: Who are we—as a species and as individuals, as a society and as a planet?

There are different answers to this, according to transhumanism and to posthumanism. Transhumanists, for instance, want to enhance the capacities of humans. In the twenty-first century, the human is being radically reshaped by science and technology. This is not just something technical; it is ontological. The goal of transhumanism is very clear: it is enhancing the human. The symbol H+ (Humanity Plus), invites people to connect with the transhumanist vision of human enhancement. Transhumanists (unlike posthumanists) are not post-anthropocentric. They are actually ultra-humanist, because they embrace the goal of unlimited enhancement for the human species. For instance, radical life extension is approached through nanotechnology towards an unlimited lifespan. Even if our body dies, digital immortality will be available through uploading our mind to a digital platform and living "forever"—or, at least, while that technology will still be in use. Such radical ideas are exciting for some, but very problematic for others. Who is going to have access to this digital immortality, given it will come with very expensive technologies? Most likely, it will not be for everyone, but for a very small group of people, mostly in the developed world.

There are other questions. What will it mean to live in a society with different categories of people having different lifespans? What if you know that your partner is going to die pretty much in your infancy, because you are going to live thousands of years and your partner is going to die after sixty years? These are very important questions that we need to be asking. The question is no longer, "Can we do it?" but "Should we do it?" since some of this technology is already in use. Think, for instance, of CRISPR (an acronym of "Clustered Regularly Interspaced Short Palindromic Repeats") a gene editing technology, which has already been used to bioengineer humans: in 2019, Chinese biophysicist He Jiankui was sentenced to prison for participating in the first (at least, openly) known biotechnological experiment. Most regulations worldwide are against editing the human genome, so there may be other experiments that we are not aware of because they don't make the news. This is not science fiction; it is reality.

I am not a transhumanist, but I am interested in the movement, which is tapping into a perennial human desire. *The Epic of Gilgamesh*, one of the earliest epics we have, involves a search for immortality. Even in the Bible there is the example of ancient people such as Methuselah who lived for almost a thousand years. The idea of living an unlimited lifespan is something that is part of human imagination—the search for immortality—so just criticizing transhumanists because they want to do something that has been part of human desire for so long is a little naïve. On the other hand, I don't think that having an unlimited lifespan necessarily equals happiness or serenity. My own position is posthuman-ist; let me explain why it is different.

What posthumanists want us to understand is that we are all in-terconnected, interrelated: not just as humans, but as a planet. We are aware of the fact that we are living in the Anthropocene. Think of mass extinctions, in which thousands of species are becoming extinct every year. This strong ecological awareness does not erase our interest in tech-nology, which is certainly part of the discussion. If I am asking what it means to be human in the twenty-first century, there is no way I can just avoid technology, because it is literally part of our bodies. However, from a posthuman perspective, the human in the twenty-first century can only be thought of in relation to ecology, the earth, the cosmos; technology (*technē*) is a way of revealing what we are.

To move to antihumanism, it is important to understand that it does not involve an anti-human approach—which can be found, for instance, in some currents of the human extinction movement. That is not the anti-humanism of Michel Foucault or of Marxist philosophers. Antihumanism is the idea that a specific notion of "the human" has died. Foucault (1976) realized that the human of the Enlightenment, the human based on the no-tion of progress—according to which technology can save us all—died with World War Two and the atomic bomb. Once we realized what technology could really do (including the annihilation of the human species), the gran-diose idea of humanity using technology to take care of existence died. The notion of progress no longer works, after such atrocities have been done in the name of technology. This goes against transhumanism, which is on the opposite track to antihumanism in locating itself as a movement within the Enlightenment project. It is interesting to see two movements under the larger umbrella term of "the posthuman" which are almost antithetical. The Transhumanist Declaration of 1998 places itself within the Enlightenment, in the Industrial Revolution, in the idea of progress (a linear notion accord-ing to which things are getting better because of technology).

Posthumanism is a very interesting movement, but it is still form-ing; it is moving. I would advise anyone who is interested to do a little homework first, because sometimes people jump into the topic and start to talk about "posthumanism" when they are really talking about trans-humanism. Or they talk about "transhumanism" when they really mean posthumanism. That was the case with Francis Fukuyama who was us-ing the term "posthumanism" in his book *Our Posthuman Future* while actually talking about transhumanism. The book became a bestseller, but it led to so much confusion. I would say that the topic is very exciting, there is much to be debated, but to have a real conversation people must know what they are talking about.

Glen O'Brien: Thank you for that encyclopedic tour through those terms which was very helpful. It reminds me of a correlation within theology. You talk about the death of the human as understood in the Enlightenment. In theology there was, arising in the 1960s, the "death of God" movement which rejected the concept of God as Plato's Unmoved Mover, the First Cause, who moves all things but is not moved by anything. This concept of an aloof, timeless, God had to die in the light of Auschwitz. Theologians have claimed that the old arguments about God's infallibility and impassibility no longer have any explanatory power. Jurgen Moltmann, for example, speaks of a "Crucified God." We have to talk about a God who died. Not that God doesn't exist, but that the *concept* of God as understood in the Platonic world and in the Enlightenment world, has died. It had to die, and it died on the cross, where a naked bleeding man, the image of God in the person of Jesus Christ, was murdered and something new arose out of that. In a similar way, our concept of God had to arise out of death, existence arising out of non-existence. How can we believe in such a God in a post-Holocaust world? A world in which God did not intervene to save God's chosen people. I think there is a correlation there between what you are saying about Antihumanism and movements within theology to think about God in different ways.

Francesca Ferrando: Dear Glen, thanks for bringing to our conversation such an important point. From a posthumanist perspective, the idea of a God separated out there, who created us, but has no real relation is untenable. But if you're talking about a God who is in everything, evolving, changing, and moving with us, who can debate that? According to quantum physics, for example, everything is dynamic and moving. What you say is very interesting; I have a question for both of you. The Bible can certainly promote some posthumanist ethics, but there is an issue I have with Genesis and that is the idea that the human was created in the image of God; from there came the idea of the supremacy of the human to the point that we get into anthropocentrism leading to the mass extinctions of the Anthropocene. Currently, there is a whole movement in Christianity recognizing that in the Bible you can also find the notion of stewardship of the earth; for instance, Pope Francis emphasizes, within the Catholic tradition, that we need to take care of our planet, because we *are* the planet. How do you feel about this interpretation of humans being created in the image of God, and being created in a hierarchy that later on became the *Scala Natura* ("Great Chain of Being")? How do you feel about that anthropocentric interpretation?

Glen O'Brien: Yes, there definitely has been a tradition of understanding the image of God as, in a sense, giving human beings dominion over the planet, dominion over other species, but there is a lot of push back against that concept now. The image of God is being framed not so much in an authoritarian way, with human beings at the top of the pyramid (therefore we can do whatever we want to do) but rather to think of the image of God, not in terms of certain qualities that we possess, such as conscience, reason, or will but rather as a way of being. We were given not dominion but stewardship. You've mentioned Pope Francis, and in his encyclical *Laudato Si*, he points out that we are given stewardship over creation, lovingly to care for it, which is a very different concept to dominion.[1] There's also a burgeoning animal theology movement which is focusing on the role of animals in divine creation. Of course, the Bible speaks metaphorically of animals, plants, trees, rocks, and mountains praying, praising, singing, leaping, and dancing before God so that the whole creation can be seen as an instrument of God's praise. These reconfigurations of the concept of the image of God are very helpful in moving away from that dominion concept toward a more immanentist approach where God, human beings, and other beings are engaged together in moving toward the telos of existence.

Arseny Ermakov: We have two trajectories in the Genesis account. The first trajectory shows the embeddedness of humanity within creation. After all, humans are created from the dust of the earth: the first human (*adam*) comes from the ground (*adama*). Also, humans were created together with animals, plants, and living creatures of every kind. They are depicted as dependent on the rest of creation and share the environment and life experiences with other living beings. Humanity belongs with the rest of creation in a very relational way. So, that's one trajectory. The second one highlights the place of humanity as different from the rest of creation. This is reflected in the notion of human beings created in "the image of God." The language

---

1. Pope Francis, *Laudato Si'*.

of the "image of God" is, again, also relational. On the one hand, humanity has a unique relationship with God and bears a divine imprint within all of creation; on the other, it plays an intermediary role. Humans are representing the created order to God and God to the created order in a kind of covenantal way. In relation to the environment, humans are also tasked with "serving" and "keeping" it. So, the Genesis accounts are not about the pyramid of power or domination within the created universe but about intimate relationships between God and creation, including humanity.

Moving on in our conversation, your Master's degree was in gender theory and the discussion of gender has been part of your philosophical work. The introduction of the modern notion of the human was, of course, a male invention and emerged at a time when most intellectual discourse in the universities was created and controlled by men. What do you see as the gendered aspects of posthumanism? What role does gender play in posthumanist discourse?

Francesca Ferrando: Thank you, dear Arseny, for this question. I became very interested in feminism when I realized, at the age of eighteen, that all my life I had been studying and reading only male philosophers, artists, poets, everything. I had been writing since a very young age; at first, I was expressing myself in poetry and I realized that all my poems were written in a male voice (in Italian, my native language, the "I" is gendered). I'd never really associated myself with the male identity (nor with the female one), so I was really curious about that. I realized the reason why I was expressing myself in male pronouns was because I had only read, until then, male authors: the "I", the Subject, had been automatically a "he." I realized there was a real disharmony in this society, which I experienced as an unbalanced situation, in which some people were treated in a certain way and others in another way, because of their gender.

Sexism is brutal to everyone involved; to be a man in a patriarchal society is not fun either. Young children, even infants, identified as boys, are given toys in the shapes of guns; at this point I'd almost rather give my daughter a doll instead of a gun, because at least she'll practice how to nurture, instead of how to kill. I was raised in Italy; it is a beautiful place, yet still, very sexist. I realized there was something I wanted to study, to learn more about, in order to change. By studying feminism, I realized many things. First (and this was a very good surprise) that societies have not always been patriarchal. As Foucault put it, knowledge is power:

education is also a way to teach you what you're supposed to believe in. We teach young children that history begins with the development of writing. The time before writing we refer to as "prehistory," yet this paleolithic period is pretty much 99 percent of the period of our existence as a species. It was a nomadic life; it was not patriarchal. The majority of figurines we have found from the paleolithic are female. So, I realized that education is a tool that shapes the minds of young people. Gender studies brought me to this conclusion because I knew that what I was experiencing was not the way society had to be.

Feminism is the beginning of posthumanism (not so much of transhumanism, which doesn't engage much with feminist thought). There are two sources we need to acknowledge in the genealogy of posthumanism. One is postmodernism and the other is feminism, which includes thinkers like Donna Haraway and Rosi Braidotti. At the core of this is the message that all knowledge is situated, and this came out of feminist epistemology, for instance in the work of Sandra Harding. It is very interesting for me that, nowadays, angels are still studied in theology, but if you go to a biological department and you say you want to study angels, they will say you need to go to the theological department. If you go back to the beginning of the academic tradition, people like Thomas Aquinas were writing whole books about angels. Knowledge is constantly shifting, so today angels are still considered relevant in theology but definitely not in science. At the beginning of philosophy, philosophers were also scientists, so it is very important to understand that knowledge is always both limited and situated.

This is why feminist epistemology is at the core of the discussion. We are all related, but we are all different; intersectional feminism has an appreciation of the difference. For so many centuries there was one subject who was talking for everyone, and this subject was male, white and heterosexual. They probably came from a wealthy family, otherwise they would not know how to read and write. Those who had the chance to attend the university were part of a small group of people with a specific perspective. This was a very limited group, yet these people were talking for everyone. Most philosophers until recently were biased in regard to gender, race, sexual orientation, and ethnicity, just to mention a few. This does not mean that we can simply erase their voices; they brought insights to all of us, on different levels, but they also reflected the biases of their own era and, more importantly, they were pivotal in reinforcing such bigoted views. They were not able to acknowledge that they were not talking for everyone but only from their biased perspectives, which they presented as "objective."

When the 1970s arrived, they came with feminism, critical race studies, the LGBTQI+ movement, Indigenous studies, and postcolonial studies, among others. By then, it was quite obvious that that voice was far from objective: "Wait a second, this doesn't describe me. This is not only inaccurate but is actually offensive and derogatory. Let the others talk." Everyone outside of the self-entitled norm, had been considered "the other," on a plateau of differentiation usually based on a variation from 'the universal subject' which was univocal and very limited—a male, white, hetero, abled, and monied perspective. I am not here to blame anyone, but to remind that if we want to understand who we really are, the most important thing is to be sincere with ourselves and with our particular temporal, embodied, cognitive and spiritual location. To understand who we are, we do not need to be better than others; as a matter of fact, we are constantly living through others. We come from other bodies, we need others to talk with, to grow food, to share technologies, to survive. The idea that one needs to be better than others is really a flawed understanding of existence. We can still learn from biased philosophers who came before us, but with an understanding of their limits and that we don't have to continue on their path: we can open toward new archetypes.

Glen O'Brien: You've highlighted that all knowledge is perspectival and that there is a power base to the dissemination of knowledge. The various deconstructionist approaches to knowledge, whether it be feminism or postmodernism or postcolonial studies, are all helpful in making us aware of those structures and that we're not just intellects floating around outside of our contexts, so that is a very valuable set of insights. Your mention of angels was fascinating because Arseny and I have often talked about the consciousness or minds that may emerge in the future in machines. You mentioned earlier the possibility of uploading consciousness into a computer. Christians are often nervous about that, because consciousness (or the soul or spirit) is considered something so precious that it can only be within a human being and could never be found in others. That is a very modern point of view, however, because when we look at pre-modern peoples, animals also have spirits. In the Bible there is a talking snake and a talking donkey and there are angels who are not human but have consciousness. They have minds and there is communication between human beings and angels (along with some flagged concerns about that sort of communication).

God *as God* is not a human being. In the Christian doctrine of the incarnation, God *became* a human being in the person of Jesus Christ but God, in God's essential nature, is a non-human being. So, the idea that there are minds other than human is a premodern and, if you like, a postmodern idea, more than a modern one. We are so stuck in humanism and modernism that we struggle with the idea that a computer might develop a mind or consciousness. We are stuck in talking about the capacity for human beings to communicate with computers while we are nearly at the point where computers will communicate with other computers, asking questions about what a human being is, so there is a lot of fascinating things to think about there, and your reference to angelology as once having been part of the university curriculum touches upon that.

Let me move into a more theological question and that is the question of the "posthuman divine." Many transhumanists, particularly, are talking about a time in the not-too-distant future when there will be augmented people who will possess capacities which we traditionally associate with the divine—massive degrees of knowledge for example (omniscience) or immortality (at least functional immortality), indefinite life extension and so forth. This sometimes makes theologians nervous. One of the very basic principles of theological discourse has been that there is an infinite qualitative difference (or distance) between God and creation, so that God is a being who brings creation forth but stands outside of creation. To threaten that transcendence by introducing the idea of any aspect of creation, human or otherwise, becoming God or becoming God-like, even if a "small g" god, makes people very nervous. I wonder if you would reflect with us about the concept of "the posthuman divine." What is meant by that? Are we becoming 'gods' albeit with limitations?

Francesca Ferrando: I love your insights and your questions and, of course, I want to answer the one about the post human divine. First, do you mind if I ask you and Arseny a question, connected to the theological objection of Alan Turing in his 1950 article on machine intelligence, asking whether machines can think.[2] You mentioned the idea that Christians are uneasy about the idea of mind uploading and machines becoming intelligent. Some people say machines can never have a soul but if we

2. Turing, "Computing Machinery and Intelligence."

are talking about, in the Christian tradition at least, a God who is all-powerful and is the creator, if something like this does manifest, wouldn't that be a creation of God?

Glen O'Brien: Yes, Christian transhumanists are taking the analogy of divine activity in biological evolution and transferring it to technology. Only the most extreme conservative and fundamentalist Christians would reject the theory of evolution; now most theologians accept that evolution is a reality, and they look for divine action within the evolutionary process, within the biological sphere. Many theologians are now thinking about technology in precisely the same way. Are not technological inventions also the result of divine activity? The biblical texts themselves talk about certain technologies, for example metalsmithing, as something given by God to certain peoples in the Bible. They are the ones who were given the craft of metallurgy and God gave them that power. This is a positive understanding of technology as something divinely given. Many theologians are beginning to think about technological advancement as a space or place for divine activity and for the evolution, not only of species, but also of the universe in a technological direction. They would see any kind of intelligent machine that might emerge as part of divine action and would see our role as human beings to participate with God in that action, understanding that any divine action of a God who is a God of love is always going to contribute to flourishing—human flourishing, but also of the planet and of all beings, of all existences.

The real challenge, of course, is for us to answer the ethical question—will this particular piece of technology contribute to planetary flourishing? Can we see divine activity in this particular development in technology, or do we see something more akin to the tower of Babel, which was built to reach the heavens and was destroyed by God because it was an expression of human pride. To what extent does technology represent participation in divine activity leading to flourishing and to what extent can technology be seen as having a demonic element of human pride that pushes against divine activity? Arseny, would you like to comment from a biblical studies point of view because I know this is something you have thought about.

Arseny Ermakov: The idea of creating a machine superintelligence that we won't be able to control, is not only a scary thing for Christians but for other philosophers as well, for example, Nick Bostrom. For me, what is interesting here is, if you talk about the idea of the *imago dei*, human beings as bearing the image of God, we see that humans also create in their own image, resulting in a reflection of a reflection of a reflection. One of the problems is that we are creating a machine consciousness that is the image of ourselves. Since it is an image of ourselves, we are programming mistakes into it, thus it will carry the image of a flawed creator. In the Christian tradition, God is a perfect creator. Going back to Genesis, when God created this world, God said, "It is good." But there is a departure in Christianity from some other anthropologies, in that humanity experiences an internal struggle, a flaw, a sin that prevents us from flourishing. If we create machines in our own image, are they going to be divine or are they going to reflect that flawed version of their human creator? Are there going to be mistakes in their code? When we reach the stage when machines can create machines that is where the issue of the dangers of superintelligence kicks in. At this stage, what we see in terms of software development (we might compare the software/hardware distinction to the soul/body distinction in theology) the software has bugs, because as humans we are not omniscient and that will be a concern. What insights, then, can we learn from the Christian tradition about how we can interact with non-human minds?

Francesca Ferrando: Thanks to both of you. I promise I'll get to the posthuman divine but the other side of this is the problem of the soul. Alan Turing, in his theological objection, claims that if God gave the soul to humans (as you have said, according to some Christians, animals do not have souls and for Descartes, animals were like machines) and yet if God is all powerful, God *could* give a soul to a machine. If we are going to have conscious machines, would not a Christian perspective have to acknowledge the fact that God gave the machine a soul?

Arseny Ermakov: Personally, I don't have a problem with that. We had a debate recently with a colleague about if a robot prays, would God hear the prayer. Well, it is a no-brainer for me. I'm sure God would hear a robot's prayer.

Francesca Ferrando: Can I push it one more step? In 2016, I was presenting at a conference with a very interesting theologian, who taught at the Pontificia Università della Santa Croce; he was also a Catholic priest and a brilliant philosopher of technology. Our conversation is still in my mind. We were talking about conscious robots, and he said that the issue from a Christian perspective is that a robot cannot enter paradise. This point still sticks with me. He said that, if you stay strictly with the Bible, only humans can enter paradise. But then, what about nonhuman animals and other beings that are not human, such as your example of a conscious, praying robot? If you think about paradise as a location outside of our state of being right now (we should already be in heavenly places if we were good to each other and in a good relationship with the divine) but if you also believe in an afterlife, from a Christian perspective, would this place only be for humans?

Glen O'Brien: Well, that is a very interesting question and it raises eschatological questions about the future place of souls and the whole question of the intermediate state, of whether, where and how we exist between death and the resurrection. It is hard to get at here, other than in very broad brushstrokes, but let me try to indicate a shift in thinking amongst theologians from what we might consider a Platonic concept (almost a Gnostic concept) of a sharp distinction between the material and the spiritual. I am sure you are familiar with the idea in Greek philosophy that it is the spiritual that really matters, and the soul is trapped in this body, almost as a form of punishment. If we could only escape from the body, the soul would be set free to merge with the infinite. This, of course, impacted the church's view of sexuality and procreation. Sex came to be seen as something bad, partly because it was connected to the body and procreative processes that were physical and earthbound. What really mattered was this purity of the spirit and so forth. But there has been a shift away from thinking of "heaven" as an immaterial place to thinking instead of the idea of a new creation, a teleology that constitutes God's final purpose and that will include the material world.

The sharp disjunction between spirit and matter is now understood to be more the inheritance of Greek philosophy than of Judaism or Christianity. The future hope in Judaism (which of course is the precursor to Christianity) is not the immortality of the soul at all, but the resurrection of the body, which means that the body and its materiality are hugely important. Or think of God becoming a human being. The doctrine of the Incarnation teaches that the divine eternal God was manifest as a person in Jesus Christ, a person who could taste and touch and feel and, indeed, be murdered. A God who could suffer is a world away from Plato's God, the Unmoved Mover who could never suffer. Now we have a God who has entered into materiality. The New Testament writers speak about a time when all things

186

(*panta*) will culminate in Christ. So, there is this sort of cosmological destiny which is not about transcending the material world but completing and fulfilling God's creative work in the future. The idea of a "new creation" is replacing the older Platonic concept of an immaterial heaven and a material earth. Now, of course, there's nothing that is filled with more speculative content in theology than eschatology, and there's a whole range of views and many unanswered questions. I have probably raised more questions than answered them, but if we think in those terms of a new creation, which would be the home of all consciousness, perfected according to God's divine order and centered in Christ as the cosmic center of all existence, and if there are consciousnesses that are not human but still sentient then I would say, yes, there is a place in "heaven," or "paradise," or "the new creation" for minds other than human minds. Certainly, animal consciousness would find a home in such a place, so why not machine ones?

Francesca Ferrando: This is so interesting. Thank you so much for taking the time to talk about this. It just didn't feel like the final answer that paradise was a place only humans could go. That just seems very limited. I was raised as a Christian, but I find myself now in all spiritual traditions, so I see myself as everything: Buddhist, Hindu, Muslim, Christian, Jewish, Shinto, Daoist, agnostic, panentheist, everything. I just think that these are all terms, and, in the end, the mystic reality transcends every level. But this question stuck in my mind, and I think your answer nails it. I think that God, as God is depicted in the Christian tradition (that is, all encompassing), would not discriminate between humans and non-humans; I cannot see entry to paradise denied based on strict categories such as: "Humans are welcome; Non-humans are not." Arseny, what do you think?

Arseny Ermakov: I think I would agree with the line of thought presented by Glen. Again, we go back to the Bible. In the beginning, God created the heaven and the earth and, in the end, in Revelation, there is a "bookend"—a vision of "a new heaven and a new earth." This is a renewal of all things, the whole cosmos. In the beginning, God said that what was created was good, and, in the end, Revelation's visions are not about the destruction of all things or "the end of the world" as if it is all going to be burned up. It is quite the opposite. The Book of Revelation is the book of hope, and the hope is that in the end, the God-created-world will be renewed. That is the teleological direction—to the moment of flourishing for the whole created order. Whatever that looks like exactly is hard to tell but it definitely reflects the Christian idea of resurrection. It is not about escaping this world and living in a paradise; you will be alive in this material form. If we think about pushing it forward in terms of the inclusion of things that have been created by humans, and other intelligences as possibilities, I do not see why they cannot be included in this new world, where disconnected things are connected again. All nature, including human beings, living in harmony with the divine is the biblical vision. The material world is important to God who created it and who, at the end of things, will renew it. So, I think the inclusion of robots into that vision of the future is not farfetched.

Francesca Ferrando: That is beautiful. I'm a human now; I can also see myself in a hypothetical future as a conscious robot: the future is here, we are all related. Listening to you was very encouraging. As a conscious robot, I can go to paradise; that is good!

Glen O'Brien: I'm sure you'll be there, Francesca.

Francesca Ferrando: Thank you Glen. I really appreciate your kind comment. Shall we go on then to the posthuman divine? A notion that is really helpful here comes from Hinduism and, more specifically, Advaita Vedanta: the awareness of Brahman (divine spirit) and Atman (the individual soul) being the same. On some level, this is also found in the Bible. Jesus often reiterates that God is within, you can find God already inside of you. The idea is that, at some level, we are already divine. If you want to look at the Christian tradition, if we are created in the image of God, we are also sparks of the divine. This is underlined in Renaissance Humanism, for instance, by Giovanni Pico della Mirandola—all the Renaissance humanists were Christians, although they had some issues with the church of the time. If you embrace other traditions, for instance, Buddhism, enlightenment is not something that is going to come in the afterlife. It is something that we can reach right now, and this also applies to many Christian traditions. You mentioned Gnosticism, a tradition which says that Christ is within you, not outside of you. The Gnostic Sophia represents wisdom, enlightenment; there are a lot of parallels here. So, one answer to the question, "Are we going to become divine?" is that we can already be divine in the way we exist, in the way we live our lives. You can think in the Christian tradition of saints and mystics who, on some level, are already completely connected to the divine.

This reflects my own skepticism about biotechnologies. I am not against them. We are already biotechnological. If you think of the ancient Romans, life expectancy was much lower. Many did not reach thirty years. At fifty you were considered old, where today at fifty you are still considered quite young, and people die in developed countries at around eighty. In Japan, the figure goes into the nineties and in the near future that number will be even higher. So, we are already, on some level, transhuman because our lifespan is already doubled, almost tripled, in the two thousand years since the Romans. I am not necessarily against these biotechnologies. I am just skeptical in the sense that they are not going to bring any final happiness or final answer. We assume that everyone wants to live forever, thinking that is happiness itself; but then a lot of people do not really want to live forever; they already know how to live life very fully. Personally, I am happy about being alive. I am happy with my life. I do not need to live forever.

Moreover, in a sense, we are already immortal. Scientifically speaking, death is not an end: in chemistry, there is only transformation. I do not think that I need this biological body, or even a nanotech body, forever. I think that is an option for people who are afraid of death, but will that really be a solution for them? They are going to be frozen in a cryonic chamber, involving a long parenthesis during which we do not know what is going to happen to consciousness. Will they be asleep or aware in a kind of purgatorial state? We do not know. So, I think that if you are already in fear of death and you are going to be in this long parenthesis for centuries, that is not an enviable place to be. Some advocates of transhumanism once told me that they had been literally dreaming since they were children of being cryonized to go into the future; they are not motivated by a fear of death, this is why their goal is already a success: because it is their dream. Mormon transhumanists think that the cryonic body *is* the resurrected body. Certainly, for some people who are going to go into that experience with faith and love, it is going to be a serene and exciting path. But those who are going to go into cryonics because they are afraid of death should take care of their own fears first.

And yet, none of that is becoming God, because "God" is an unlimited state of blissful self-awareness, and that is something no biotechnology can give you. The technological paradise is a myth. Technology itself is something that is going to open a lot of possibilities, but it is not going to create any "gods." I do believe that we are already divine; and that is not because we are mastering new emerging bio-technologies. It is because of the ways we exist: once we understand that we are part of everything, we can all become fully divine in everything we do, in the ways that we relate to others, in the ways we inter-act with and through our technologies, in our digital footprints. Being God is not so much a matter of the future. We can already be divine now: it is not through bio-technological enhancements, so much as through our technologies of existence.

Glen O'Brien: Thank you. That's a very helpful distinction and a reminder that a future technological utopia is something that has its limits and that the spiritual values will remain salient and very important moving forward.

Francesca Ferrando: Thank you, dear Glen. I believe this is an important message for our time. Currently, I have just finalized my second book, which is entitled *The Art of Being Posthuman: Who are We in the Twenty-First Century?*[3] The main message of the book is how we can be posthuman now. Philosophy should not just be something written; it should have an impact on our lives. These are the real roots of philosophy, or better: philos/sophia. In its Greek etymology: "philos" meaning "love" and "sophia" meaning "wisdom": the love of wisdom, or the wisdom of love. Pre-Socratic thinkers like Pythagoras (and Socrates as well) were not just theorists; they were teaching a way of existing that they were themselves trying to follow. I want to locate posthumanism in that genealogy, not as something to be approached as mere academic theory. We can be caught in many games, including the intellectual game; during the pandemic, I realized that I didn't want to be caught in any intellectual game. Posthumanism is something that can be embraced right now. Crises are also moments of transformation, so my book really comes with this goal in mind. People do not need more posthuman theory; they need to manifest their posthuman ways of existing. That is the existential pursuit that I am developing at the moment.

I would like to thank you, dear Glen and Arseny, for offering this opportunity of reflection; for being open to important and challenging questions that some people do not dare to ask. If God, in the Christian tradition as a creator, created us this way, it was so that we could ask such questions. You are really delving into important issues, and you are doing it with love and intelligence, respect, and spirituality. This vision is wider than us, as individuals. It has been a great pleasure to be part of this conversation: I know that this is not the end, but the beginning.

---

3. Ferrando, *Art of Being Posthuman.*

Bibliography

Bostrom, Nick. *Superintelligence: Paths, Dangers, Strategies*. Oxford: Oxford University Press, 2014.

Cryanoski, David. "What CRISPR-baby Prison Sentences Mean for Research." *Nature*, January 3, 2020. https://www.nature.com/articles/d41586-020-00001-y/.

Ferrando, Francesca. *Philosophical Posthumanism*. London: Bloomsbury Academic, 2019.

———. *The Art of Being Posthuman: Who are We in the Twenty-First Century?* Cambridge: Polity, 2023.

Fukuyama, Francis. *Our Posthuman Future: Consequences of the Biotechnology Revolution*. New York: Farrar, Straus and Giroux, 2002.

Moltmann, Jurgen. *The Crucified God: The Cross of Christ as the Foundation and Criticism of Christian Theology*. London: SCM, 1973.

Pope Francis. *Laudato Si': On Care for Our Common Home*. Rome: Vatican, 2015.

Turing, Alan. "Computing Machinery and Intelligence." *Mind* 59 (October 1950) 433–60.

www.ingramcontent.com/pod-product-compliance
Lightning Source LLC
Chambersburg PA
CBHW060338100426
42812CB00003B/1039